6766/88

This book belongs to

Nigel & Steffan MacKay

84 DICK ST.,
Reefton

I'M NINETY-FIVE... ANY OBJECTION?

Christine Hunt

Illustrations by Bardi Ivory

RM

REED METHUEN

Also by Christine Hunt:

Something in the Hills: Yesterdays in Central Otago
Speaking a Silence

First published 1985

REED METHUEN PUBLISHERS LTD
39 Rawene Road, Auckland 10

ISBN 0 474 00040 0

Design and production — Paper Dart, Auckland
Typesetting — Saba Graphics Ltd, Christchurch
Printed by Singapore National Printers (Pte) Ltd, Singapore

THE AUTHOR

Christine Hunt (now Christine Daniell) was born and brought up in the hill country of Nelson province. After graduating MA (English) from the University of Canterbury, she travelled abroad, spending three years working in isolated rural communities in Europe, where her interest in national folklore was given special meaning.

On returning to New Zealand she worked in radio at Wellington, then moved to Central Otago where she researched and wrote her first book, *Something in the Hills*. Then followed a return to her home territory, Golden Bay. Her second book, *Speaking a Silence*, was the result of seeking out and talking in depth with the old people of that area.

During the next three years Christine worked with young, unemployed people at Nelson Polytechnic as a tutor on the Young Persons' Training Programme. In her holidays she toured the South Island, gleaning material for her new book from old people whose memories reached back nearly a century. She now lives in the hills north of Masterton, with her husband Derek, baby Jessica and a dog Buffalo.

For the South Island,
your land and your people.

My thanks for your time, for all that talking. My thanks, too,
for your practical kindnesses, for beds and sofas and floors, for hot water
and endless cups of tea and eats. And thank you, above all,
for your ready acceptance and moral support of a total stranger
with her questions and crazed scribbling.
Thank you for all those hours.

Contents

Introduction

Wattie was typical of the characters in this book. He'd lived ninety years in the bush above Ringaringa Bay. He was blunt yet welcoming: "Come on in and I'll boil the billy." He listened politely enough as I outlined my objective of fossicking out folk history, but he was clearly sceptical as he poked the wood range, waved aside blowflies and heaped big chipped cups, condensed milk and gingernuts on the table.

Wattie was happy to talk, but he needed to think about this folk history business. What was it? He was respected locally for his quiet, first-hand knowledge of plants, birds and sea and preferred to be remembered as a practical, logical sort of chap. He was intolerant of opinion or abstraction, the personal thoughts and feelings shot through every move a man makes.

But my convictions were ingrained, like Wattie's. I knew there were all those personal responses inside him, waiting: an intricate tapestry of facts and feelings and home-grown philosophy, shrewd perceptions and tomfoolery and fantasy and faith; the essence of folk history.

Eventually, one morning Wattie sprawled back in his kitchen chair and made his statement: "Yes, all those blooming personal bits and pieces you keep talking about — they're important, too. After all, we don't know what William the Conqueror had for breakfast, do we?"

We do know much about William's heroic deeds, but next to nothing about the domestic details of his life or his feelings, the "personal bits and pieces" that flesh out the heroics. Yet someone at the time *did* know what William the Conqueror had for breakfast. If it had been written down, we'd know, too. The same could be said of our own legacy of half-preserved history. We don't know what Arthur Wakefield or Hone Heke had for lunch. It's no doubt too late to worry about the day-to-day details of Wakefield's life. But it's not too late to flesh out Wattie and Marama and Jess, the generation born late last century.

None of the men and women in this book did startling, heroic deeds in the eyes of the world. Yet in their own, uncluttered way,

1

they're all significant. They're survivors.

So Wattie talked and allowed the "personal bits and pieces" to stand as they should stand, twined around the concrete details of his life history like clematis on a beech tree. He slipped easily into my concept that folk history is not obsessed with dates and figures and hard facts. It is authentic to flavour rather than fact. Folk history reveals the ordinary person, not necessarily the hero, and it considers not just what happened but how and why it happened, how it *felt*.

Yet, like Wattie, most of these old people were dubious at first about the value of their ordinary brand of remembering. Alf was pottering in the back yard when I first called and he insisted he had nothing worthwhile to tell me; he might as well not even turn off the damn tap. His wife said we'd have a cup of tea anyway, and that got old Alf talking. The memories flowed and I listened, trying to absorb the flavour of what he was saying, and at the same time trying to concentrate on what I wanted to ask him next, what he said half an hour ago, how he phrased that old-timer's expression about the swaggers on the road, and trying to get down notes about it all. Then later on I'd have to make sense of those copious and often indecipherable notes and Alf's haphazard pattern of remembering. I'd have to transplant myself back to Alf's porch and shape a story that faithfully recreated his character as well as his words.

I never used a tape recorder or machine of any kind for recording the stories in my books. I have always believed that a tape recorder is a glaringly modern gadget to most ninety-year-olds, and an intrusion. I hate them; why shouldn't they? Eva was afraid of electric washing machines and refused to have one in her house. There was no way she'd talk comfortably into a mike, and I had no intention of hiding a machine in my pocket or somewhere so she didn't see. I wanted our communication to be based on trust, not pretence.

Albie was of the same breed. He soon told me that the newspapers had tried to prise stories from him, but he didn't tell them much, "And I wouldn't of told you all this either, lass, if you'd turned up with one of those tape recorder outfits." You talk "nicely" to a sophisticated reporter. You speak carefully into a mike. But I wanted to allow the remembering and the flavour of the old words and phrases to flow freely from these old people. I was a stranger yet I needed their trust, their realisation that our communication was very ordinary.

So it suited us all to chat informally around the kitchen table with the inevitable cups of tea, or out the back while we dug around the cauliflowers or picked plums and made chutney. There were, of course, types I couldn't *stop* talking. They'd have talked into a tape recorder or an eggbeater! I had to listen my way through days of detail, sometimes touching, sometimes fascinating, but hopelessly irrelevant — the latest news on their arthritis and bunions, what all the grandchildren were doing, what Aunt Lil said when Jack called in last Wednesday. But I was more interested in those who'd never told their stories before, who'd hugged their feelings to themselves for nearly a century and felt shocked, or grateful, at exposing a vulnerable part of themselves. I was constantly astounded by their simple and very direct appreciation of our talking and found it humbling, but reassuring, to identify with their confessed pain, doubts, satisfactions, regrets, insights. Those raw emotions are precious because we've all felt them.

Some of these old people were surprised at their own outpourings. Wattie admitted, "I don't tell anyone about all this as a rule — it's baring the soul — but you've got me talking." Stan said of his wife Vera: "You know, she's not a talker as a rule. She's told you things she hasn't told me," and he concluded, "You know more about me now than I know myself."

Others were grateful for a fresh ear now that the family were tired of Gran going on about the old days again. Charlotte constantly reminded me of this: "I'm enjoying this because I've got no one here to talk to, not really. It's all superficial," and "All this talking's doing me a power of good; it's bringing all sorts of things back. It's like having a plough-up. And it's making me consider things I wouldn't say to anyone else."

Some wanted to confess, some understated, some didn't believe in spoiling a good story by sticking to the truth. Folk history allows for this, for bits chopped off and tacked on as stories are handed down from father to son to workmate at smoko. Wattie spoke clearly about this: "It's just like when a man comes home from hunting, the wife's busy poking around cooking and bathing the babies . . . he has to say the boar charged him and whatnot to get the story *across* to her. Well, us men tend to do the same sort of thing about the war."

We all tend to exaggerate and select, especially when we look backwards, and folk history allows for that human failing. I am not too interested in "the facts" anyway, in what ship Ellen's grandfather came out on, when the first church or school was built at Waikari and where. All that's probably recorded somewhere. It's safe. But I am interested in Ellen's thoughts and feelings, which aren't preserved: what it feels like to be ninety-five, blind and almost deaf and looking back over not only your own century but also your grandmother's memories of Kaikoura during the early 1860s, when there was no wharf, no coast road and only three white women in the area; while outside in "the world" we're breeding test-tube babies and docking in space. I'm interested in what life felt like for Marama, one of a family of eighteen children, and in how Harry and Kenny responded very differently to the realities of war, especially the psychological pressures on coming home. Kenny felt condemned to remain a bachelor, struggling with his third-rate land and his pride. He still regrets that struggle: "I couldn't ask a woman to share what I had here." It is this response to living that I have tried to recapture in these stories.

For my previous books I spent a year each in Central Otago and Golden Bay. I worked in the regions, fossicked out and talked with the old locals by the day and wrote their stories. For this book I made a journey. I set out from Nelson with my dog, my Volkswagen Beetle and a big bag of biros and jumbo school pads and slowly made my way around the South Island. There were advantages and disadvantages in this approach. I felt frustrated by my sense of skimming the surface of this huge, creased island, rushing past places where I knew there'd be interesting old people and stories stashed away in the bush and down the back streets. But I'd already spent time in that area, or already heard too many goldmining or fishing or mustering stories.

This negative aspect was balanced by unexpected bonuses. I was on the road, following my nose, roughing it. I was living uncertainly, from day to day, as those people had done. None of them knew I was coming. All accepted me. Many insisted I stay with them, and intimacy grew from the sharing of space and food and everyday concerns like who would have the bathroom first, where my dog would sleep and what time to get up in the morning. The closeness of those connections was still there when, long months later, I sat down to organise their memories. This sharing is reflected in deeper, more rounded stories.

Others accepted, or respected, my desire to sleep sometimes out under the trees or on the beach, to have a tent fly but no tent — the need for a "modern" to take an occasional break from civilisation, to rough it and perhaps taste something of the old way of life. Amy laughed at me, insisting I was more of a pioneer than she was: "Look at you, you're even more primitive than me, lass. I slept in a tent; you're sleeping outside under the trees. I'd say you're a breakaway from the young generation, lass." Amy's motive for living in a tent was necessity. Mine was whim. Yet we understood one another.

Only seventeen of the old people I met appear in this book. Those whose conversations I didn't shape into stories were in no way rejects, they were simply another example of a "type" of New Zealand character I couldn't keep repeating in a book like this. There were any number of bashful old retired miners with their coats hanging on a nail on the door. There were raw yet romantic old musterers, reminiscing over dogs and camp-oven bread and river valleys; and old women with their hair up in buns, recalling large families and washing days at the copper. There was Jess of Kanerie, born and married at the top end of the road and not ever wanting to shift; wanting to die there at the bottom end of the road. At Kaikoura there was Ted, an old fisherman, a classical Kiwi do-it-yourselfer, a character. The inevitable roll-your-own stuck on his bottom lip as he talked and all the words merged together into a tide of noise. Their stories are precious, but there just isn't room here.

Those who do appear are unique yet representative. They have so obviously gathered to themselves a strength made of resilience, hard humour, vulnerability and vision. They had to have this strength to survive. They battled with each other, as we do, and they struggled with the elements and the land. But they didn't push them around. They adapted to their surroundings, whereas we try to force our surroundings to adapt to us. They spoke of their struggles, mostly without bitterness or coyness. They demonstrated the lack of resilience our soft civilisation breeds in us today.

Above all, they spoke before it was too late. Our experiences and memories go into the grave with us when we die, unless we preserve them in images: words, music, art. Yet memories and thoughts are such frail, complex, organic things, like cobwebs. We tend to brush them aside, neglect or destroy them. Their potency, their colour and smell, is so easily bruised out. Ellen recognised this frailty: "Yes, now I'm remembering things I didn't know I remembered; they were buried. I sit here now on the sofa, I go off dreaming about the past and they come back, all the memories. One sparks off another; they're all linked up like a train. And I want to pass it all on to you. I've got that energy."

I smelt New Zealand in these old people of the South Island, in their conversations and in their tussock ridges, their hurling West Coast tides, their sofas and scones, their freesias and cabbage patches, in their old institutions: kerosene tin buckets, crinkly tubes of condensed milk, plum duffs and dumplings with golden syrup, walls plastered with cut-outs from the *Auckland Weekly*.

These stories are my gleanings.

ELLEN

'I'm not a creeping kind of an old lady'

Ellen was sitting in the porch untangling bindertwine when I called. She had bits in her hair and all over her dress. She was direct and welcoming: "Come along in before you say another word."

Ellen was ninety-five and, in her own words, four-quarters Irish. All four of her grandparents, her father and her husband were Irish, and they'd gathered together quite a clan on the dairy-farming land fondly named Donegal Flat, just north of Kaikoura.

Her husband was long dead. She'd been cared for for many years by her daughter Theresa. Both Ellen and Theresa looked fresh from Cork or County Clare, with their lovely fine faces and their hair wound in plaits around their heads or coiled up in a bun. They had slow, soft voices, flowing up and down like water.

Ellen was clearly aging. She had worn-out hands and a wrinkled neck. She had cataracts in her eyes and couldn't see well, but a quiet, fine energy swept through her. She was very talkative. Her eyes shone despite the cataracts and her face was remarkably unlined and smiley.

We spent many days together, in the porch or in her lovely big wooden farmhouse kitchen, complete with wood range and black kettle. Ellen was quick to light a fire even though it was mid-January, and we had tea in big white cups, "for a good cup of tea", and soggy fruit cake; she always had fruit cake in the tin. She sat on the sofa, backed up to a pile of cushions, a shawl around her shoulders; we talked and laughed a lot. Ellen had a darting, shimmering sense of humour. The wry Irish wit flowed from her and she loved to share someone else's laughter. "We need a bit of humour, need to give our lives a bit of a tilt now and again."

Yet there was another, very thoughtful side to Ellen. She had a poignant sense of the tragedy of things. Her age and her sharp wit had mellowed this into acceptance: "Now my faculties are sliding, all the senses merge. I don't know where to start to judge things. My eyes are going . . . my daughter's got to see if my ears are clean!"

Ellen and Theresa were quick to offer me their living room to sleep in when the weather turned bad, and fresh eggs from their hens. A family phrase kept coming out, like a chorus: "You're more than welcome."

Theresa insisted she drive me around the district to all their old haunts: her grandmother's and mother's old homes, the church, the school, so I could understand their stories better. Ellen loved retelling all those stories; she knew the value of them: "I'm filling Theresa up with them, because they'll be gone when I'm gone. I don't want to go off and have them all with me, the old stories."

Three months after I left them many things happened in the family. Theresa died suddenly. Ellen became frail overnight and unable to care for herself. She lost her memory and was put in the Kaikoura hospital. I received a letter from her foster daughter, saying Ellen and Theresa had often spoken of my visit and Ellen would love me to call when I was next down her way.

Ellen's vitality was still ignited, though fading.

I'm ninety-five, yes. Any objection? I was born in 1888. It's a long time ago; it's got to the stage now it's almost too long. My eyes are going and I can't see so much; it's all rather foggy now. Then my hearing isn't as good as it used to be, I've very little taste and there's lots of flowers I can't smell. Feeling is indefinite, too, and I have to feel with my hands a lot more now my sight is going. You could say there's a slackening off all through.

Then when you lose your sight there's another thing happens — you can't walk properly. You've got to creep along. It does annoy me; I'm not a creeping kind of an old lady. My arms are skinny, but my legs and feet are still good . . . are these old women's legs? Even the doctor commented on them. It's strange, I've had tired enough feet all these years, hours and hours on the concrete milking cows, but it doesn't seem to have hurt my legs and feet. If it wasn't for my eyes I'd get about everywhere, freely. But now I have to creep about. You'd think I was a thousand years old!

No, old age isn't so funny now. I have no ambition to be 100. No, it's not a desirable attainment. When you're that age you're on somebody's back; you're a burden to yourself and other people. No thank you, no telegrams from the Queen. Poor Queen's got enough to do without worrying about me, even though it's not her that sends the telegrams; I know that.

The ones that don't worry about dying are the ones that live the longest? Yes, that's the awkward part of it. But if Father Time turned up, I wouldn't say a word. I've had the best of it all.

And another thing, I think that over the last year or so I'm remembering back better. I'm losing my grip on the present, can't remember where I left my boots, but I can remember way back to when I was a girl. I never troubled about it, before that; I was getting on with it, living. But now that I can't see properly I can't occupy myself the same so I think back, try and recover some of the memories for my daughter. Got nothing else to do . . . can't occupy my hands. So perhaps it really is a deliberate thing, casting my mind back to entertain myself. There's nothing more for me to look forward to, so I must look backwards.

I can remember all my grandmother's stories, too. From the time I was a child my granny and grandfather talked a lot about their lives, then my mother talked about it, kept it in my mind. So I've got the whole lot of it. And I'm doing the same with Theresa. I'm filling her in with all those stories. . . . I always did like talking, had the gift of the gab. Only thing is, nowadays I can't get people to listen to me. But you're such a good listener. . . .

I was born here, a little over a mile up this road, and my mother and grandmother lived here before me, up the top of Mt Fyffe road. There were so few people here in Grandmother's day; she was the third white woman in Kaikoura. Three of them arrived here within a few weeks of one another. It's a romantic story, the whole thing. Grandmother went to school with Grandfather in Ireland. They were always friends, then they fell in love, but they always felt their differences. She was temperamental; he was stubborn.

Then the potato famine and black plague hit Ireland badly. People were dying everywhere. Life was appalling, and yet there was this fire between Grandfather and Grandmother. Then when she was nineteen Grandmother saw a notice posted up at a fair. The Australian Government was offering passages to young people, especially young women. Grandmother's married sister and her husband decided to take up the offer, and Grandmother and Grandfather had quarrelled so she made up her mind to go with them. Her father didn't try to stop her as times were so hard in Ireland; maybe a new country could offer her more. So they set sail and landed in Melbourne in 1852, after four months at sea.

Grandmother got a position in Melbourne with an English couple, and one day she was hanging out the washing when a voice over the fence called out, "Annie". It was Grandfather. He'd come over the seas looking for her. Grandmother went straight into his arms, they married and he worked on the Jim Crow gold diggings until they earned enough money to sail to New Zealand. Grandfather worked for several years as a sawyer in Wellington, but there was no future there and he was always on the lookout for a bit of cheap land. Eventually, he heard there was plenty of land to be settled in Kaikoura so he arranged a job at Cheviot Hills, south of Kaikoura, and in 1860 Grandfather, Grandmother and their two children — a two-year-old and a six-month-old baby — sailed out of Wellington on the *Spray* and headed south.

They called in at Kaikoura where at that stage there wasn't even a wharf, but a whaleboat took them ashore to the whaling base set up in 1843 by Robert Fyffe. The whaleboat tied up at an iron ring fastened in a rock — you can still see that ring at low tide

— and a woman met them on the rocks. She was the late Robert Fyffe's housekeeper, living in the home he'd built of pitsawn timber and bricks from Australia. His house is still standing there above the rocks today; it's being lived in and restored. But it was the only house in Kaikoura when my grandparents called in in 1860. The only other dwellings were just rough shacks.

The woman took Grandfather and his family up to Fyffe House, made them a cup of tea and helped make the babies comfortable. Then on they went to Cheviot Hills, but they worked there only a short time in the end because the executors for the late Robert Fyffe engaged Grandfather to work on the Kahutara run, out of Kaikoura. They left their heavy luggage to be brought up on the boat whenever she chanced to call again and rode up to Kahutara on pack-horses, carrying all their essential goods plus the two babies. No road up the coast — that road wasn't formed until I was at school myself. If you wanted to go to Christchurch you had to go fifty-two miles inland by coach to Waiau, spend the night there, then go on by coach to Domett and on by train to Christchurch.

No, in Granny's time there was just the beach or rough tracks over the hills, and she'd never been on a horse before! She got off and walked whenever possible, and the rest of the time clung on to a blanket strapped in front of the saddle and closed her eyes going down the hills. It's a romantic story, romantic all the way through, really. The men took the children in front of them and off they went again, up and down hills and up to Kahutara house where Grandfather was to help with shearing and anything else that was going, and Granny was to be cook and general housemaid. When they arrived that night she was very sore and tired, but she had to set to work and wash for the baby. She had so few clothes, she said she was always at the wash-tub.

But Grandmother was tough. She'd come through the hunger and the plague back in Tipperary; she went through all this like a Briton. She was a very small lady, only five foot high, size-two boots, but she was healthy and active; even when she was in her eighties she'd drive the horse and buggy over three miles down to the Kowhai church, then back again, and she lived to be just over 100. Granny always said: "I had been brought up to expect hard times, so you must not imagine I thought I had any reason to complain."

All she had to cook on there at Kahutara was a colonial oven — an oblong box about thirty inches long, ten inches high, eighteen inches wide. A wood fire was kept burning on top of the oven and when a good heap of red coals had built up they were shovelled underneath the oven — very hot on your face, stoking and cooking on those colonial ovens in the summer-time. You needed a lot of dry, hard wood, too, but there was plenty because one of the big worries was clearing enough bush to get crops planted.

But always there was the lure of the land for these immigrants from Ireland, and the Government had announced a very attractive contract: you could buy land for two pound an acre, or else you could take up £100 worth of ditching on Mt Fyffe road, which was the first attempt at a road around here. As it turned out, it was seventeen years before they could put any shingle on that road; it just wasn't stable enough.

Grandfather got the land up there at the foot of the mountains, put in potatoes and other vegetables and early in 1860 started work on their whare — slow work, as all supplies had to be carried by back from the whaling base. No timber around, so the whare was built Maori style: spars and poles, thatched roof and walls, mud lined and a clay floor. He built two rooms but they lived in only one and stored food, tools and farm equipment in the other. In the living room Grandfather built a large fireplace. All the cooking was done in a camp oven over that fire, and their beds were made of long manuka rails. The men pulled and stripped bulrushes for the mattress. They just stripped off the top black bit and used it as we'd use kapok, but it doesn't last well — loses its life and goes flat and dusty. It had to do though. Grandmother made a cover for the mattress and there was a comfortable bed. But Grandmother said she was glad she had a large counterpane, because the bed "certainly wasn't a thing of beauty".

Granny used to say: "With all our makeshifts I often wondered if we were any relation to Robinson Crusoe. But the fact that they were our own made us quite contented." The furniture was rough and homemade, too. A circle cut from a huge fallen totara tree made quite a good table; they just chopped off a slice, like a slice of bread. Four foot six it was, at its widest part. It wasn't perfectly round, but that was all right. They put the flatter side against the wall, and I remember clearly Granny talking about the legs of that table. They were lovely pieces cut from a clean spar; they shone beautifully.

The potatoes and some big cabbages in the garden were ready to eat by the time the whare was finished so two men loaded up their possessions and off they went again, Grandmother with a toddler at her skirt and the baby in her arms. One of the young boys threw down his swag and showed her how to carry the babies Maori style: he took her shawl, wrapped the baby around her back and that left her with two hands free to help the toddler. They walked all day with many stops for the children, through heavy bush but over mostly flat land. That evening they reached their home: "A poor thing," Granny said, "but all our own."

Then for the next three years she was never off that place. She went nowhere, saw no one . . . only the occasional man who called. Often she saw no one for six months or a year, it was that isolated; no house anywhere near them, and just swamp between their place and the sea. Only woman she saw was a Mrs Keene who came to the area in 1860, same year as they did. She'd settled at Swyncombe and made a habit of riding around and seeing all the isolated women. She was no doubt lonely, too, but it meant a lot to Granny to have her call.

Next thing was, Granny had another baby. Grandfather wanted to get in another woman to help at the birth, but there was no woman to get! When the baby was born on the mat by the bedside, he fainted. Grandmother told me: "I just had to lie there and wait until he came round, then he lifted us onto the bed." He insisted on going to get a Maori woman. It was a long, rough walk, four miles through the swamp, but she came. When she saw Grandmother in bed with the baby in her arms she turned to go. Granny tried to get her to stay but she wouldn't; said her husband needed her! She couldn't see what the fuss was about; the mother and the baby were healthy. So Grandfather brought Granny in a basin of water. She washed the baby and a day or two later she got up and did her work as usual.

They were still fearfully poor, couldn't even afford a cow, but then a wonderful thing happened. They were given a goat in milk. Granny was thrilled to bits. It was always her lament she never had enough milk for the children, and they bred several goats from that nanny, until they could afford a cow.

But generally, food was never short. They got in fowls as soon as possible and there were plenty of trout and wild pigs, pukekos and wekas. They thought pukekos were nice to eat but wekas were oily, more useful for softening leather. Ate the pukeko and weka eggs, too; and gathered up gulls' eggs by the bucketful during the laying season, but used them mostly for cooking; they were strong-tasting on their own.

As for bread, at first they just cooked damper in the hot ashes or in the camp oven, then later on they made yeast and baked yeast bread. But it was the whalers made the loveliest bread; they were the first ones around here to perfect the art of deep-frying. They cooked their bread in boiling whale oil, in the tripots!

But it was fertile land. You'd poke a peach stone in, or a branch, and it grew. Then some of the runholders gave away fruit trees to anyone who wanted them, and soon peaches were so plentiful from Goose Bay to Oaro that the wild pigs lived on the surplus that rotted on the ground. Beautiful big peaches — you'd take the bathtub and bring it back, full up. We'd bottle them and make jams and sauces and pickles. Then suddenly the peaches got some disease and died out.

But all sorts of fruit grew very well up there at Granny's place. They put in gooseberries, blackcurrants, pears, plums and all kinds of apples that aren't known today. Yes, they grew nearly everything they needed. All Grandfather had to buy was salt, sugar, tea and flour. No shop in Kaikoura until 1867; they had to order what they wanted from Wellington and it all came down by boat.

But gradually more settlers came to the area and they started pitsawing timber for building homes, so soon Grandfather and Grandmother made a decent home and the old whare became the shed. This new house had two rooms with a floor and a shingle roof. It was mud-lined inside, up- and down-boarded outside. A local ship's carpenter made them a table and chairs. They bought two iron bedsteads and feather mattresses and installed a colonial oven and a "fountain", a six- or eight-gallon kettle with a tap instead of a spout, hanging on a chain from an iron bar up the chimney. That was the hot-water supply!

Grandfather got all these new gadgets up to the house on a sledge, which was real progress, as before that everything had to be packed in on a horse. Another important thing Granny had brought in on the sledge was a forty-gallon cask which Grandfather cut in two, for washing the clothes. Made two good washing tubs, except that sometimes splinters came out of the wood and pierced Granny's hands. But before that she'd been doing all the washing in a small baby's bath and a bucket, with a kerosene tin for a copper. She was often short of soap, too, so she invented a substitute: she'd line a large box with fern or hay, pile in dry wood ashes and pour over a kettle of boiling water. The liquid that dripped out was quite good for washing, she always said, but severe on the hands. Made all her own starch, of course. She'd grate a few potatoes, strain them through muslin and use the liquid. It stiffened the clothes well but gave them a poor colour. They thought up all sorts of things, the old pioneers. One young chap told Granny he'd ironed his shirts with a square gin bottle filled with boiling water.

Yes, I remember all this old stuff Granny told me. It's just part of me.

By 1865 they were getting along quite well up there. They had a mare and foal and a yearling filly. They were also milking two cows by that stage, and they set the milk in pans, skimming off the cream and churning butter. Any surplus they salted in a small keg, then when the keg was full they'd send it by boat to Wellington where it sold readily. Their eggs also brought them in a small income at the same market.

Yes, all this appealed to me, the hard but romantic lives of Grandfather and Grandmother. But there was also tragedy came out of all that hard living. Grandfather was drinking too much in Wellington, but he'd controlled it down in Kaikoura, then after their sixth child died he became terribly upset and took to the drink again. Grandmother always objected very much to his drinking, then when he really went to town after the baby died she wasn't going to stand it any more. She was a fiery old girl, very impulsive. She jumped on a boat, went up to Wellington and got a job helping out in a Quaker family. But she was fretting, homesick for her family, and in the end the Quaker woman sent word down to Grandfather; she slipped a note in Granny's letter and told him his wife was fretting for them all. Up he went and got her back to Kaikoura. Yes, it's a romantic story through and through.

Some of my earliest memories are of my granny's house and her stories. She used to walk the cattle tracks all round the district with a baby on her back, helping the women with their pregnancies. All the women adored her. All the men hated her; she used to give them lectures on how they treated their wives like kept slaves. Granny said it was quite funny though. The women would be in bed with their babies, smiling; the men would be out the back, scowling. But they couldn't say anything. She was the only one around who could help out at the births.

Many of the Maori men helped confine their daughters — midhusbandry you'd call it! But most of the white men would run a mile rather than face it. They were so ignorant about birth; it was never talked about openly so it left them hopeless. Birth and sex were never talked about. It was all taboo, even between a man and woman. Same thing in my day; we were taught nothing at all. Blind innocence. Then you got married, and Nature's a great teacher.

Even the doctor didn't seem to know about planning children — safe times and that. But then some women are never safe — one baby a year no matter what you do. And in our day the need for population was an acknowledged thing; there were too few people in the district. A dozen people would make the start of a crowd! And when girls grew up there were plenty of men to court them; the bachelors far outnumbered the spinsters. That's why there's always been so many old hermits and bachelors in the hills.

But you never ever talked about having children with a man. It was all blanketed. Too much talk about sex and birth today? No.

I think there's still more talking to be done. There's no dead secret about it. Never was. At least, it's one that can't be kept. But what bothered me was the terrible time a girl got if she made a mistake and got pregnant. Poor, innocent girls, they knew nothing. No one had ever talked to them about it in their lives. But they were branded for life, shunned. And what kills me completely, it's a crime for the girl, but it doesn't matter a bit for the man. No other girl would turn up her nose at him. That was never quite fair. Mind you, I think now the women expect a bit too much; they're pushing men into the background. It's a reaction to thousands of years of being just an accessory. There should be as many women as men in Parliament; we're equal in population as well as in everything else. But women are working the equality the wrong way to my mind.

How it can be done better? I don't see another way. But I see it's just a bit over the balance. I think in married life there's got to be a head. You can't always have two opinions working against one another and then expect harmony. The real secret is how much each one cares for his mate. There's no trouble if there's love between them. I was lucky. I had plenty of love, but it was steady. Granny and Grandfather had passion, up and down.

Granny was a dignified old lady, but fiery, full of fun. I've got that, too; it was in the breed. All four of my grandparents were Irish. Then I had an Irish husband, to cap it all off. He came out here from northern Donegal when he was twenty-three. I was twenty-nine when we married, late in life for those days. We waited four or five years, until he got this place paid off. But it was all unspoken; we just had an understanding. He never asked me to marry him. I knew I'd say yes and I knew he wanted me and that's that. Yes, we're still in the romantic story business!

Before we married, my husband had a hard life, on his own. He'd milk sixteen cows by hand every morning, take the milk up to the factory in the old horse and cart, drive back to clean the cans, then come inside and cook breakfast, wash his clothes, do all the domestic chores; a hard life for a man on his own. But he did it for years and years, and it gave me time to gather up a lot of stuff for the house; yes, my glory box. And I've been here ever since, on this block of land. I was happy — it's somehow happy land around here. I've had a lifetime of getting up early and milking cows. I was up before the sun every morning for twenty years, except for once when I had mumps, and when the babies were born. Other than that I was up at half past four or quarter to five every morning. I always helped in the milking shed. We'd have a cup of tea, I'd change the baby and feed him, then I'd take him out to the shed

16

in a basket and get to work, milking. On it went. I'd come in and
get the breakfast, my husband would take the milk up to the factory
and I'd get on with the housework.

I was six years married before I had a living baby. I had one
stillborn, that was a shock, and several miscarriages. In the end
I had two children living, and we adopted a first cousin. No, I
wasn't lucky with my children. But we always had a lot of love
between us, me and my husband. I didn't go into hysterics about
it, but it was a solid place in my life. My husband was a good
man, and such a simple thing took his life. He was coughing hard
one day and broke a hernia. It didn't give him much trouble at
the time, but years later a clot developed. It's twenty-four years
ago. . . .

I was going well, too, until last year. I was gardening and all
sorts. I usually keep a fruit cake on the go. I make all my own
orange and lemon peel and cook them up in the wood range. I'm
going to give up making cakes though. I can't see the measurements.

There's still things I want to do, plenty of them, but I've sense
enough to know I can't, not unless I get this operation done on
my eyes and they improve my sight. I can still spin, though. I
always liked spinning . . . done it for nearly a century! And I've
taught a lot of people to spin, from one end of New Zealand to
the other. It's all in fashion now, isn't it? I've knitted a lot, too,
especially men's big jerseys. That was my line, not the fine things.
I don't do white; I go for the browns and blacks. White's no good
for the working ones. When I was young I did a lot of embroidery
— embroidered a christening gown for my sister when she got
married and she used it for all her children, and I did a lot of
blouses and things. Seems strange doesn't it — rough old hands
from the camp ovens and black stoves making those delicate, lacy
white things? But the other side of a woman's nature demanded
something of that kind. You couldn't live at the tough level all
the time.

Clothing those days was something you wore until you wore it
out. Working dresses were made of galatea — a very strong, fairly
solid cotton material in bluish grey and white stripes; it wore and
wore. Best dresses were woollen, made of cashmere or melton cloth
and lined throughout. They were all down to the ground, even
the working dresses you wore for working in the hills. They dragged
in the mud and were hard to clean. You'd have to hang them out
to dry, then brush the dirt off, and us children often had to do
that job; we'd have a go at them with a stiff brush.

Every adult woman wore corsets too, every day, in the house and
out. I did, too, in my day, but I had sense enough soon to throw

it away. All that nonsense — girls fainting with the tight lacing. Mind you, they were warm in winter. Then we always wore waist petticoats and black woollen stockings; sometimes you'd have a cashmere wool pair for good, but mostly you stuck with the black ones. You never ever went around bare-legged; that was shocking.

Those days they always had boots, too, never shoes, and they always wore hats and gloves. Funny how things change. And we all had long hair; I've never had mine cut in my life. First time I ever saw a woman with short hair was this librarian from Wellington who came here to retire. Us kids all called her Uncle Emma because she had short hair; no one around here had ever seen a woman without long hair. The last man I saw with the old-fashioned long hair was the Singer sewing-machine man. He had long, brown hair twisted round and round in a roll at the back of his head. How he had the nerve to keep it on, I don't know; none of the other men had kept that fashion, and later on even he cut it all off. We're going back to it again now, though. You've got more of a chance of seeing a man with a ponytail again these days.

I've seen a lot of changes all right. Been through three wars. The Boer War was on round about the time I left school. I really understood what was going on, then there were the two world wars. During all those wars we lived on the edge — couldn't go to the post office or see the postman without being anxious. I had brothers and friends go to the first war. A lot of them never came back . . . .

I think war ought to be outlawed. You won't believe some of the shocking things done to men. I was thinking about the case of a man who did some petty offence; I don't know that I ever heard exactly what he'd done. The officer ordered him to be shot, ordered four of his mates to shoot him. They all refused and all got shot themselves. These things came out after years and years. My brothers told me that story and all sorts of other shocking things. But mostly the men who came back didn't talk freely about the war. There was too much else happening that interested them, or they pretended they were interested. It wasn't so much they wanted to forget; they *needed* to forget.

My mother? When the wars were on mother kept quiet. Never discussed it. It was better not discussed; too much talking leads you on, gives you further thoughts. Better to stifle them, work it off, keep yourself busy. One cousin of mine was killed in France. He'd had a very bad time over his last three weeks. No decent night's sleep, just leaning against the trench, up to his knees in mud. When his parcel of personal effects was returned to his family, they found all his things covered with mud. Someone picked up his watch and it started to tick. That broke my mother up. It was a pitiful thing, a direct link with the boy. She said nothing.

Then when peace was declared after World War I there was the usual fuss and kick-up. They had to have a welcome back. But there was too much sorrow at the back of it to make a big fuss. For a lot of the men it was hurting badly; you could see it on their faces. To my mind there's a lot of injustice in the world, some queer old rules. I want to push the war years aside.

But I'll tell you one thing I think. It's about time there was a law passed about plastic bags. You don't know what to do with them. They don't decompose; you've got to bury them. Who wants to go out and have a funeral everyday? We'll all be strangled in plastic bags before we're done. And look at the number of people making a fat million with those plastic bags. I detest them.

The world's changing too fast. UFOs? I don't think anything about them. Never seen any. Yet some people are so sure about them, and some of them just like to get up a fuss. I went out when the UFO display was at its best down here; I went out to have a look. Fishing boats! People just wanted some excitement. No, I'm a calm one.

Space travel? I don't know. I ask myself what's the use of it, and I've got no answer. I'm not well-informed. It feels right? No, I'd forget it myself, unless we can find a good place to put our pollution and our surplus population. The whole world today, it's too fast. You take little children. They aren't little children these days; they're old men and women. Before you know it they're talking like adults, using big words and reading and writing; they're up on their feet and away. In our day children stayed babies for much longer. And the increase in wages, that's astounding to an old one like me, but all that money won't buy anything. I take it in my stride. I say, what are you going to do with all that money? You can't eat it, can't take it with you. It doesn't bother me. I'd have to worry if I didn't take it in my stride, and I prefer not to worry.

But you've got to be very quick to survive in the world today. And that's where Kaikoura gains. We're very small. We'll never be a forward place unless they discover gold or oil or something. There's no active work going on in the district that calls for speed. People just live . . . and us old people don't like rushing. I don't take a rest during the day, but it's only because I wouldn't sleep at night. I just put my feet up for a while on the kitchen sofa of an afternoon. So we carry on talking, you and me.

I'll say this: if I know anything, I know this area well. I was born here, at home. I was a fully grown woman before there was ever a hospital here in Kaikoura, and that's a day or two ago. I went to school here, got my proficiency when I was twelve, and those days after you passed the exam you more or less left school. But I stayed on a year. I was still young and I was considered to be fairly bright at school; it was no trouble to me. Then I left school and quietly took up algebra. I simply loved it, got all sorts of algebra books. But then circumstances changed — there was work at home to be done, so I had to give it up. They were here for years and years, those old algebra books of mine, then I gave them away.

So after that I just helped out at home, milking cows, cooking and sewing. There was no other work for girls around Kaikoura those days, apart from being maids for the big farms, and wages were scandalous at first — half a crown a week.

Next came the war and marriage, children, then the Depression of the 30s. During that Depression we had our farm freehold. We were producing nearly all of our own food and my husband was working sixteen hours a day, but still we weren't able to keep our heads above water. There was just no sale for stock. They had to cut the calves' throats when they were born and drive sheep over the bluffs; couldn't sell them and couldn't afford to keep them. You'd send bullocks or steers to the market and all you'd get back would be the bill for the transport. During one year of that Depression our total income was £200 and we had to pay all sorts out of that: keeping the place going, tax, unemployment tax, food for the five of us.

Of course, there were lots worse off than we were. Some families around here couldn't afford to buy bread. They might have a cow and a few vegetables, maybe a few hens, but then the problem was to feed those hens; they've got to be fed well to lay well. Many families like that struggled fearfully in the Depression. The father would cut firewood and go round in a horse and cart trying to sell it. The mother would walk way down to the hospital, more than four miles away, and do a day's washing; she'd get a decent meal there in the middle of the day. We'd all pitch in and give them what we could — a sack of swedes or potatoes — but most of us didn't have much to spare either. Their kids would run home from school at lunch-time and all they'd get was a plate of swedes or potatoes. They'd have to run home a mile for that. And then they didn't learn much at school, couldn't concentrate with no decent food in them. To this day you can see the starvation on those people. Their flesh never plumped out; it still looks hard, as if it never got the chance to expand. And those poor kids didn't even have a proper pencil or anything for school, just a butt end of a pencil they'd found somewhere.

I laugh when people talk of depression today. We really knew what it was like to ration. At one stage sugar was very short so I made up my mind I'd go without sugar in tea. I did that for three months, then I gave up tea! Just drank hot water after that. Then during the war petrol rations got down to three gallons a month, just enough to go to town once a week and do your shopping. There was sheer hunger around during that Depression, especially in the towns where they couldn't grow their food. The Government announced that anyone who had a shepherds' hut or shearers' cookshop was to let people use them in return for work of some kind, and the Government would pay a nominal price towards their food. One farmer near here took on nine or ten men. He picked them up from the station in his wagon. One chap fainted on the platform, through hunger. There were all sorts came — doctors, accountants, dentists — and the farmer said that for ten days he couldn't give them enough food; they just couldn't get enough. He got tired of rounding up sheep and killing them for food so he went out the back and shot a huge wild steer. That lasted them a week.

Yes, we wasted nothing those days; hung on to anything that was reasonable. Mind you, a lot of the stuff we have today isn't really essential. In my day houses had no cupboards to speak of, just a wardrobe or two and a pantry if you were lucky. Those wardrobes weren't built-in jobs either; they were ones you could move around, and most bedrooms just had a row of nails across the corner with a curtain across and a shelf above, if you were lucky. That was your wardrobe. Then for many people the wardrobe was simply under the bed, or a nail on the back of the door!

Our bathroom was a tin dish on the verandah. It was always there at the back door — a tin dish, with a piece of soap and a towel hanging on a nail, for washing your hands. You'd fling the water into the ditch when you'd finished. Pollution you'd call it nowadays! Then we had an old oval galvanised bath; we used that for washing clothes as well as bathing ourselves. You'd put it in front of the fire to bath the kids, then take it into the bedroom for mum and dad. Those were the days.

Forty-seven years ago we built this house, for just under £600. The whole job cost only that much, including materials, labour and some of the pathing. Timber was so cheap those days — eightpence a foot if I remember rightly — and that included bringing it down from the West Coast and landing it here on the site. All the windows and doors and doors on the cupboards cost twenty pounds; the stained glass fanlights in the kitchen, sitting room, bathroom and one bedroom cost six pounds ten; that was a big expense.

There were thirteen of them built our house, in less than seven weeks, and they had to take down the old original home, put in new foundations and build the new one. I'd take them over morning and afternoon teas — batches of scones, that sort of thing. I clearly remember the first day we came over here. I lit the stove and in twenty-five minutes I had scones on the table — a house-warming. And there was our new house: five rooms, hot and cold water, a bath, everything. . . .

I had everything I wanted. And the quiet life — the slow pace here suited me. My husband was the same — a very quiet man, from Donegal. They used to call this area Donegal Flat because there were so many Donegal people here. Donegal people, it's a habit our family have. We often married relatives, just like royalty do! At one stage there 120 people in the area had our surname, including twenty-seven women, and they were all first cousins. Then they even started doubling up on the christian names so we'd have to give them nicknames. There'd be old David, long David, new chum David, Davey of the Rosses, Bucky David. They gave their farms Irish names — Carrickfin, Coleraine — and sang all the old songs. There's still a lot of Irish descendants here in Kaikoura and round about, but we don't stand out in any way. We're just New Zealanders.

Your pen's running out. I always was a big talker!

Yes, now I'm remembering things I didn't know I remembered. They'd been buried. I sit here now on the sofa, I go off dreaming about the past and they come back, all the memories. One sparks off another; they're linked up like a train. Sometimes words trip me up — names of people and objects. I might forget "teapot" or something I'm familiar with. For the moment I just can't pick it up. I'm a bit vague. Today and yesterday, they're just on the surface, they go away easily. But right back, that's branded on me. And I want to pass it on to you; I've got that energy.

Why I'm so healthy? I've always been healthy. Never had a sickness in my life except for the mumps. The nature of my life did it; I wasn't the type to get excited about nothing. I was full of fun, yet always calm. You mightn't believe this, but I never ever remember losing my temper, and I've lived nearly a century. Yes, I've had a placid life. Mostly work. You had no entertainment; if you had any go in you at all you worked. And I was happy in it.

But now I'm the only one left of my generation. It's not a happy thing. There's no one I can talk to on the same level. You might say it's a bit lonely. Still, I've got a lot to be thankful for. The older I get, the more I pity old people alone, left with nobody. I don't know how they manage, especially the men, doing for themselves as well as being lonely. But the women get lonely, too. And it seems to be that always some old girl will rush up and help an old man on his own. They think he needs mothering or wifeing or something; they rush up with pies and puddings and things. Don't seem to do it so much for an old woman.

Then there's the old people who go from the country to the city, end up living in flats so small you've got to go outside if you want to change your mind! No, I like it here in the country — plenty of room, fresh air, fresh fruit and vegetables. I get up at half past 6 every morning, perhaps a little later in the winter. I'm awake and I want to get out. I've had a lifetime of it.

I'll be right again as soon as my eyes are done. I'll be jumping about like a lamb. Perhaps they made a mistake about my age!

WALLY

'They called me Barbed Wire Wally 'cos I'm hard to handle'

The locals at Havelock all said: "You should go and see Wally. He's a real character." There was fondness in their eyes and also mischief. I soon found out why. The first thing you notice about Wally is his sense of humour. He bustled me through the door of his cottage and straight into a tour of inspection of the wines and liqueurs he was brewing on the kitchen shelf and floor and all over the living room.

Wally was used to getting his own way; always has been: "You sit down and do what you're told girl and have a tomato sandwich."

We then inspected his poems, his plants, his family photos, all at top speed. We had many sessions and became buddies. Wally never hesitated to give advice: "It's no good being single. I want an invite to your wedding. I'll make up a piece of poetry and recite it." And always his sense of humour came pouring out — as he talked, as he jumped up and down checking the wine, watering the plants, brewing up tea and eats, quoting passages from articles and books. Wally had no time for people who were chronically serious.

Wally talked about all the jobs he'd tried, but the focus fell on his years at the Wakamarina goldmine and down the Sounds, scrub cutting. He reminisced and toasted his old mates, he philosophised and recited jaunty verses he'd written about them. But beneath all the banter was Wally the thoughtful and contented man, recognising his failings yet also aware of his contribution to the world. He was awarded the M.B.E. for his forty years of work with blind children, but Wally had no reverence for the piece of metal: "These are my real medals — the thank-you letters from private homes and institutions, wherever there's a blind kid I gave funds to."

Dylan Thomas had a philosophy about old age:

Do not go gentle into that good night.

Old age should burn and rave at close of day.

Wally was burning and raving.

They reckon I'm the oldest bloke around Havelock, the oldest original. Nothing wonderful about that. Nothing clever about living to an old age; you're just lucky. You've got to have something on your side. I don't know what it is, religion or what. I don't understand it. Some people go to church all their life, they're very good and they die young. A little girl walks out on the street and gets killed. An atheist lives to ninety. I can't work it out. All I understand is life is as it is. If you play the game and help other people and keep an open mind and trust in nature, you'll be all right. I reckon so.

I'm happy here in Havelock. I like a place where there's hills and water and bush and birds. You take someone out of Woolworths, they'd be no good here; they wouldn't survive. I've lived in plenty of big towns — Sydney, Melbourne, San Francisco, London. They're all right. They're beautiful: pretty buildings and museums. But the people, they've all got their noses to the ground; they don't look up and smile. You know nobody. Some old lady falls over in the gutter . . . people say she's drunk. Here in Havelock the kids would pick her up. You give me the country any time. You wake up in a town and you hear a bus rolling past. Wake up in this place and you hear the trees or the birds singing, a whole orchestra of them. Don't hear them in the towns. What've they got to sing about?

I was born here in 1900, in Fuchsia Gully. Went to school here, worked in the blacksmith's shop down the road, then in the Wakamarina goldmine way in from Canvastown, then in the bush. When the bush ran out and the mines closed down I went to sea. Sooner or later I met a girl — the natural thing, bound to happen. The birds were singing, the moon came up, next thing I was married and raising kids in Wellington and working on riggings for buildings or testing power stations. The years rolled along, then my wife died so I came back here to roost. Just like a seagull, I came back to where I was born.

In all that time I never worried about getting a gold watch. Other men get gold watches after forty years at one steady job. Good on them, but they'll die in a rocking chair. I liked taking on a job I enjoyed, then when I got sick of it I threw it away. That's what we did out here, those days. I started work when I was thirteen years old, had just left school. I more or less didn't leave school, just ran away; I hated it. I tell you what, girl: I learnt nothing at school. Teachers those days were stand-over teachers; they tried to drive education into us, and that didn't suit my nature. Ask me to do something, I do it. But I won't be driven.

So if I got the chance to wag, I wagged. There was no argument about it. Then later on in life I found I needed to be able to read and write so I could get a job in the railways, and that's what I did. I went back to night school and learnt to read and write, and to type and take shorthand as well. Learnt everything when I left school. Took a lot of guts, girl, going back to learn reading and writing, but I got there. I can write letters, compose poems. I have a go at everything; you've got to have a go.

My first job was sharpening picks in the blacksmith's shop here in Havelock. I was the striker. The blacksmith would get the pick hot, then tap on the anvil to show me where to hit with the hammer. I had to "draw" the pick out to a point again. Two and six I got, working six days a week. I was thirteen years old, but I was a man, going off to work. The other kids would be walking to school; I'd stand at the smithy door and smirk. I put everything into that job. . . .

I stayed there at the blacksmith's shop until I heard there was a job going at the Wakamarina goldmine — the Golden Bar we called it those days. It was a big mine at one stage there with a great, long fluming system bringing water from creeks six miles or so back in the hills and a big battery, stampers going day and night. The whole place would shake. And thump, thump — terrible noise, you couldn't talk to anyone. Then if the battery ever stopped at night we couldn't sleep! Go there now, you wouldn't think there was room for the whole outfit. Nothing but fern, blackberries and a few pine trees.

I went up to the Wakamarina when I was sixteen. I joined the team of about six men timbering inside the mine. Dangerous work in there; she caves in all over the place. She had to be timbered properly: props each side of the tunnel and one over the top, then stays to hold the roof up.

We worked hard — six days a week in those conditions for thirty-six bob; you could take Saturday off if you liked and lose a day's pay. So we didn't ever come out much; it's a long way, eight miles or so out to the pub at Canvastown. No trains, no buses or taxis, too rough for a bike, so we only walked out now and again, or got a lift with the butcher or the grocer who came up once a week.

I'd say there were about forty men altogether at the mine, living way up the valley there in huts or tents. I was in a hut with my mate Jack. He was a miner and a lot older than me. We had this system: he did the cooking; I did the cleaning of the hut and getting the wood in. Hardest job of the lot was getting the clothes dried — everything got wet through in winter. There's a lot of rain in that valley. Rains like hell most of the time in winter and it's wet inside the mine, too, dripping water all the time. What you had to do of a night-time, you had to keep the fire going all night to dry out the clothes for next day. Chuck a decent log on, that was the story; none of this flimsy stuff.

Blooming cold way in there, too. It got that cold of a day you'd be walking along in the sun and your shadow froze on the ground. Yes, my grandmother's Irish! But it was frosty as hell. The Wakamarina valley lies north and south, so of a winter's morning the sun would stagger up the eastern hills at 9 o'clock and by 3 in the afternoon he'd be dipping down behind the western spur. So the air had all that time to cool off, and boy, those frosts. There'd be icicles high as that table along the sides of the road. The kids would have sword fights with them. Then the north and south winds would funnel up the valley as well. But it didn't matter; you had to go to work.

It was all open fires up there — no stoves, no hot water. We heated up water over the fire and washed our clothes in a kerosene tin or a bucket, anything that was going. We just slept in blankets. No use having sheets; they got dirty. Couldn't see the dirt in the blankets. And we cooked with a camp oven swinging over the flames; cooked everything — goats, pigs, deer or mutton, all in the camp oven. Doesn't take long to learn. You get hungry; you soon learn to cook. We'd cook up a good feed at night-time — roast meat or stew, that was the standby, and if you made a stew those days you made it so's it'd last three or four days, and there'd be a bit to have on toast when you got up in the morning. Or else you had pork fat on toast for breakfast, with salt; boy that was good — beats butter on toast — and plenty of strong tea. You want tea with a bit of kick in it.

We'd take our crib into the mine with us: a cut lunch wrapped up in newspaper, cold meat, stew or bacon sandwiches and tea. Milk was a bit of a problem at times; no milk powder those days. We lived on condensed milk or a billy of real milk from a nearby farm if you were lucky. I'll tell you what was good: we'd get a slice of bread, spread condensed milk and raspberry jam on — beautiful. Good for hard work; good and sweet. We made camp oven bread, too — beautiful. I'll tell you what, if half these young kids today had a billy of goat or mutton stew and a hunk of camp oven bread — boy oh boy. You get a piece of bread today, hold it up and you can see through it!

We'd make dumplings, too, fried up in the camp oven. Buggers afloat we called them; Christ, they were good! And what the hell did we call the poached eggs? A pair of bastards on a raft, and we'd have tits on toast — belly pickled pork on toast. I still use those old names; everyone laughs at me. I like a bloke with a bit of wit about him. I can't work or drink or knock around with a bloke hasn't got a sense of humour. Complainers, hell, they upset me. I won't knock around with those jokers. And you must remember in those days if you could create a joke or put one across the other joker, that was thought a pretty good quality in a man. That was our entertainment; no radio or TV of a night-time. We sat in front of the fire and told stories and lies. Didn't matter if they were true or not, 'long as they were good yarns. We might visit one another, have a game of cards — crib, euchre, poker — then we went to bed. Nothing else to do, and most nights we were damn tired, we wanted to go to bed. No music except the odd mouth-organ, tin whistle or accordion. We'd play all the old ballads. *I'm Trying So Hard To Forget You,* that was our favourite.

Then sometimes of an evening we'd all meet up at the boarding house, right near the gold battery. We'd have one or two beers and play cards or hang around the maids from the boarding house, and there was a piano so we'd have a sing-song. There was always someone could play a tune. I used to, then my fingers went on me. Now and again we'd polish up the floor and have little dances. There'd be dance programmes with pink pencils, and babies in clothes baskets out in the supper room. . . .

Some of the miners lived in tents or huts like me, but got all their meals at the boarding house. Not me. Those blokes were either a bit lazy when it came to cooking up a feed, or they didn't like the style of living on their own. I liked it. Mind you, it was good tucker at the boarding house. Cost you one shilling for a big dinner — soup, meat and vegetables and pudding — two and six if you wanted to stay for dinner, bed and a big cooked breakfast of porridge, bacon and eggs, chops, toast and marmalade.

That boarding house was famous for beefsteak pudding, something you don't see these days. You'd get a pudding basin, line it with pastry dough rolled out thin, pop in the partly-boiled meat, cover the top with pastry, right oh. Then you wrapped the whole thing in a tea-towel, tied her up and boiled her in a pot. It's beautiful, girl. You can have all your flash food; if you haven't tried beefsteak pudding. . . .

You got good plum duffs over there, too — big fellows boiled up in a tea-towel — and bread and butter pudding. Good tucker to work on. Then if you wanted morning or afternoon tea it cost you sixpence and you got tea and scones, big yellow jokers with eggs in them — you don't see them like that today — and plenty of butter and raspberry or plum jam. Crikes they were good. And pikelets: they'd roll them up with butter and jam, like asparagus rolls; blimey they were good, too. You'd get about three of those jokers, you were right.

The boarding house also had a little store, sold a bit of everything: tea, sugar, boots, dungarees, stiff collars, china, kerosene, biscuits, drapery. And they ran a taxi, too, a 1918 Ford T. Those days if you wanted to run a taxi service you just went ahead and did it; no taxi licence, no car licence, no registration, nothing. That taxi got used mostly for taking the miners down to the pub at Canvastown, or to the three pubs over at Havelock.

Some of the miners went to the pub, drank till their wages were gone, then went back to the mine. They'd be fighting at the pub and fighting in the taxi on the way home, and the ones walking back up the valley would get half way, fall over, have a fight; some of them would still be in the ditch next morning.

But nothing to see now at Wakamarina, only blackberries and scrub growing over our old mining shafts. Don't you go walking around up the old mine, girl, or we'll never see this book published; she's puckered with holes up there. And nothing to see now at Deep Creek, where the township was. In our day there was a main street called Queen Street, another one called Camp Street, a hotel, courthouse, school, post office, hall, and there was also another township further up, at the Forks. Gone are the days. Nothing much happening in the valley now.

The Wakamarina was quite a small field, but the gold was always considered quite easy stuff to get. The nuggets were concentrated in crevices in the bedrock, and the word soon got round. Mind you, miners don't let on how much gold they've got. You don't talk about it until you've cleaned your lot out. You're a bit secretive, a bit suspicious.

You could say the goldmining was the spark that set the whole Wakamarina valley alight. The miners cleared and settled the place. The timber mills sprang up at practically the same time because the miners needed timber, but nearby valleys like the Rai were much slower and later developing because there was no gold in them. Then when the mines and mills started to fade out in the Wakamarina a lot of the miners and timber hands bought land there under the Government scheme.

That valley's also been a great place for people to come and be a recluse. All sorts of hermits lived up the gullies; never came out. They'd put a note for the grocer in the box at the bottom of the track. The grocer would come, never see them. They'd just leave their money there in the box; he'd leave their stores. Home was just a little bit of a shack. They'd cart sheets of iron up, one or two at a time, cut posts out of the bush, put iron on the roof and make an open fireplace at one end. That was it. Strong, tough men; you can't beat them. But you won't find many city types can understand why they lived like that.

I'll give you an instance. One old miner lived way up the valley. He might come out to Canvastown once every three or four weeks for stores. One day a local bloke and a city type were watching him putting his stores into his sugarbag, struggling to shoulder it and walk off up the track, eight miles to his hut. The local bloke said: "You know, that chap has to carry his tucker eight miles into the bush before he reaches his camp tonight." "Gosh," the city type said, "couldn't he eat his food without carrying it all that way?" No understanding.

A lot of those old jokers got bronchitis or pneumonia types of things when they got old so they'd be sent off to a hospital somewhere. First thing the nurse would do was give them a bath, then put them to bed by a big open window. But those old chaps just couldn't stand it; they'd been living all those years on tobacco and strong black tea in old, damp whares, black inside with smoke. Put them in a bath; they probably hadn't had one for years. Then put them by an open window; they'd get a chill quick as look at you. Many of them died within a week or two. Good thing, really. They'd be out of their element away from their whare and their old way of life. They'd never be happy.

We liked listening to their stories. They'd be full of tomfoolery, but they'd be worth listening to. Like old Jack: he always used to say that when the first possum poisoning came in he saw a weka pick up a poison bait. Down it went. But then it flapped its wings violently and two wekas raced up, got his wings in their beaks, picked him up and worked him backwards and forwards. They were working the poison out of the bird's system, like a drunk man working out his beer. We listened to those stories for their humour, but there'd also always be something in them.

In a place like this everyone's a character. You take the old miners, chewing tobacco and smoking a pipe at the same time. Old Paddy Flaherty, he could do it. They always reckoned he could spit and kill a blowfly twelve foot away. Old Paddy's teeth were always as black as coal, from chewing tobacco. That much is the truth, anyhow.

Then there was old Charlie Pickering. He was a well-educated man, a real gentleman, but he was a character all right. He lived with his big family, way up the hill behind here and later on in the Sounds and up the Rai. He was like a gypsy, but different, and he was definitely eccentric; he'd have people on at the drop of a spanner. Tell you what he used to do. Instead of buying a pipe he'd hollow out a carrot, fit a straw in and smoke that. Whether he was having people on in the pub and that, I don't know.

Then he had his own special method of stumping. It was always a big job to get rid of tree stumps around here and they'd get in the way when you were ploughing. So what old Charlie would do, he'd dig a few holes around the stump with his crowbar and drop in some dried peas. His pigs would get the smell of these peas, they'd keep rooting and rooting till there were none left and wasn't long before the stump was rocking on its foundations and old Charlie could just push it over. That was his own idea; beat having to buy gelignite! Then you might see him riding up the road on his bull, just like anyone else rode a horse. No saddle, just a bridle. All the kids would rush out and climb the fence to see the sight. Yes, and laugh like hell. But it made sense. He had to have a bull because he had dairy cows so it was practical thinking; he only had one animal to feed, and he could ride it as well!

If Charlie had been a young man today he'd be a great inventor of something. I don't know what, but I'm picking he would have been. He was always thinking things up. Whenever he went away from home he'd put his valuables in a milk can and a swarm of bees in with them; he left it to the bees to do the protecting. It took a brave man to touch those valuables. Then he concocted his own water system. Nowadays people lay water pipes. Charlie had nothing like that, but he'd have water running to his house, water running uphill, water running everywhere. And he put a fence around a big paddock — great big poles about fifteen foot high. No one knows how he fitted those poles and got them up there on his own, but he got them up. His purpose? No one knows. Old Charlie could quite easily have been a spaceman. Those types are gone.

His job? He did all sorts. You ask me what Charlie didn't do, that'd be an easier question. But tell you one thing: see how they've drained this harbour? Well Charlie started to do that seventy years ago, with a shovel and a wheelbarrow. He was going to reclaim it, but the tides and floods beat him, and they've only now got round to doing it, what Charlie started seventy years ago. A very clever man, that one. When I was a young bloke I used to sit and listen to him. He had visions of things: what members of parliament and heads of nations should have done at the time, that sort of a thing. When I look at it now, we'd have been better off if we'd taken his advice. You couldn't beat him on world affairs. I don't know where he got it from. I think he must have been a deep thinker at some time in his life. All his family were brilliant, too — businessmen and that. No duds among them.

You'd be surprised what Havelock has produced. Lord Rutherford went to school here and also William Pickering, the nuclear scientist who's in the States now. An uncle of mine, born over the bay, was world-champion cyclist; he won the world title in Salt Lake City in about 1920, won the New Zealand road race and the Australian road race before that. We've also had the world title cross-saw pair, a champion wood chopper, top boxers, all from Havelock and the Sounds.

Me? I've always kept fit. Played all sorts: football, boxing, everything. I'm not a New Zealand champion at anything, but I had a go at it all. We were always on the go when we were kids. Lived in the hills and mountains and in the water, knew nothing else. Soon as we came out of school, first thing we did was dive into the water. No swimming baths. Swam in the drink: sea, creeks, river, whatever you felt like. I can live anywhere there's hills and water and bush and birds. Missed all that in Wellington, all those years; but I've come back to it. I'm in my element here. It's freedom. One stage there a chap and me took out a claim in Snow's Gully. Worked there nearly two years, prospecting with a pan and a sluice box. We didn't make a million, but they were good days — crikey yes. Out there is freedom. It's the greatest thing in the world, freedom. Someone says "politics", "unions", "Muldoon", "inflation", you don't worry. The world can go by.

I think that's what kept me out of jail, freedom. It's too good, this kind of living. I'd die if I was locked up. For a feeling of peace, what's better than sitting in the bush of an evening and listening to the birds, or sitting by a stream. I could write poetry all day about it. To think of all the worries I had in the cities and this was all here, all along.

In Wellington I had a three-bedroomed house, a car. When my wife died I walked back into the house, no one there. So I said, I'm going back down to Havelock, and look at me now — all I've got's a bed in the living room, a kitchen and a wash-house. That's a big come-down to some people's way of thinking. Not to me; it suits me down to the ground. I've got no worries in the world; my kids are all doing all right, I've got plenty to eat, plenty of mates. If you go through life and end up with no money but a good bunch of friends, you've got wealth, and I've got that.

I haven't got anything at all in the bank; I put my money in the post office bonds, then if I win I give it away; there's plenty of charities to give your money to. I give mine to the blind. I got known as the organiser of the Mayor of Thorndon Blind Kiddies' Appeal. Did it for forty years. See, I was blind for eleven months myself; a bit of machinery blew up in my face. I know what it's like to be blind. Eleven months soon teaches you. Got the M.B.E. in the end, for helping the blind kids for forty years, but medals don't mean a thing. I get two to three hundred letters of thanks a year, those are my real medals.

We'll have a cup of tea now, girl. You have a couple of slabs of this fruit cake. An old lady here in Havelock makes it, another one brings me scones, another one pikelets. They all come up and see me, the old ones. They come up for a yarn about the old times. They like it because the young people can't talk about that.

Mind you, people chuck off about the young people today. They're all right; they're just different from what we were. They're not hopeless. It's the world that's hopeless. Easy to say: "Why don't they get out and work like we did?" We *had* to work, because if we didn't work we weren't fed. Every family was on the breadline; no social welfare, no dole, no domestic purpose this and that.

But the women were great women those days; they worked damn hard — washed clothes in half a beer barrel, chopped wood, made all the bread and butter. I've seen my cousin carrying two four-gallon pails of water on a yoke on her shoulders, uphill from the well. Hard yakker for a woman, living those days. If she had a family and then her husband died she'd pretty soon have to find another man to marry. Feelings didn't come into it; it was simply common sense, and she'd take the first decent offer that came along. No way she could make a living alone. She could grow some vegetables, but vegetables take some time to grow and the kids would be dead by then.

One good thing, though — those women had a great feeling for cows, and there's the old saying: "If you've got a cow you can feed your family" — plenty of milk, cream, butter and cheese. Somehow they got along well together, women and cows. The women were by far the best hand milkers. And cows were so easy to keep. Even in the days before there was much grass about the cows could look after themselves in the bush; five-finger is remarkably good cow food.

No frills at all in life for anyone, those days. No money, no electricity, no radio, no chewing gum. I was nine before I ever saw a banana or an orange; got them for my ninth birthday. The silent pictures came once every two or three months. It was all excitement. You'd hear the kids scream: "Look out, he's behind you." Everyone went; cripes it was good fun. Then the circus came once every eighteen months. That was *big* entertainment. You didn't want anything more, didn't know anything different. Once you turned thirteen or fourteen you got a job, in the mine or the timber mills, perhaps fencing or fishing. We didn't question it; what else was there except hard work? No McKenzies here in Havelock.

After the three years in the goldmine I could see it was soon going to pack up so I went off scrub cutting. I'm a horizon man; there's always something just over the horizon. I'm not too keen on anyone telling me what to do, couldn't stand being regimented. I'd be no good as a horse! And that's why I never ended up being a fisherman. I had a go at it because I liked being on the sea, but no, if I'm not the boss of the boat it's no good to me. So after the goldmine I went off cutting bush in Pelorus Sound, way down Puketea and Garden Bay — takes you three hours in the boat. You go down there and you don't come out for two months.

I was right in my element down there — plenty of birds and water, plenty of fish. We got pretty hungry, working up in the hills. Tough job, that scrub cutting, but once you're used to it you're right, and I'll work hard, long as I've got good mates and good tucker. We always cooked up plenty, too right girl. The owner of the property gave us half a sheep a week as part of the contract. We'd walk four miles over the hill to get it, and into the camp oven she went, roasted, fried, stewed, anything. Tons of fish, too — blue cod and snapper. If you were the cook you'd knock off at half past 3, get the fire going back at the camp and put the tucker on. Then when the other two came home at 5.30 we'd eat like mad. Only got supplies in once a fortnight on the mail boat — if the weather was right, that is — so'd make yeast out of spuds and cook up big round loaves of bread in the camp oven; cooked up all sorts.

If anyone got sick we had to walk four miles over the hill to the farmhouse, but you didn't see many people sick those days. If they did get sick, generally that was the end of them. Today people get sick all the time, but it's not surprising; they eat tinned stuff and instant this and that. No, we were rough as guts, but we were healthy. And I like roughing it; that's my life, no one's rougher than me. I'm not too keen on that drawing-room business.

As for entertainment, one day I remember a bloke on a fishing boat called in and told us there was a dance on at a settlement five miles away. That night me and my brother tied our good shoes around our necks, got the old hurricane lamp and set off down the steep track to the dance. Got there at half past 8, knocked on the door and found everyone in bed. "It's next week," someone

yelled out. So we had a cup of tea and walked the five miles home.
No, we didn't go again the next week! That was our outing.

We were used to making our own entertainment anyway. George
had a Jap fiddle, a one-stringed fiddle with a horn attached to it
— I've never seen one since — and he could sing, too: all the
old English songs like *Goodbye Dolly, After The Ball Was Over,*
and what the dickens was the other one? *Only A Bird In A Gilded
Cage.* Songs those days were so descriptive; they told a story. Today
they've got no words, just a few lines repeated over and over. Then
I made up songs and poems. That was entertainment, too. I can
make a poem up anywhere — the old back country-style poems.
I could make one up on you.

I wrote a poem about the scrub cutting at our first camp down
there at Puketea bay. Take a look at this:

> *Gather round you chaps and I'll tell you a yarn*
> *When we pulled tawhina, down on Harris's farm.*
> *Well from Havelock we sailed one mid winter day*
> *And we pitched our first camp in Pukutea bay.*
> *We made up our bunks the best way we could*
> *And piled up the fire with birch and beech wood.*
> *For months we put up with hard work and poor grub,*
> *And now I'm wasting my money at this pub.*
> *When I came to town I was healthy and strong*
> *But my health, like my money, won't last very long.*

I sat in the old Masonic Hotel at Havelock and I wrote a whole
poem about that scrub cutting. I'll fish it out and recite the whole
darn thing for you. It's what you'd call a memory. But then when
we'd cut out all the bush and scrub I disappeared from the area.
Had to go away; the mills and mines were closed down so off I
went to Wellington. My first thoughts of Wellington? Ask yourself.
I wasn't very impressed. But, you stick your finger in the fire, you
get used to it — like marriage. I adapted. I think I could adapt
to anything; I could become secretary of the mother-in-laws' picnic!
Put it this way, I didn't hate Wellington. Only two things I ever
hated in my life were school and caraway seed cake. Mother used
to make it all the time and I just can't eat it; I'd starve rather
than eat caraway seed cake.

Funny you turning up like this. It's taking me right back to the
old days. And I like going back to the past; I could write poetry
about it all the time. I go into the pub, the blokes are talking about
scandals. I turn it back to the old days and the yarns and jokes;
that's what I like. In a place like this, if you can't take a joke you'd
better shift to Blenheim. You walk into a room, someone'll have

a go at you. No use being a prude, and no use being someone you aren't.

Tell you what, I'm an official Bastard; a member of the Australian Order of Bastards, registered in Sydney. Here's my membership card and my number: "Wally Townsend, Grand Old Bastard", that's what it says. We're a real registered outfit with a list of qualifications. The marital status of your parents is irrelevant, but your drinking habits must be hearty and jovial. What happens is this: if a Bastard comes into a pub and slaps you on the back and says, "Hello, you Old Bastard," you've got to produce your membership card. You can't say, "I'm not a Bastard". You've got to admit it, and if you can't produce your card you're sunk; you've got to shout for him and any other Bastards in the room. I got caught once; didn't have my card with me and it cost me seven dollars. Never again. And you can also be reported to the Arch Bastard of even excommunicated. I tell you, we're higher than the Masonic Lodge or the Catholic church!

Why I'm interested in the whole thing? All the money goes to charity. Last year we got $47,000 through membership and donations and fines. Costs you three dollars for life membership and you get fined for this and that, or you can make donations and buy badges and key-rings and things, to prove you're a Bastard. A cop might pick you up, but if he notices your badge he might let you off. We have our rules! And we're everywhere, us Bastards; you've got to be careful, got to carry your card. There's not many Bastards around here, but I've nominated two. You don't ask to join; you've got to be nominated, and you've got to be someone who's done something. We've got everything from a boxer to a priest. I know an Italian opera singer who's a Bastard, a sergeant of police, a priest and a high-up solicitor I know is nominated; he should have his card any time now. Some pretty prominent people are Bastards and we're all proud of it; it's an honour.

Tell you what, I'm going to nominate you. We have all different sorts: Rotten Bastards, Stupid Bastards, Right Bastards, Arch Bastards; you've got to rise up through the ranks. Nearly every publican in New Zealand and Australia is a Grand Old Bastard, like me, or an Arch Bastard. I'm near enough to one of the founding members. I've been in it damn nearly fifty years. Twenty-six years I was president, at Johnsonville Workingmen's Club, and I'm a life patron now. But I'm not an Arch Bastard yet.

I like all that sort of thing, people having each other on. I like to keep things on the go. No wonder they always called me Barbed Wire Wally, 'cos I'm hard to handle.

You sit down and do what you're told, and have a tomato sandwich.

I haven't got much of a place but I always have plenty of good tucker. When you're old you've got to look after yourself. Those old jokers who live on bread and jam, they don't last long. I've got pickled pork on and there'll be new potatoes, new peas and beans. You've got to keep active, too. If you sit in a rocking chair in front of the fire, your brain goes. If you sit down and don't mix with people and don't take any notice of kids, you'll die off. I get plenty of visitors: family, friends, the local kids. The kids love coming here; they all call me Uncle Wally. I make cakes and toffee for them and pikelets, scones, soft drinks, all sorts. They're not allowed to wreck the place, but they can feel at home here. You've got to be easy-going; once you get regimental in life you've had it. I'd say one of the greatest words ever coined is tolerance. Then comes love.

Yes, I'm happy here. I've got everything I need. All I want is one of these books, when you get it finished. You might be able to knock up a bit of a story out of all this. I'd say, if you can go through a life like mine and end up happy then it's all worthwhile. I'm not religious, but I still think I must have had someone on my side, somewhere along the line.

It's away from the world, of course, here in Havelock, but it's freedom. And I don't care what Muldoon and Thatcher and the oil kings are doing. I like to live simply, the way nature intended it, and I've got to be near the sea; don't mind if the mudflats stink. This is peace, down here. I think even the people in the cemetery are happy, here in Havelock.

STAN and VERA

'She's the best girl
I've ever had'

I answered their "Come in" through the open door of their cottage in Springfield, at the foot of the Alps, and there they were in front of their coal range watching telly — an earthy, no-frills old couple in their mid-eighties. As Stan explained later: "It worked out well, us two. There's not much we haven't done, the two of us together."

Stan was a dog-trial man, a musterer, a hard case, proud of his wife, his eleven grown kids and his reputation as a hill country man. He was well organised and used to being in charge. We kept jumping up and down to inspect his dog-trial trophies and certificates, photos of his dogs and his huge vegetable garden, still thirteen-in-a-family sized.

Vera sat with her feet up on the sofa, her white hair coiled up in a bun, new loaves of bread cooling on the bench. She had a habit of leaving the talking — and the limelight — to her man. But she warmed to the chance to air her feelings about birth and mothering and death: "We knew nothing at all about birth control. One stage there I thought we were getting too many children; we had six and we couldn't afford to look after any more. So I asked the doctor what I could do. 'Oh, nothing you can do about that.' *That's what he told me. So I had five more."*

Stan was surprised at Vera's outpourings: "You know, she's not a talker as a rule. She's told you things she hasn't told me."

At each of our sessions I experienced the humbling feeling of being in on a discovery. They were exposing things to one another, as well as to me. And we were all learning from it.

41

Stan: Tell you what, girl, if you have as good a life as we've had you'll have a good one, and a lot of fun, too. Vera, she's the best girl I've ever had. It worked out well, us two; we fitted in together. Vera liked anything that came along. When I was out felling gorse she'd be raking up. If it was haymaking she'd be out there, too. Then when I got in cows we'd be out milking together at 5 o'clock in the morning. There's not much we haven't done, the two of us together.

I'm a back country type. I liked it in the hills, but I was actually a town boy, born in Christchurch. When I was fourteen I went off to the hills, off to work at Kaituna out near Akaroa. Why I took to the farm life in the first place? It was the only place I could get a job. Milking cows. Earned ten bob a week, working from half past 4 in the morning till 7 at night, milking 140 cows between three of us boys and the manager. Milking your own cows is all right; milking for anyone else isn't. And I always wanted to be a shepherd so I went off to Double Hill station at Hororata to learn shepherding. That was my first real taste of the back country and hell, girl, I liked it. The back country was my life from then on, till I left it to come here to Springfield and start farming on my own account. We were out in that back country for thirty odd years, me and Vera, working around all the stations. You get to know those hills; they become part of your life.

Vera: Even today he stands and looks out the bedroom window every morning. He looks and looks at Mt Torlesse.

Stan: What I'd like right now is a horse and a dog, and I'd ride up in the mountains. It gets in your blood, the back country — the air and the sun. I've seen very special sunrises on the snow. You're up there 6,000 feet above the smog, the sun comes up and it's beautiful. All that, for nothing.

I met Vera out the back there at Mason Hills station in north Canterbury, when we were both twenty-three. I was the shepherd, she was the cook; we had nothing else to do but fall in love.

Hell, at this rate you'll know more about me than my mother does.

Vera: I also started work when I was fourteen years old, just like Stan. I had a job doing housework and cooking for farmers. We really had to work, too. I'd get up at 6 o'clock, make a cup of tea and take it to the master and mistress in bed. Then I'd have to cook breakfast for everyone — the family and the working men — a big breakfast of porridge and bacon and eggs and toast. Next would come the washing up and baking scones for morning tea, and all the cleaning: doing out all the fireplaces, scrubbing floors and tables with scrubbing brushes and sand soap, washing and ironing and starching. Then after every meal I'd have to clean the knives and forks and things, with powder on a board. The cutlery wasn't stainless steel those days, so it'd rust; and there'd also be all the silver to polish every week. Everything had to be perfect, not a speck of dust anywhere. The old coal range had to be cleaned out once a week, too — black leaded and polished. That was a whale of a job. I did practically all the cooking at that place. Now and again the mistress gave a hand with the fancy stuff for visitors, but the rest of the time she just did a bit of sewing, a bit of gardening and entertaining.

They had a little four-year-old boy, too, and I had to look after him most of the time, entertain and feed him and take him to the beach three afternoons a week. Just me doing all that work, except for some help with the washing. It was all done with a washboard and a bar of soap, too; no washing machines and Persil. The sheets and all were done on that board and put through a hand wringer on the tub. Everything had to be just so. All the blankets had to be washed once a year, all the tablecloths and that had to be starched and ironed with the old Mrs Potts iron on the stove. You'd spit on it to see how hot it was; if it sizzled it was ready. Then you'd have to rub it on a cloth wiped with candle-grease to make it clean and smooth; a real carry-on.

I had to wear a uniform: a holland dress in the mornings — fawn sort of stuff made up into a dress; and in the afternoons I had to have a black dress with a starched apron and hat. I hated that, having to wear the uniform and take in afternoon tea to the lady visitors — rich fruit cake and scones and pikelets. You know "Upstairs and Downstairs" on the telly? That's what it was like. They were wealthy farmers; I was the maid. The farmer fancied his house girls, too. Not me! He was frightened of me. I always had a stern look, so they all said.

Stan: I was frightened of her, too. That's how she got me.

Vera: I'd finish up at 7 or 8 o'clock or later at night, when I'd done all the washing up. I'd be tired out. No time to sit down all day, and I had bad feet — they'd sweat and ruin my shoes. And all that work for seven and six a week, with only one afternoon off. In the end, after I'd been there five years, they were paying me seventeen and six. But times were hard. They couldn't afford to keep me on and in the long run they had to sell the farm and move away. The little boy pined for me for months.

From there I went to a nursing home in Waimate and earned two pound a week, cooking. Big money, that. Joves, I'd practically forgotten all this, till you came along. Then I moved on to cooking at the Waimate tearooms, and on again to cook at the hospital. Two pound ten a week I got there. I thought I was wealthy, and it was easy work as I had two other girls to help peel the spuds and that. I was still just a teenager myself at that stage, but I'd been out working for all those years. I've spent all my life cooking and washing and mending.

Stan: I'll tell you the best joke I ever heard. When I was courting Vera up there at Mason Hills, there was this rule: the shepherd wasn't supposed to go out with the girl of the house. So she'd sneak out, I'd sneak out and we'd go for a walk of an evening. The master would be spying around, seeing if anyone was out. One night there we knew he was creeping around — we could hear his old torch whirring — so Vera ducked inside. I didn't have time to hide so I jumped in the meat safe. I was crouching in there with the roasts and shanks and that, scared to breathe. The old boss knew something was going on; he knew I was there somewhere. He waited around for half an hour, but he couldn't work it out. He never ever guessed I was in the meat safe.

We're bits of wags, us old high country ones.

Courting those days? Hell's teeth. You'd take her for a walk of a Sunday evening. You walked to church, you walked up the hill and sat in the tussock. No such thing as cars and going to the pictures and this and that. Just walking and canoodling.

I'll leave you two to it. It's beyond me, this sort of thing.

Vera: You didn't expect to be taken anywhere; never thought about those sorts of things. And we never thought of flatting or living together and that. I think that's gone too far, myself. Some of them live together for two or three years and then they turn around and get married: a big ceremony, fancy clothes, the lot. It's a joke. And a good lot of them don't last after they're married; there's such a lot of unhappiness. Any theories why? Well, they want too much I suppose. Don't expect to work hard. Money problems. They're not mature, live together too young. I feel sorry for kids today, actually; they don't have the fun they could have.

We had eleven of a family, me and Stan — two sets of twins. We were pretty darn innocent about babies and sex and birth control and things. I didn't know anything at all about sex when I got married. It was all sort of a forbidden subject. Parents didn't talk about it; your husband didn't talk about it. Even things like periods, you didn't talk about them either. It was all hush hush. I remember when I was a young girl I had a terrible pain. The chap I was working for said I just had "the women's complaint" and gave me half a cup of whisky. I'd never had alcohol before; it hit me hard. The smell of whisky today makes me ill. Anyhow, I knew it wasn't my period causing all that pain so I rode five miles to town on my bike, up and down hills. When I got there my appendix burst. It was touch and go for four or five days; they didn't know whether I'd live. Burst appendix, that was a big operation those days. Certainly not "the women's complaint"!

Today the kids know all about periods and sex and that long before they've left school. Better? I don't know if they're better off or not. It's taken as a matter of course today, sex. It's nothing special at all, doesn't seem to be sacred any more. But at least they know what's what today; we just had to pick it up as we went along.

Stan: It just came natural to her, the kids, no trouble at all. The day the babies were born she'd be out working, burning gorse or something. Then she'd go in to the nursing home at night. It was all in the day's march, just like the ewes in the hills.

Vera: I wouldn't go and see the doctor till I was four or five months pregnant, then I wouldn't see him again till after the baby was born, if then. The nurse delivered all but one of my eleven babies. You didn't worry about doctors those days. Both times I had twins the doctor didn't know; but I knew — I could feel them. Ever worried things mightn't be right? I just accepted it. I never got into any difficulties having the babies. I didn't rush things and I didn't worry. I've wondered, but never been afraid. You just didn't talk about birth those days, even if you *were* afraid. And the men got as far away as possible.

Our old grocer used to come round. I'd be there one week, nine months pregnant. Then next week there'd be another baby in the kitchen. The old grocer would say: "Oh, I didn't know you were having a baby." No one noticed, only the woman having the baby. You didn't talk about it at all. Then you had to farm out all the other children to relatives and neighbours when you went to have the new baby. Couldn't leave them at home with the husband; he wouldn't know what to do. Did you ever change the babies' nappies, Stan?

Stan: I don't remember. . . .

Ever there when they were born? No. I didn't hold with that business. I've seen animals in distress, giving birth. I wouldn't want the memory of seeing my wife in that distress. That's what I feel about it. Put it this way, girl: if I saw her in that distress I wouldn't want her to go through it again.

Vera: That's the idea of it! We probably wouldn't have had so many if you'd seen what I went through each time. But I wouldn't want anyone around, definitely not.

Stan: You've learnt a thing or two today, girl.

Vera: So have you!

My first baby was born in 1924, last one in 1947. I spent twenty-three years having babies, and then how many years rearing them all. . . .

Stan: There were six, then a gap of five years, then she decided to have another go. But she wasn't satisfied with one; she had five more!

Vera: I'll tell you what really happened. We knew nothing at all about birth control. Even if you asked your doctor he told you nothing. One stage there we thought we were getting too many children, we had six and we couldn't afford to look after any more, so I asked the doctor what we could do. "Oh, nothing you can do about *that*." That's what he told me. Didn't even explain about the monthly cycle, when it's safe and when it's not. So I had five more children.

Talk about it with Stan? We didn't those days; we just didn't talk about it. Stan's mother used to say: "Poor Stan, another baby," as if I was the one to blame. And no "Poor Vera".

Stan: You know, she's not a talker as a rule. She's told you things she hasn't told me.

Vera: Yes, if I told you, you'd know everything about me. I'm the strong, silent type. And I was that healthy, the babies just grew. My first one was born in July. There was frost and snow all over the ground. I remember my granddad had to take me to the nursing home in the horse and cart at three in the morning. The horse was slipping all over the place, trying to keep its feet. The baby was born at three in the afternoon — a big nine and a half pound baby. Funniest part of it was hearing a couple of the nurses there talking about babies. One says: "It's a funny thing, Vera's baby came in the afternoon, but most of them happen in the middle of the night." "Well," the other one says, "that makes sense. They're

usually started in the night. And that doesn't say much for Vera."
Imagine me in bed at 3 o'clock in the afternoon!

Yes, I just went on having babies. I was forty-seven and my oldest
boy was twenty-two when the last one was born. So that boy was
away from home and working; he hardly knew the little ones.

We used to wonder at times how we'd manage to look after them
all. We were pretty hard up, but they never ever went hungry or
barefoot. The Plunket nurse always used to say they were the best
babies around; they were solid, healthy kids, very contented. They
never looked flash, but they were well cared for. We'd make toys
out of nothing at all — hockey sticks cut out of the gorse hedge,
that sort of thing. Makes a good stick, gorse, if you can get a piece
with a bend in it, and manuka's good, too; and you'd find an old
fruit tin for a ball. Our kids' footballs were always pigs' bladders,
blown up; they lasted ages and ages. Then they'd get great fun
out of an old hoop and a stick; they'd just make the hoop themselves
out of an old bicycle wheel. Or they'd make bows and arrows and
shanghais, or rag dolls.

Stan: Of a Sunday she'd take them out shooting, for a hare or
a rabbit. She could shoot like one thing, Vera. You see, girl, she
had a terrible lot of time on her own when I was out mustering.
No telephone, nothing. If anything went wrong she'd have to walk
thirteen miles to Mt White station with the kid on her back. We
had this system: I had to report in to the station every Saturday,
unless someone had seen me during the week. If I didn't report
they'd send someone out to see what'd happened.

No, I never failed to report. Only time I ever got myself lost
was in Christchurch, last Christmas Day. I never got lost in the
mountains, even in the fog; I had bush sense. And the dogs have
a natural gift. If you've been to a hut or a camp once, the dogs
will get you back there all right. If you're caught out at night,
girl, you don't say anything at all to the dogs; you just let them
wander along in the dark. They'll get you there.

Lochinvar was one of the most isolated stations around. It was
run together with Mt White. Beautiful country, you could ride sixty
miles from one end of it to the other and one stage there they
shore 40,000 sheep. No one in there at all now, at Lochinvar; a
lot of it's national park. And Mt White's a different cup of tea
altogether, only about 12,000 sheep and it's all fenced up. In my
day there'd be sixteen or eighteen permanent men working at Mt
White, and in winter they'd be out boundary riding, keeping the
stock from going too far. There's none of that now.

Lonely? No, I was never lonely. I always had my horses and

dogs, and I was always interested in what I was doing and what I could see. I liked it way out there. From Lochinvar I moved over to Grasmere station; I was head shepherd there for eighteen years. It's all changed now as far as I can make out, that back country life. In my day everyone worked in together for mustering and that. My headquarters was Grasmere, but I'd go from one station to another, leading the mustering, from Craigieburn to Flock Hill, Castle Hill, Avoca — all over that area. And I'll tell you something pretty surprising, girl. When I first started mustering, our dogs got fed only twice a week. The boss gave you a quarter of a sheep twice a week and you had to share that up between your team of dogs. They work pretty damn hard, too, those mustering dogs. Takes a lot of believing, that, doesn't it, girl? Nowadays dogs are fed pretty well every night.

Us musterers worked pretty hard, too. We shifted camp each day, moved on till we got back to the station with the sheep. We had a packer who carried our bed-rolls, cooked our breakfast and a meal when we got in at night. Our main fare was mutton, spuds and rice — all good, wholesome tucker, but the same thing over and over again. No veges much, out at camp, and no porridge. You'd get a couple of greasy chops at three or four in the morning and a hunk or two of bread and butter and tinned jam. At night it'd be stew and spuds, and now and again a bit of plum duff. But there you are, I was quite happy, I work best on mutton.

You just slept on the ground, out mustering. Some places had huts, but most of the time we were just in tents, and no such things as sleeping bags. All we had were canvas bags; you opened them out and put a couple of blankets in. Mustering's a very different thing these days. They go out in a Land-Rover, come back to the homestead at night. And they don't cover the big high country we used to muster. Half of it's been closed up, with erosion and that. They reckon they're resting the country, but it's still eroding. A lot of erosion is done by wind, rain and frost. The deer and rabbits have done some damage, but not as much as some of these blokes'd have you believe. I'd say the worst of the erosion has been caused partly naturally, by the elements, partly by poor management — stupid burning, in the wrong place and at the wrong time of the year.

Jove, I liked it out in the hills though, girl. Now'n again, I'd be camped out at Cora Lynn for ten weeks at a time on my own, at lambing time. I was a whale of a lot happier looking after myself than having other chaps up there with me; I was too fussy about keeping the hut clean and tidy. I'd even clean my boots every morning, polish them up. That's what I'm known as: the musterer who cleaned his boots! I'm a bit of a crank, I suppose. But it was just my way of doing things. I'm a perfectionist in everything: my dogs, my garden. My wife? Yes.

Vera: Yes, I had to come up to scratch. I'd have been kicked out years ago if I wasn't tidy.

Stan: Lots of those musterers were pretty rough and ready; it's surprising how dirty they get. No need for it. I'd tell them, "You clean the hut up." Same thing with my clothes: they had to be just so. I'd get in the creek, wash myself down, wash my clothes and socks and hang them on the bushes.

Then after shearing I'd be way up there at the back of Grasmere, boundary keeping. Just me up there at 5,000 feet looking after the sheep, spreading them out each day through the basins and gullies. Mind you, nowadays you wouldn't be allowed to have a man up there by himself; if you had an accident there'd be no one to help out. It's a law now, there's got to be two men on the job. Same thing at Lochinvar: I wouldn't be allowed to go away and leave my wife by herself for a week or so at a time.

Vera: Didn't worry me, though. I was fairly realistic, didn't get frightened. I accepted Stan would be away a lot; he had to earn the money to keep us all. Meant more work for me, of course. I was like one of these solo mothers, rearing the children, cooking, milking the cows, feeding the pigs, chopping wood, looking after the garden.

Stan: We always had to have a terrible lot of vegetables growing, to feed all those kids. There'd be cabbages, caulis, carrots, spuds, peas as high as that mantlepiece, pods four inches long. We grew them all, even way up at Lochinvar. Vera had a great garden going up there on the edge of the bush. I diverted a little creek. That helped things along, and I had to fence it off from the wild goats and pigs. But other than that, things just grew quite happily way up there — no Maxicrop and sprays and that. My wife can grow anything; she puts a stick in the ground and it grows. No wonder we've got all these kids!

Vera: I was a jack of all trades, master of none. While we were at Grasmere the women from all round would come and ask me for help with their babies and miscarriages and things. Or I'd walk over to the Cass railway settlement in the middle of the night and help deliver babies.

Stan: We'd have dances at Cass, too, in the railway kitchen. Everyone from round about went along, in the horse and buggy. You'd wrap the baby up in the horse cover, to keep it warm, then you'd get on with the dancing and beer and supper. People think we had no fun those days; we had real fun. We were all one big lot. You danced with every woman in the room and you knew all the old dances — waltzes, one steps, lancers, valencias, square dances, alberts. Nowadays you don't really dance; just shuffle around and cuddle one girl all night, don't you?

Mind you, a fair bit of the time we were living too far away from anywhere and just didn't see anyone. We might be six to twelve months on a place without going to town. Might go over the river to see the neighbours. You'd run your dog against their dog, the women'd have a yarn and swap recipes and that. But you didn't go anywhere else.

Vera: That's something I think about now. I had no time for myself. We had to work all the time; didn't make any friends. Comes to now . . . we're old, we've got plenty of friends, but nothing really close.

We just had to keep going, working. Many times we had nothing much in the pocket. We didn't even have a buggy, just a horse; we were lucky to have a wheelbarrow. Stan and me never ever bought anything unless we could pay for it, and we've kept to that. We didn't have a car till late in life. Paid £100 for it, secondhand; a Sunbeam Talbot, a beautiful car. I made all the clothes for the kids on my old Unity treadle sewing machine — got it in 1925 from the Farmers' Trading Company in Auckland. Cost five pounds and got delivered free on the boat, but we had to save and save to get it. It's still out there, still goes well. I don't like those electric ones. And it did all sorts, not just clothes; I'd make cow covers and double sacks for sleeping bags and musterers' oilskins. The old Unity did the job.

Then during the Depression all our clothes were made from something else; you cut down one dress, made something else from it. We never threw anything away; still don't. If there's something wrong, I mend it. I never ever had a washing machine till I had my seventh child. Just washboards up till then, and carrying water from the tank, lighting the copper, stoking her up, boiling the whites.

I've spent a lot of my life sewing and washing and cooking. On those back country stations I'd have to cook for the shearers, too; that kept me going. It went on for weeks and weeks those days, the shearing — up to six weeks when we struck bad weather one year there at Grasmere. I'd be cooking for about twenty men — shearers and rousies, musterers, station hands and cowmen — and all I had was a wood range.

You'd be at it all day, that cooking. If Stan was going out to muster in more sheep for the shearers they'd be up at 3 o'clock for breakfast; chops and eggs and toast. On an ordinary day the shearers would be up at 5 o'clock for a cup of tea and a rock cake or a bun, they'd do a run before breakfast, then it'd be chops and eggs at 7 and tea, sandwiches, scones or rock cakes for morning tea at 10. Everything had to be exactly on time, at shearing. Then came dinner at midday — mutton and veges and pudding — afternoon tea at 3, and another big meal at night — cold meat or stew, fried potatoes, scones and rock cakes. I don't know how they worked with all that food inside them. Then came supper, at 8 o'clock!

I had just one child that year. I'd pen him up a bit, but he'd wander off after the men or get in the water race and I'd have to change all his clothes. One day he went in three times; he was mud all over. Yes, I was ready for bed when I got there.

Stan: Mind you, we were lucky to have a job those days, during the slump. A bad time, that. I was head shepherd on a sheep station, with a wife and five kids, and earning one pound a week. Then when the slump got really bad they couldn't even afford to pay me that much, so they had to let me go. I'd get a day's work here and there. I'd go up to a lady who had a rest home for invalid children: I'd beat the carpets for five bob (no electroluxes those days!) or I'd split a load of wood for five bob, or climb up forty feet and top pine trees and split them up for firewood, for eight bob a day. During the slump you'd crutch sheep for four bob a hundred. Now what do they get? Well over forty or fifty *dollars* a hundred. Then if you were unmarried you might just work for your tucker, no pay at all.

But today? I was watching four jokers down the road here the other day; they were supposed to be pruning trees for the council. But most of the time they were breaking bottles and chipping a tree with a knife. They were getting $150 a week for playing around like that. My conscience wouldn't allow me to do that; I'd have to do a reasonable day's work. This paying people to do nothing is no good.

But those slump days in the '20s and '30s, they sorted us out all right. I remember there were big gangs of men building the ramp for the Bealey bridge, over the Waimakariri river. That ramp was built with wheelbarrows and shovels, two men to a barrow, taking turns wheeling. One penny a barrow load, that's what they earned; the very best men could earn eighteen bob a week. They came from all walks of life, those men. There were teachers and bank clerks, all sorts. Just lived in tents down on the Klondyke flat; there'd be snow and frost on the ground in the winter. Some mornings up there I've seen boots all frozen you couldn't get into them. You'd have to get a coal from the fire, wrap it in a piece of sack or something and poke it into your boots to thaw them out.

As for the big snows we had, like the 1918 snow, it was up to the top of the fences. I remember it well. Flock Hill lost 2,000 sheep in that 1918 snow. All sorts can happen. I've seen sheep held up in the snow so long they start eating the wool off one another's backs. They get that wild and desperate, they actually gnaw at one another — and the wool's no good for them, binds them up. Then the keas get after them. . . .

You get to know about the snow and clouds and winds and that, living in the hills like we've done.

Yes, I've been in this area a long time, shepherding these hills for nearly sixty years. Then we got a small place of our own here in Springfield and milked cows. Started off with two cows and Vera set up a milk round; she'd go round on a bicycle with two gallons of milk. The women would come out with their jugs and she'd deal it out by the pint. Twopence a pint, that's what we sold it for, and cream for threepence a half cup. It was really good cream, too, not like the stuff today that looks like milk when you pour it. We'd make butter, too, and sell it for sixpence a pound, and sold eggs for eightpence a dozen. We even made our own cheese, both the soft type with caraway seeds in it (the German type of cheese) and also hard, round cheeses. Then we'd get salmon down the river and bottle it; keeps for years and years.

No fridges, nothing. But we had our own system of keeping things cool; we'd dig a hole in the ground, make a box, set it in the hole and fill up the gap with cinders or charcoal and sprinkle a bit of water over. You'd just put your butter and cream and milk and stuff in the box, close down the lid and it all stayed sweet as a nut over the summer, so long as you threw a bit of water over the cinders every now and then. The cool box, that's what we called it. Joves, I didn't think I knew as much as this about the old days.

We lived off the land, me and Vera and the kids, and had no luxuries. Had to be self-supporting. The hippies are doing it nowadays; some of them are doing it quite well, too, and they'll teach the others. I think before too long the world will turn back again to the old ways of doing things. Then gradually we built up the cows till we had thirty in the end and were delivering sixty gallons of milk a day. Our son's taken it over now, and it's one of the biggest milk runs in the South Island. He picks up the milk in Christchurch at 2 in the morning and finishes by about 10.30.

How I feel living on the flat after the hills? It's all right. I can look at the high country and go up there for a drive. I miss the hills all right, but I'm done for it now.

Vera: I'm better in the back country, too. I'm not used to towns and shopping. I get near shops and I forget what I want; not used to it. I'm used to growing things, making things. We even made our own candles; had a stand that held a dozen moulds and you'd put the wick up the centre, tie it up, pour in the melted fat and let it set. Take it out of the mould and there's a candle. They used to smell a bit, but we couldn't afford the wax candles. Our kids don't believe we had to do those sorts of things, but it was a regular job. Made all our own soap, too.

Now? I don't mind doing all that old-timer stuff, but it's not necessary. And half the time it costs more to buy the materials than it costs to buy the thing, ready-made. Even bread, it's a toss-up whether it's cheaper for me to make all our own bread, but it keeps better. Can't stand this bought town bread — it's too soggy, not cooked thoroughly. It's just whipped through the oven; it sticks to the roof of our mouths. We have a job to eat it, Stan and me. I always bake bread twice a week. I've done it for fifty-eight years anyhow, ever since we got married and went up to Lochinvar.

I've just baked a couple of loaves; we'll cut into one for lunch. But flour today's not what it used to be. When I was a girl we always grew a patch of wheat and the flour we got was good flour, properly ripened. But today they don't let the wheat ripen; there's still moisture in the grain so the flour's not so good. I don't think so. Bread and buns and cakes and things certainly tasted better with the cured flour we had. We'd make beautiful yeast buns five inches high or so. The men used to call them "half acre buns"; you'd split them in four and butter them.

The butter isn't as good now, either. I don't know whether we're getting pure butter or not. You don't know what's in it, do you? It doesn't bake the same, anyhow.

It's hard to change over to the new ways of doing things. It's even taken me a long time to get down to cooking for just the two of us, after thirteen. I still make too much, but then if anyone comes there's enough. I still use our coal range in the winter-time; it makes better bread and cakes and I like it for meat. But coal's getting very expensive. The electricity's cheaper in the long run.

I keep on saying this, but it's the truth: I was always working, cooking or washing or making something. But you're far better if you're working, doing something all the time like we were. I used to think it'd be nice to be able to sit down. Now I wish to Christ

I had something to do. I can't knit any more, my hands are gone and I spoil the wool. I've still got my garden, though, and the telly. I've got bad knees, don't get around the garden terribly well, but as long as I'm left alone I'm all right.

Stan: That's why we're still going strong, us two. We're always doing something. People round about ask our kids: "How is it your dad is always so well? He never seems to get any older." They say: "He's always interested in something, always doing something." I find things to do every day, interesting things.

My main interest all along was sheep dogs, for mustering and for dog trials. I've spent a whale of a lot of time training dogs. All these cups and championship certificates here and all those trophies in the china cabinet, the crockery and stuff, are from the dogs. I got Champion Dog in New Zealand twice over, with Ben and Roy; there's Ben up there in that photo.

It's been my interest, dog trials, but it's been more than that. Don't know how we'd of managed wasn't for the dogs. We'd be wondering how we were going to feed and clothe all those eleven kids, then I'd go to the dog trials and win some money. Yes, I *had* to win. Got twenty pound for an open event. If I didn't win I couldn't go, what with the cost of entry fees and travel and that. Then when you're winning you sell your pups well, too — four pound or so apiece.

Yes, you could say they've been a big part of my life, dogs. Each year we had a big dog trial here in Springfield, a whole week of it. It was a really big occasion, the dog trials. All the women looked forward to it, got a new dress and that. All the shepherds and musterers came out of the hills — plenty of booze and high jinks. Every house with a spare room had someone staying in it.

There'd be dog trials all day, then a do at night. One night there'd be a smoke concert, men only, smoking and drinking and telling yarns; one night there'd be a ball; one night presentation of trophies and a dance. You went to it all. You had enough for a while after dog trial week. For the ball the ladies got all dressed up — long dresses and gloves, the works. We'd dance till daylight; the wooden floor of that old hall would really shake. Ashley Atkinson'd be there on the piano and Ned Rogers on the violin and old Cliff Smith, he'd play the concertina. You've missed a lot, girl; you can't have the fun today that we had. We loved dancing, me and Vera. We won dancing competitions together. Wouldn't think so now, would you?

Vera: Stan was very light on his feet. All the ladies wanted to dance with him. But he always danced with me in the competitions. Yes, he was a perfectionist at dancing, too. We won the waltzing competition several times; got a prize of some sort — a box of chocolates or hankies or a tie.

Us local women always used to cater for the meals at the dog trials, too. We'd have a great big open fire, outside, to boil up stews, potatoes, swedes and carrots and that in great big pots. I'd have to stand and stoke the fire, keep things going. There'd also be a big copper boiling up the water for tea, and we'd have scones and pikelets and sponges and things. All the puddings we made at home and took over — apple pies and jellies and fruit salad. We'd set it all up on tables in a big tent, serve up the meals and make a bit of money for plunket or the church. Nowadays there's a great big building over there for the catering, a range to cook on, tables and that inside. And then again, people have cars. They come in the morning, bring their lunch with them and go away again in the afternoon.

Stan: Yes, they bring their dogs, they run them and away they go. That's the sort of thing we miss a lot now, us old timers, the social part of the dog trials. They only go for two days now, the Springfield dog trials. That's it, finish. And it's a different life up in the back country stations. The musterers and shepherds all have cars. They can come out at weekends or whenever they want to. It's not the social event of the year any more, the dog trials.

There was one old musterer from Waikouaiti, way down south, he always came up to our dog trials. He could swear for twenty minutes and never use the same word twice. One day he was going well, showing off all his words, but only thing was there were two ladies painting nearby. The poor ladies were embarrassed. They started kneeling down, and in the end they were *lying* down so no one would see them. They were hearing too much to want to be seen. But then again, if they were well brought up they wouldn't know what he meant, would they?

There were plenty of characters about the place those days, girl. Another well-known dog trialist was old Frank. He had a very good dog but he'd get very drunk and spoil it all. One year he made a bet that if you went down to Christchurch and put an Indian Runner drake on the river bank near the Bridge of Remembrance, his dog would stop it from getting in the river. So he did it; he got his dog to work the duck just like he'd work a sheep, and it couldn't make it down to the river. But the SPCA got hold of old Frank and took him to court. The magistrate told Frank that the case was a clear one: "The dog bit the duck." But old Frank stood up for his dog. He told the magistrate just what he thought:

"If that dog bit that duck, that bloody duck bit that dog first." The magistrate then turned round and fined him ten pound for bad language!

I'd say not many around now would remember Frank; he's dead long ago. A lot of us old musterers are gone now. I'm one of the lucky ones who's survived through it all. We're not that ancient, me and Vera. We're in our eighties, but we never expected to live this long. When we retired from the farm we were pretty well worn out. Thought five to six years would be all we'd do.

Vera: We were seventeen years on the farm; never had a break except when I was in hospital for a few weeks and he had a tractor accident and got put in hospital, too. That's the only holiday we had — if you call it a holiday! We were pretty healthy all along; didn't have time to be ill. Biggest problem was toothache — a terrible lot of people had rotten teeth those days. Only the wealthy people could afford a dentist, and no such things as dental nurses; our teeth just weren't taken care of. I never ever had a toothbrush till I was fourteen and went out to work.

Stan: Same for me. Then I had all my teeth pulled out when I was sixteen and got false teeth put in. Terrible thing, eh girl? But couldn't afford them till then. Cost me ten pound to be knocked out with chloroform, to have all my teeth pulled out and another set made, and I've still got those bottom ones, too. The top ones got cracked in a fight, so I had to get them to put a new lot in.

Vera: I lost all my teeth when I was twenty-eight. We all had rotten teeth and terrible toothache. You'd see people going around with their faces puffed up, or rubbing pain-killer on a tooth, or cloves or iodine or salt — anything to try and stop it. Many a time I walked the paddock at night; couldn't sleep for toothache.

Stan: Or you'd haul the tooth out yourself, with a pair of pliers or a string tied round the door knob. Sometimes you broke the tooth in half. You'd leave it there as long as you could and it'd go rotten.

Vera: I'd say dental care is one of the greatest improvements I've seen in the world. Kids today have beautiful teeth. We just had to do things the natural way. I never ever had any make-up, just soap and water.

Stan: She's good looking the way she is.

Vera: No shampoo, just Sunlight soap. Then we'd get some rosemary or camomile from the garden, pour boiling water over, cool it and use it as a final rinse to make your hair shine. My hair used to be curly, but it went scraggy and straight with all that feeding of the babies.

I would say we've had our ups and downs in our life, me and Stan, but nothing dreadful. Long as you stay in your own category you're all right; long as you don't try and be something you're not. My aunt always used to say: "Don't be a poor copy of a great person. Be yourself and try and become somebody." You've got to stay at your own level and do your best there. Some people like to climb up and up. But we're just what we are, me and Stan. If people don't like us, that's all right, too.

I'm going to tell you something. I've never ever envied anyone. Never. And I never wanted anything I couldn't have. I'm just content to go along the way I am. One thing, though, I'm not good at conversations and going out amongst people.

Stan: Yes, but she's been a hell of a good girl. A great partner.

Vera: Not good at talking. I think a lot, though. Yes. And I keep coming back to that thing: what's the sense of striving, longing for things you haven't got. Our children's attitudes different? Yes, but we don't interfere. They were brought up out here in the country with good, solid country values, but some of them had to go away, to work. If they need help we can give it. Otherwise they're on their own.

And that's where this women's lib business falls down. In a certain way it's all right, but they're going a bit far. A lot of married women are going out to work, to get things they yearn for but don't really need. Luxuries. It means their kids are neglected, too. And it also means there's a terrible lot of young people unemployed because the married women have taken up the jobs. That's happening even here in Springfield. In a time like this it shouldn't be allowed. The country's got to turn round and pay all these young people the dole; it's just no good. I don't see how the country can improve that way.

Stan: Phew! We've never had anyone put us through the mill like you have, girl. I'll tell you something that'll amaze you. My mother and father couldn't read and write, couldn't sign their names. They couldn't help me with homework and they'd make a bit of a joke of me when I was trying to read books. Then if you got three mistakes in your spelling at school next day you got the cuts; the girls, too. I'd be out the front reading. I'd get to the big words and I couldn't say them properly — I'd split them up wrong. The teacher would whack me with the cane and all the kids would laugh. It's been a handicap all my life, not being able to spell.

Vera: I got my proficiency all right, when I was fourteen, which was pretty young. But those days only the wealthy kids went to high school, so once I was through proficiency I was sent out to work.

Stan: Anything to do with my hands — woodwork, painting, drawing, writing — I was tops. But reading and spelling, they were a nightmare; still are. If I can't spell a word I use two or three little ones instead. Still, I've had a lot of rewards in life — breaking in dogs, breaking in land. I can look back and say "I did that and did it well." That's a way of life, isn't it, girl?

Vera: And we've been very comfortable here in this wee cottage. The likes of this old-fashioned sofa of ours, it's very comfortable to lie on; you can really sleep on it. And our coal range and old wireless. See, I don't believe in waste, turfing out old furniture and buying new stuff just because it's more modern. Then some of them are frightened to use all their new things. I call that show.

You can't realise the way the world's changed for us old-timers. We're from the age of chopping wood and growing veges and feeding cows on the road when the feed got short; grazing the long acre, that's what we called it. It's a big jump to computers and calculators and things; you'd think the brain would give up. It's confusing, all the scientific stuff. We haven't even had the telephone on for long, only about fifteen years. It's very handy — and very expensive. You start talking on the tolls and you don't know when to stop. And me and Stan don't understand the new measures. I just stick with the old way, for baking and that.

No, we're quite comfortable here in this wee cottage. I can't look after things quite as I used to, but long as they're clean. . . .

I'd like to die here, working away. Old people's homes aren't for me. I never want to go there. You see some people get lonely living on their own, so they go into a rest home and they just lose their identity. Actually, I wouldn't like to live with any of the family, either. I wouldn't like them to have to look after me. Old people get cranky; they get their own little ways of doing things. No, long as I can crawl around, I'll be here in Springfield.

Death? It's never worried me, death. I've no fears of it. It's nearly come two or three times, but I've missed. They found me not so long ago here on the sofa, unconscious. I was nearly dead. I remember I was up in space somewhere. People were standing there, holding me down, and I was fighting, fighting. The doctor said I'd had a stroke, but it wasn't a stroke. And I wasn't dead out; I didn't know what was going on, but I was fighting all the time. Seems I wasn't ready to die just then.

No it's never worried me, death. Sometimes I think about the others here, how they'd manage. Once I was unconscious for three days, and I wasn't fighting at all. I remember Stan came down and grabbed hold of me. He said I wasn't to die. The family still needed me.

Stan: Yes, we needed her. But it's the one thing you can't shirk, death. It comes; that's all there is about it. You can shirk everything else, not death.

Vera: We're getting on though, me and Stan. A while back our kids and their kids all decided to have a get-together for my eightieth birthday. There'd be 120 or 130 of them, if they all came. We've got forty-six grandchildren and twenty-something great-grand-children. So I decided not to have it; it'd be too much, the accommodation and that. We'd over-run Springfield! I said, you can have one when I'm ninety. I won't be taking much part in it then, will I? Yes, true, then there'll be more great-grandchildren to cope with! Some of them are just down the road at Oxford and that; some are away in Christchurch or the North Island. Some we haven't even seen; they're way over in Australia.

Stan: You think about them. Not much you can do about it.

Vera: We could take a trip. But then I don't feel up to travelling. I can't walk long distances and I can't stand about. Don't think I'll have to worry much about my ninetieth. . . .

Stan: Phew! Your pen's nearly run out, girl. And I'd better go over the shop and get you a new writing pad. If anyone told me a young lady was going to come in and get us two talking like this, I'd say nonsense. I think you're a bit of a character, getting a fellow talking this much. You know more about me now than I know myself.

GEORGE

'A masterpiece of understatement'

George was, quite rightly, dubious when I first turned up. Who was I? What was all this for? Why him? And we had to arrange further sessions around his work at the library, his gardening, his bowls.

But George warmed quickly to our talking. He loved to tell stories, approved of my "adventure" as he was an exceptionally spirited man himself, and he liked my dog. Above all, he loved laughter. He wanted to expose the funny and the ridiculous, the quaint side of the old days. He loved to have someone on. He tested me at our first session; I was far too gullible for George.

He was a city man, an executive in a mercantile and coal company in Christchurch, but he was also drawn to the mountains. He loved too the challenge and clamour of the new inventions of the day: motorcars, trams, trains. George responded passionately to the drama of modern transport: "No Warrants of Fitness those days, no parking meters, no locks; no one would steal your car because no one could drive. You didn't have to know any road rules — there weren't any!" He described with great gusto one of his early motoring trips, up the Waimakariri River: "We took three cars up the Waimak, from the Bealey hotel up to Carrington hut. Delinquency you'd call it today."

George was just into his eighties, brown and wiry and very active. He waved his hands about a lot as we sat talking on the verandah of his house at Sumner, where he'd lived with his wife since 1945. He thought very fast, talked even faster; it was tormenting trying to capture in note form his flow of tales and quirky comment. But George's knowledge and experience, spiced with his wry humour, were far too precious to be ignored just because I couldn't keep up.

George, I have done my best to recapture the flavour of your remembering.

I started driving a motorcar in 1917 and I ran into trouble straight away — got fined for going too fast, twelve miles per hour. The ticket says I was guilty of driving a motor car "at a speed in excess of eight miles per hour, to whit estimated at twelve miles per hour." That's what it says. I don't know how the policeman estimated it — no radars and things like they've got these days. And I'd be had up for dawdling today.

Anyhow, the policeman brought the summons around and off I went to court. I was just a schoolboy, fifteen years old. I thought the magistrate would look down and see my bare legs and be lenient on me, but he didn't even look up; just fined me. I was that annoyed. Fined me two pound plus ten shillings court costs — a lot of money those days. I didn't have that much money, so they sent the Lincoln policeman around to arrest me for not paying the fine. That cost my father another three bob travel cost for the policeman!

You didn't worry about drivers' licences those days — all you needed was a certificate of ability. Cost you five bob and lasted forever. I'd had my certificate of ability about a year at the time of the fine; all you had to do was fill out a form, tell them your age and that, then the county clerk took you for a bit of a test. No oral or written questions; you just drove around the block, stopped and started a few times and put her in reverse. Then for the hill test you went down into a shingle pit and had to drive up again, a total climb of about thirty foot. Half way up you had to stop and re-start, then drive on out. If you could do it you were thought competent to drive up hills.

You didn't have to know any road rules — there weren't any! All you had to do was keep to the left, for your own safety, and look out for traction engines and animals. Car lights were very dim and poor those days. Wandering cows and sheep were the biggest problems on the roads; there was nothing else on the roads . . . so few cars to get in the way! If you hit an animal on the road you just took it home for tucker — that was an unwritten rule. Half the time you didn't know who it belonged to anyway, and it was tidier than leaving it on the roadside.

Then the steam traction engines were a real hazard at night. You didn't see them, with the poor lights on the cars, and you couldn't hear them because cars made a lot of noise those days and there was the din of the wheels on the shingle as well. So you'd run into the back of the traction engine; lots of people did. One thing, though, you could watch out for hot coals falling out of the fire box and onto the road. They were very useful as they told you there was a traction engine ahead.

The policemen controlled the traffic as well those days — no traffic officers about except for one in Christchurch later on, in the early 1920s. McIntosh, he was the sole traffic inspector; it was quite a while before they got a second one. But I remember McIntosh all right. I had a motorbike at that stage and I was riding along, one brother in front of me on the petrol tank, one behind me. It was illegal here in Christchurch to have a passenger on your bike; not illegal in Wellington. Daft, isn't it? Well, I rode round the corner and straight into McIntosh coming out of his gate in Hereford Street. He put up his hand to stop me. I said, "What's the matter?" He said, "You ought to know boy." He took my name down — spelt both my Christian and surnames wrongly — and brought the summons around to my dad. The local policeman had a look at it and suggested, "I wouldn't accept this summons if I were you; it's incorrectly spelt." So nothing was done.

Later on it became legal to have one passenger on behind, but those old motorbikes . . . no real gears, just one belt gear, and you pushed her down the road to start her. And roads those days! Even on the main south road you couldn't go fast; it was all shingle and dust. If a car passed you had to slow down to let the dust settle or you couldn't see where you were going. Then every couple of miles you had to slow down again for a water race; there'd be a white post to show you where they were. If you went through at twenty miles an hour you'd break the springs.

Driving at night was quite hazardous. All you had were acetylene headlamps and kerosene side lights — parking lights you call them today. You had to light both sorts with a match. The acetylene lights faded out pretty soon; you didn't get much light, so no one went too far at night.

Most of the rivers and creeks had no bridges. Only the Waimakariri and the Rakaia were bridged on the main road south; for years and years you had to ford the Selwyn. Even in the 30s, if you were going over to the West Coast from Christchurch there were no bridges after the Avon until you got to the Taramakau. You spent half your time in the rivers, being stuck in the mud and soft shingle. You'd always take along a heavy hammer, a crowbar and a block and tackle to get you out of the rivers. Then when there was heavy rain you couldn't travel at all.

But driving was hell of a lot more fun than it is these days. Cars are ever so much better now, but they're just a means of getting from A to B — no fun at all. In our day the getting there was the thing. And it was like the old horse and cart days — you had plenty of time to think about things as you went along. You could see things so much better, too. You were way up in the air. You saw over the hedges and fences.

Old open cars; you kept the hood down unless it was raining hard, always wore an overcoat. We were used to it. And you always carried a tin of water because the cars would boil now and again on the hills, and you *always* had a tyre repair outfit with you. It was unusual to go thirty miles without getting a puncture; the wheels and the roads were both pretty substandard. You'd simply all jump out and mend the puncture on the spot — put on a patch with rubber solution just like you'd patch a bike tyre — and off you'd go again.

Yet we'd do some pretty courageous trips in those old cars. No motels or camping grounds — we just pulled up at someone's farm and they'd let you pitch your tent, or we'd pull in to the side of the lake and move in with our tent, even at Queenstown. You'd be fired off the place today.

Yes, those motor trips were all action, from start to finish. In my youth we took three cars up the Waimak, from the Bealey hotel up to Carrington hut; twelve miles, straight up the river bed. No road, no track, nothing. Our first attempt was in 1938, in a Ford motorcar we bought for five pound. It had no registration and no brakes, so we had to sneak up in the dark so no one could see us. Then on the steep bits on the way up to the Bealey we had to get a hand from one of the other cars. We'd tie on a rope so we could pull back and stop the Ford running away on us — a safety precaution because the Ford had no brakes . . . not much else either.

The Ford only got about a mile up the river from the Bealey. The clutch kept slipping — everything was slipping — then the whole outfit caught fire and the hood got burnt off. We reckoned it'd suffered a lot in depreciation after that; it'd be worth only about thirty bob. So we took off sufficient parts to recover our five pound, then we pushed it over the side of the road, between the Bealey and Klondyke corners. We did it just as the train was coming up the river. There must have been a reporter on board as a few days later we read in the paper: "Some unfortunate young men lost their motorcar over the bank up at the Bealey. . . ."

Next time we tried to get a Dodge truck up the river, in 1939. The brakes worked this time, but it wasn't registered, so once again we had to sneak up at night. Got a long way with the Dodge — ten miles up the river; only two miles from our destination, Carrington hut. At that point the magneto ignition got wet and we stalled. Got her out with a rope. I got the mag out, dried it and put it back in, but I timed it incorrectly and the vacuum tank caught fire. I can see it now. We had all the cartridges for our guns on the floor and they kept exploding. We had to get out of it, up into the bush until all that business finished. Then we dragged the Dodge up to higher ground and came back in two weeks' time to get it. When we got there, nothing to be seen. The river had risen and changed course, took away the car and the trees and all the country they were on. So that was the end of the Dodge.

But we were back at it by Easter 1940. We bought a Buick three-seater — an expensive car; cost us eight pound because she was registered so we were able to drive her up to the Bealey in daylight. She went beautifully, too. Took us two days to get up to Big Bend, with all sorts happening en route, of course. The carburettor would get full of water, but that didn't stop us. I'd just take it out, tip out the cockabullies and off we'd go again. Only held us up a couple of hours. Anyhow, then we had to stop in mid river to shift some boulders, and the car wouldn't go again. Petrol tank was empty! We were eight miles from the petrol station, four miles from our destination.

We walked back to the Bealey hotel, bought two gallons of petrol and one gallon of beer and did the eight-mile walk back to the car on the one gallon of beer and the next four miles up the river on the two gallons of petrol. Got within sight of Carrington hut and what happened? A stone went through the crank case and we stopped dead; we walked back out to the Bealey. That was the finish of our motoring experience up the Waimak. The car was up there at the hut for years, too. The wind polished her up and she looked like new, until the larrikins shot holes in her. Finish.

All this might be a bit in the paddock. Some of the details might be a bit out — the dates and miles and things. But it's all within the boundaries, the general gist of it. It's not romance. I did a movie film of it. I've got forty foot of film recording the three attempts — that shows I'm the real thing, doesn't it? Mind you, everyone thought we were mad, but they got used to it. I've been doing mad things all my life.

And we thought it was the height of modern living to actually *have* a motorcar; we were real pioneers. I remember when we finished having a horse and gig and got a motorcar, in 1914 or 1915; it was an outstanding event in my life. Everyone turned out on the road to see you whizz past. You might get up to twenty miles an hour — a terrific speed for a road vehicle.

I can clearly remember the horse and cart days, though. Having a gig was a sign of real progress; you were getting on in life you had some land to put a gig on! And it meant you didn't have to walk everywhere, or go by tram or train. When I was a boy we'd get out the horse and cart or the dray and go off for a picnic. We'd throw in some sandwiches and a bit of chaff for the horse and off we'd go, all our family and quite often other families as well.

The Selwyn river twelve miles away was a favourite spot. It was absolutely in its natural state — no ice cream stalls, no lavatories, nothing. We'd spend two hours getting there, then we were left to our own devices. Father would swim, mother would read, us kids would tear around climbing trees and building rafts out of logs lashed together with binder-twine. Then we'd jump in the river — no togs, no towels. We'd have a swim around and lie on the bank, then we'd put our trousers on, light a fire and cook up some sausages. Drank river water, or boiled up the billy and made tea. Very simple living in those pre-car days.

As for the old trains . . . you wouldn't ride in them these days. All there was to sit on was a long seat along the side — no upholstery, just a hard, horsehair pad to sit on. In the smoking apartments there'd be spittoons on the floor — round wells nine inches in diameter, with little trapdoors opening down onto the track below. The smokers would give a spit into them now and again.

Just wooden floors, no lino and gas lamps to read by. Heating? None. Only things we had were foot-warmers — little contraptions eight inches long, eight inches wide, four inches deep and filled with some sort of chemical. They'd stay hot for two to three hours, and when you came to a station like Timaru men would come in, take them all away and bring on new ones. They'd put the old ones in a big trough of boiling water to heat them up again; took all night to get them up to their full temperature.

Then there was the dining car on the train. In the early days before the First World War you could get a lovely roast dinner and pudding for one and sixpence, or two bob if you wanted soup as well. Otherwise, most people took along a vacuum flask — thermoses you call them nowadays. The stations didn't have tearooms, not until they took the dining cars off trains during the first war and built big tearooms at the stations. Then there'd be a real bun-rush; a heck of a lot of people travelled by train those days.

66

The express used to have fourteen carriages, all chock full. Now there's only four carriages on the Southerner. You didn't have to book — just turned up, and no one ever got turned away; you just all squeezed in. The guard came round to punch the tickets. Threw you off at the next station if you didn't have one. Or if you didn't buy a ticket at the station and bought it off the guard on the train it cost you sixpence more.

Then there was the slow train that carried more goods than passenger carriages. You shunted at every station; took a whale of a time to get anywhere, 3 hours to Ashburton. A real world of its own, the old railways. And the steam locomotives would shoot out coal dust, cinders and ashes. They'd come into the carriages if you left the window down, and you half suffocated in the tunnels. Then when they were pulling hard up the hills they'd put on more coal. That'd send out more sparks and they'd always be setting the ripe crops alight along the sides of the railways.

I even remember the old horse-drawn steam fire engines; they were a great thing. The city council horses would be hitched up to drays all round the place, doing other council work. When the fire bell rang they'd be unhitched, the men would leap on, tear off down to the fire station and hitch them up to the engine. A man would be there shovelling coal in the engine to get a good steam up and off they'd go, the brass chimney belching out flame and smoke. Us boys loved seeing it. I remember the big 1908 fire in Christchurch; Lichfield, Colombo and High Streets all got burnt out. I saw the steam engine roar in and put the main fire out, but there were sparks and smouldering for three weeks afterwards.

And there were the old excursion trams. I remember there'd be a special excursion tram from the Square to Sumner at 10 in the morning during the holidays. There'd be half a dozen steam locomotives, each one pulling five double-decker trailers. Same price upstairs or down — sixpence return — but if you were upstairs getting the view you also got cinders in your eyes from the funnel. But it was very popular, going on the excursion tram. Sumner was a resort place those days with weekend baches, merry-go-rounds and helter-skelters. You'd have a real day out — take a picnic lunch, buy some hot water and make yourself a billy of tea. Nowadays Sumner's just a part of Christchurch city. You go way up to Hanmer or over to Akaroa for a day's outing.

I clearly remember the first electric trams they ran here in Christchurch, in 1906. That was one of my first memories ever, my father taking me to see the trams and watching the sizzling of the wires on the double deckers and the sparks flying off the wheels as they bumped against the shingle. They seemed like great big flashes of flame. The tram board had big tankers — horse-drawn carts loaded up with tanks of water and going around spraying the road to lay the dust, and they also got used to damp down the tram tracks, especially in north-west weather. It was a big industry all right, watering the roads and tram tracks. And there'd be a man walking along the tram lines with a shovel with a spike on the end, pushing the stones out of the grooves on the line so the tram wouldn't derail.

Yes, it was considered a very revolutionary thing to have, that electric tram system. People wrote letters to the paper saying the trams were dangerous, we'd all get electrocuted. And they wouldn't use the electric power from the first Government hydro scheme at Coleridge; they thought it was far too risky. So you see, I've lived from the horse and buggy days to the jet age.

How we'll be getting ourselves around in the future? Don't know. But I think it'll be some sort of personalised air travel. I think it's time we got rid of these great big buses running around with no one in them. And those great big 747s — the Wright brothers could just about hold their whole flight in one of those things! But all this fast travel, it doesn't make us any happier. Mind you, I don't think we're born to be happy. Life is supposed to be a struggle, but we're trying to do away with the struggle and get someone else to do the struggling for us.

I've always been an active type myself. In the olden days I did a lot of cycling, from one end of the South Island to the other. Then I always had a motorbike. Got my first one when I was sixteen — a very good one too — a one-speed Triumph with a single-cylinder and belt drive. Cost me fifteen pound. . . .

You could say I was a real outdoor type; I liked it out in the hills. As a kid, before I ever went near the mountains, I used to look at the map of Canterbury on my wall and it struck me there was very little plain and a hell of a lot of mountain. I wanted to go and see those places. Well, I can say I've seen a lot of those hills. I got to the top of Mt Cook anyhow, in 1933. There were nine of us in three parties, the biggest party ever to be on the summit. I was the first man ever to take a colour movie on the top of Mt Cook. Those damn cameras were heavy too, those days; long before we got to the summit I was wishing they were sandwiches.

Nearly killed ourselves on that trip, too. We were going up the summit rock and the rope between me and the chap above me got cut clean in two by a falling rock. Hard to believe, isn't it? I heard the whizz of the rock, and there was our rope, in two pieces. Damn lucky it never hit any of us, and lucky I was actually standing still when it happened. The slack of the rope hadn't been taken up, otherwise we'd have been a gonner. The rope was just a whole lot of ragged ends. We tied them together and off we went again. Never thought much of it at the time, but it was a near miss when you look back on it.

What got me into climbing? This chap Edgar Williams talked me into it. When I was still a boy Edgar used to come out to see my mother, and one day he suggested me and my older brother climb Mt Torlesse with him. Nineteen nineteen it was, when I was sixteen years old. We thought it was a terrible thing to do — pushbike for three hours and then all you had was a cold, steep mountain. Anyhow, I borrowed an ice axe and puttees and a pair of long pants. I was still a schoolboy; you didn't have long pants those days until you left school. The three of us loaded up our bikes and off we went. Camped the night at the base of Mt Torlesse, and the next day we went to the top.

It was the coming down that got me. Edgar said: "We'll glissade down now, George." That was my undoing, the glissading. I got out of control and went tumbling over and over, down the slope. I was damn cold and frightened and nearly crying. I took my coat off, shook out the snow and down we walked to the camp. "Enjoy the climb?" says Edgar! I told him, all right: "No one'll ever get me to climb any higher than a bed from now on." And we pedalled home to Christchurch. My father asked how our trip was. Old Edgar says: "George was okay, except he fell over and got covered in snow." Those were his words. I thought that was a masterpiece of understatement. Old Edgar Williams, I went to his funeral yesterday. . . .

Anyhow, that was the start of my climbing in the mountains. Next year I went up Mt Torlesse again, and I've climbed it thirteen times since.

What kept me at it? There's always a new horizon, always something fresh to see. I liked it out there in the wilds. A friend and I walked the Milford track one morning — right, one morning! We started out at half past 2 in the morning, got to Glade House at quarter to 2 in the afternoon, caught the steamer, steamed down to Te Anau and got the taxi to Invercargill. I remember that cost one pound — and we got to Invercargill at ten minutes to midnight that same day. We didn't stay anywhere . . . only stopped at two huts on the track for cups of tea, and we even had to swim the Arthur River as there was no boat when we arrived in the middle of the damn night.

Why we did it? We wanted to get through to Invercargill. We thought we'd give it a go. Wasn't that hard. I told you I've been doing mad things all my life.

I can say this much: I've had a good, healthy, active life. I was brought up in Christchurch, but I spent my teenage life in Prebbleton, eight miles from town. Prebbleton's a part of Christchurch now, but those days it was a country village; five trains went through a day. It's all gone. No village life today and no trains. Yet no one thought in my day that trains would ever go out of date.

I started my first commercial enterprise out there at Prebbleton, delivering newspapers — a penny a copy or a week's supply for sixpence. That's six papers for five cents, and now they're twenty cents *each*. No telephones those days. You had to go down to the post office to ring someone up or to send a telegram; that cost you sixpence, anywhere in New Zealand. You'd send a letter for a penny, a bill for a halfpenny, and a postcard cost a halfpenny, for the card plus the stamp. Two deliveries of mail a day, too, so you got great value for money. And the postman would come right to your front door. No such thing as letter boxes; he didn't mind walking to your door and poking the letter through the slot.

We had the local post office and store at Prebbleton so when I was a boy I'd deliver the pensions to the old people. I'd ride around on my bike, give out the money and get them to sign, but not one out of five could sign their names; they'd just put a cross. Ten shillings a week they got, when they were sixty-five or seventy, but if people had any money of their own they didn't claim; they thought it was below their dignity. Can't imagine that sort of thinking today, can you?

But you could live on a dollar a week those days. Cost you twenty cents to rent a wee cottage, eight cents for a dozen eggs, ten cents for a pound of butter, five cents for a two-pound loaf of bread. I can even remember the early days when it cost you sixpence, or five cents, for a four-pound loaf of bread. Then there'd be threepence for a quart of milk. The milkman came round in his horse and cart, he gave you three dippers and a half dipper of milk for threepence and delivered it right to your door.

I'd be sent down to the shops to get the meat; chops were threepence a pound, or five pounds for a shilling. Same thing for sausages and mince — threepence a pound — and bacon was one and a penny a pound. Factory butter was one and two a pound, separated farmers' butter one shilling a pound, cheese ninepence a pound. So that's how those old pensioners could get by on one dollar a week. You didn't need much money.

No street lights out at Prebbleton those days; it was as dark as the inside of a cow. You carried around a hurricane kerosene lantern to stop walking in the puddles. I remember all that very well. I can go back to World War I. I was only twelve at the time, but I clearly remember 29 June 1914 when war started. I knew what was going on, and I remember my brother reading out of a newspaper and saying, "This means war." I had a war map on my bedroom wall. I'd move the flags backwards and forwards, mostly backwards in the beginning. We were never given much information — no radio. The only messages came by telegraph. But it never once occurred to us that we could lose that war.

Then another event very impressive to me as a kid was the 1918 'flu epidemic. It started when the soldiers began returning from the war, and that summer people were going down by the hundreds. Whole families would get it. There'd be no one to look after them — no nurses, no ambulances, no telephones; we had the only telephone in the village, at the post office. Thousands died in New Zealand. In fact, that 'flu killed more people throughout the world than the First World War did.

I was lucky, I didn't get the 'flu, but my father and brothers did. I spent most of my time carting coffins from the county council office at Sockburn to Prebbleton in our family car. Then I'd have to take the dead in their coffins to a big marquee at Linwood Cemetery where they were all sorted out. I did all that when I was a boy of sixteen. Wasn't paid to do it of course; just did it because I could drive my father's car. He couldn't because he was in bed with the 'flu, and there were very few others in the village could drive a motorcar.

But any rate it was quite something for me, collecting the dead people. I'd go into someone's house, no one around. I'd go inside and they'd all be in bed, except for a dead one or two lying around. The others were too sick to do anything about them. A desperate sort of a thing; you didn't know what to do to stop the thing spreading. You could go to the county council office and get free bottles of influenza cure. Then there were old tram carriages parked around the town — inhalation chambers they called them. You went inside and squeezed something and out came a vapour that was meant to keep the 'flu away. Me? I didn't try; I was too busy! And I never once thought my work carting coffins would have anything to do with me catching the bug, or dying. It was just a job. When you're sixteen you think death's got nothing to do with you.

You could say I grew up out there at Prebbleton, then moved into the city and lived there for thirty-three years. Had my career there. I worked up to general manager of a mercantile and coal firm. We were wholesale coal merchants and shipping agents, buying a lot of coal from Australia, and we were also roofing and flooring specialists. A very varied job. I had over 300 coal miners to worry about, and we had head office here and nine branches throughout New Zealand so I got around the country a lot. Kept the whole damn outfit afloat during the slump, too, when a lot of firms went under.

Then I got the sack — retirement they call it — when I was sixty-five. I was offered more work, but I didn't take it; there's any amount to do when you're old. I've been on committees and executives of all sorts of clubs all my life. I came out here to Sumner to retire and all I do is work. Someone asks me to be treasurer of this and that club and to audit the books of such and such and be president of this and that. Doing useful work, that's what you call it.

Any rate, I built this house at Sumner as a holiday place. We came out here to live in 1945 and we're still here! As a matter of fact, my very first memory is of Sumner. I remember being here on holiday when I was five years old. One of the attractions here at Sumner for a little kid was the water closet. You went to the lavatory and pulled the chain. In Christchurch we just had a dunny — a little house way down the garden path — and the night man came round with his cart and emptied them. But Sumner was more enterprising and had the sea close by, so it had a sewerage system. Each street running down to the sea (and there were only four streets those days) had a big brick septic tank on the seashore, and the pipes ran out to sea, below the low-tide mark. Wouldn't be allowed today, but no trouble those days, and we still went swimming out there.

Anyhow, as a five-year-old I thought it was great pulling the lavatory chain; it was great entertainment. And I still love being at Sumner. I'm active out here; I play bowls, keep a big garden, do all the painting and repairs here on the house, do meals on wheels, help out at the library, work on all the committees under the sun. Then there's all the funerals; that's a bit depressing. You get old and you find life's very short, very impermanent. . . .

But I don't think death's very frightening. I was never an atheist, never thought there was nothing in this religion business, but I was very agnostic for a time there. Thought there might or might not be something in it. I'm not agnostic now. I think there's something bigger and better than us, somewhere.

No, I don't feel like dying. I feel very fit. Yet I must be fairly near it; when you're eighty you've had a good innings. There's nothing I want. When you're in your eighties there's not much you want.

But all these funerals to go to, and I'm in that class now. . . .

KENNY

'It could have been life;
it could have been death'

I arrived early one morning at Kenny's house at Awatuna, on the coast south of Greymouth. We talked all day, for well over eight hours, stopping only for cups of tea and sandwiches. Eventually my dog crept sadly in and Kenny confessed: "I haven't even let the hens out today."

Kenny was stimulated by the talking, and he was drinking far too much tea for his touchy stomach. My eyes were hurting from coping for so many hours with the glare on the paper.

At that first session Kenny acted gentlemanly, treating the lady with reverence. We then relaxed and became friends. Later this relationship deepened into our sharing of poetry, music and vulnerabilities. Kenny remarked: "I think we need another cup of tea now; you've really got me talking. And I like it. After you went last time I thought of so many things. I still suppress my emotions in some situations, but not when I'm in the company of old soldiers — or another Celtic spirit."

Kenny was proud of the Celt in him — the sensitive, spontaneous side of his nature. He loved the romance of Greece and Scotland; there were photos of Robbie Burns amongst the family photos on the wall; there were tears when he talked of friendships, Crete, missed opportunities. "There's a time for tears; nothing unmanly in it. These stiff upper lip types: when are they ever warm and emotional and human?"

Kenny acknowledged the huge importance of World War II in his life. He felt confused but finally strengthened by it: "It developed me, brought out a strength in me, something that had never been tested before, and thank God it made me more tolerant."

Kenny had lived alone since the war. His kitchen, like his spartan bachelor lifestyle, was functional and kept meticulously. But there were softer (perhaps Celtic) touches: his special big easy chair, greasy with use; the vivid tartan rug; the shelves and stacks of books and records. Above all, there was Kenny's sensitivity. Our exchange was very real, often painful. Kenny confessed his regret that he'd struggled all his life on a second-rate farm rather than accept a rehabilitation farm after the war: "But no, I wanted to do it alone. With a rehab. farm I could have made some money and asked a woman to marry me. But I couldn't ask a woman to share what I had here."

I never married, but I'm very family conscious, keep in touch with everyone. You've got to remember I've got nothing else to do now. There's plenty of us, too. Mother had eleven children; one of her sisters had eight; another one had six. At one stage I had fifty-three cousins, but a lot of them have died now. As a matter of fact, I'm the last in my immediate family. The male line is going to die out now. We don't have sons.

I follow it all very carefully. I'm crazy about genealogy. Both my grandfathers came to Westland very early in the piece, and both of them had a go at goldmining down here. My father's father was a Dutchman who settled in Australia and married a Scottish woman. By that stage the land wars were on out here and the New Zealand Government was applying in Australia for people to come out as soldier/settlers. After three years' service they'd be given a grant of land. And that's what Grandfather did — he came out to New Zealand in 1862, served in the militia up the Waikato, then got his grant: fifty acres of land out of Hamilton plus an acre in the town.

Only thing was, the wars continued and my grandmother was terrified of the Maoris, so in the end she persuaded Grandfather to leave for the South Island. He gave his land up for a song and came down here to the West Coast in 1869. Got a piece of land at Greymouth, a leasehold of about ten acres. With his two sons he cleared the bush, ran a few cattle and did a bit of goldmining, but he was far too shrewd to depend solely on the gold; it was too risky. One time early on in the 1870s he and his brother tunnelled into a hill somewhere near the house and found some gold. They got the store-keeper to grubstake them — to give them picks, shovels and food in the hope he'd be paid back later — and they worked that hill like men possessed. One wash-up was marvellous; it paid off all their debts. But that was it. They tried everywhere, lived in hope, got nothing more. The old story.

Yes, I still say this: the publicans and store-keepers were the best gold miners. They were the ones who made money; there's no question about that. Even when I was a kid in Greymouth the well-to-do families were still the publicans and store-keepers.

But Grandfather was a versatile man, prepared to give anything a go. If he wasn't successful in one area he tried something else. And combined with that he was typically Dutch — very strong-willed, very determined. I've got that, too.

My mother's father was a very different man — a well-educated university man from Glasgow, Scotland. He was a real romantic, a Celtic dreamer, and he's passed it on to me. I can be moved to tears by a song, a book, a poem. But I've also got the Dutch determination, so that's diluted it a bit.

Grandfather's family went to Australia in 1848, when he was seventeen, and worked on big cattle ranches. Grandfather became a great bushman, a great horseman and stock breeder. Then when gold was discovered at Bendigo in 1851 he dropped tools and went goldmining, but he wasn't successful. By 1857 the lure of the gold had pulled him over to Otago, New Zealand, where his life started to change dramatically. He met and became friends with Gabriel Read and when the rush started at Gabriel's Gully, Grandfather was there on the spot.

He did very well there for a bit. Each man in his party of five took out £1,000 worth of gold in three months. On the strength of it he married a Scottish woman, and in 1865 they came with a big party of settlers to the West Coast — still after the gold. Part of the lure for Grandfather was the independence of it. He had his own little claim where he called no man master. That was wonderful after the feudal system in Scotland, the lairds and manors and things. I've inherited that characteristic, too — independence. I like to be my own boss.

The store-keepers on the Coast were offering men ten shillings to carry a fifty-pound sack of flour from Arnold River to Maori Gully so Grandfather worked at that for a while, then in 1868 he went to dig at Hokitika and later on at Liverpool Bill's Gully near Stafford. Stafford was a big place those days with over 2,000 inhabitants. We used to hear the story about the first cemetery there. As the years went by they had to find a place to bury all the people, so they started up a cemetery, then someone was working alongside the graves and discovered a good bit of gold. So they thought, why not? They dug up the graves and removed the coffins to another site. This is all very early stuff, from the 1860s; I like to keep it all alive. And look at Stafford now. It's just a couple of old houses, a ghost town.

My grandfather worked there at Stafford for forty years; got almost nothing. He always thought he'd strike it rich, but that first dig at Gabriel's Gully was the only really good patch of gold he ever struck. He was just a dreamer, my grandfather. He raised eleven children, did a terrible amount of reading of history and literature. He knew Shakespeare, Dickens, Scott and Byron thoroughly. But he lived on hope and died poor.

My grandmother was forced to live in the most terrific poverty in a primitive shack: two rooms, clay floor, punga walls, corrugated-iron roof. She had to cart water from the creek and cook on an old Dover stove — just a hot top over a firebox; you could boil but not bake on it. Amazing how Grandmother reared twelve children in those conditions. She had twelve babies, all born in that shack. The midwife would come each year and help add another baby to the family. Only one died, within about three days of birth, and no flaming wonder. I'd say it was survival of the fittest. The weak ones died, just like animals still do. They inherited strength those days; now we're inheriting weakness. And we have all these cot deaths and no one knows why.

Grandmother lived until 1915. I remember her well. She knew the way to any child's heart. She always brought me a bag of brandy balls. Whenever Grandmother appeared on the horizon I was there to meet her! But she always looked back on those years in the shack with great bitterness. It was a real come-down for her as she'd come from a quite prosperous family in Scotland.

But what was the alternative? There was none. Nowhere to go. In the end Grandmother became quite bitter towards her husband, the dreamer with his great education and his books; the very qualities New Zealand desperately *needed,* but there he was with his pick and shovel looking for gold. Because of that my mother, too, was always very sceptical of education without application. She wanted all us boys to have a trade rather than a formal education. She always preached that with a trade you can survive anywhere in the world.

I only just remember my grandfather, on his deathbed. I was three and a half when he died. I remember an old man with a grey beard and an old-fashioned Victorian hat, an impression of great formality. He put out his hand to shake my hand, and that was it. A romantic, right to the end.

My mother was only eleven years old when she started working for a living. She went out into domestic service in Greymouth, she and her thirteen-year-old sister. They were just so hard up, on the verge of starvation, they had to go out to work and send a little home each payday. The two girls left Stafford in the coach, each with a little old-fashioned iron hat box with her clothes inside, off to Greymouth to go to work. My mother worked for a private family at first — peeling spuds, doing dishes, looking after children, that sort of thing. Later on she moved to the Melbourne Hotel in Greymouth, worked there for several years as a general housemaid until she married when she was nineteen.

Mother was a very emotional lady, very sensitive, and I'm like her, emotionally. I was very close to my mother. Also I was last born in the family, a long time after the other children, when my mother was forty-two; and I was one of those kids who loved hearing stories. Always loved reading; still do. Mother started me off, reading Walter Scott to me. She'd fill me up with *The Bride of Lammermoor* and *Kenilworth*. I was swept off my feet with romance. Mother was only educated to standard two, then she went out into service, but she read all her life. She kept our house full of books, just like this one is.

My father was very different from Mother, emotionally — rough and ready and boisterous. He was a drover, a wonderful horseman and dogman. He had a great understanding with animals and they adored him. Mother and Father reared us eleven kids in our old house. There were just four bedrooms for the whole lot of us until the older boys grew up, learnt carpentry and built on two more outhouses. No telephones, not even any hot and cold water supply when I was young. It was a marvellous thing for my mother the day we got running water in the house. Mother was never free of babies, but of course some of the older children had moved away by the time we were born; there's nearly twenty-two years between my oldest brother and me. But when the whole thirteen of us sat down to dinner, at Christmas and that, it was something worth seeing. Mother used to say: "It's lovely to see them all come, and heaven to see them go."

All that extra work, the meals and washing and that. Yet I still say there's something nice about the large families — a very deep family feeling. As my mother said, the children rubbed the corners off one another. The parents didn't have to hand out all the discipline because the older ones kept the younger ones in line. Yes, and kept them entertained. No radio, no TV those days, but we'd get the neighbours in and have singsong evenings; they were lovely times.

In those big families the feeding was a task on its own. We weren't well off, but we were always well fed. Had all our own milk, cream, butter, eggs, meat, veges.

Mother was a marvellous housekeeper, and one of my sisters was, too. I think she got a bit of the Dutch blood. She was always scouring and polishing and dusting. They'd scour the doorsteps with sand soap till they were like snow. The men were afraid to come into the house it was so perfect. All except my father; he ignored it and came in with his boots on. He didn't care.

But you think of all that washing up, all those plates and pots. The girls did it. Us boys weren't expected to, but then as the girls married and went away we had to take a hand at the washing up, and the cooking, too. That's something that fascinated me when I went into the army: a lot of the boys were only sons, or had doting mothers. Some of them couldn't light a fire or cut kindling or blacken their boots.

Then there was all the washing and starching and ironing. You had to have very white sheets and starched aprons and ironed shirts. No drip-dry this and that; everything had to be ironed. There was a sort of ritual about it. A woman prided herself on the whiteness and crispness of her washing. I remember Mother's tubs — cut-down beer casks — and the old copper. They thought those days that all white things had to be boiled up in the copper — sheets and shirts and aprons and that — then they'd be rinsed and put into blue to make them even whiter. Mother used to buy unbleached sheets and bleach them herself, with gall bladders from the bullocks.

My word, you've led me astray today. I'm talking and talking and drinking tea. It's not good for my stomach, tea. Dates back from the war. On 12 September 1939 they asked for enlistments. I enlisted 13 September. And I can say this: the war experience has been the biggest achievement in my life. Definitely. It developed me. Brought out a strength in me, something that had never been tested before, and thank God it made me more tolerant. Now I can respect people on the other side of the fence, whether it's a political fence or a religious or whatever. I can respect them as long as they're decent people. It's everyday conduct that matters to me. I guess I'm a humanist, if anything.

I'm also grateful to the war for the friendships it brought me. When we meet up again, us old soldiers, there's such a close link. People outside don't understand. We all had this experience. It could have been life; it could have been death. You saw your mate experience danger, dying, agony. We learnt to share not only respect but also warmth, affection, a really deep, deep feeling. It's never died. I think yachtsmen and mountain climbers get it, too, that feeling. Danger binds people. Of course, their danger is voluntary and they're fighting nature. The serviceman's is another sort of danger. He's fighting another human being. That man over there is going to shoot you if he can. It also demands another type of courage: sticking it out, despite the conditions. It's a moral thing, isn't it?

I had over five years overseas at the war, serving as a quartermaster — the bloke who deals with cooks, rations, clothing, boots, that sort of thing. I was pitchforked into that job quite against my will.

I was always criticising the cooks so the Colonel thought this man has such a lot to say, let's see what he'll do. It's a real experience to have to do the job you've complained about. You learn that any fool can criticise.

Us quartermasters weren't fighting men, but then when we were in action we had to come from the rear and into the shellfire, taking food and water in. We felt we weren't really fighting, but we were.

Every morning I had to go to the regimental quartermaster storeman and pick up the rations for our company for the day. I delivered part of those rations to the cook and retained the rest for the other two meals. If we were in action in the field the cooks prepared the meals, put them in hot boxes, like ice boxes in reverse, and we had to go forward and deliver them. The men would come over, in small numbers in case a shell fell, and eat. Mostly it was porridge or stew in the field, and we were lucky if we could go forward once a day with hot meals, so the men were also issued with dry rations — bully beef or meat and veges, and biscuits.

The mid day meal in camp was sparse: tea, sometimes soup and a couple of slices of bread with margarine and jam or cheese. We got marmalade till we couldn't look at it, and apricot or fig jam; and you know what figs do to you! Once again, the quartermaster got the blame. Then in the evening we'd get stew and rice, sometimes also dried apricots or prunes. We had rice and rice; we hated it. The rude things said to me: what to do with the rice . . . *and* the bully beef and stew. Some of the men, the very nervous ones, got extremely sharp and nasty about the food. Others were steady and calm. They didn't complain about the food or the sparse rations; took it all.

As for water, every man was entitled to half a gallon a day, for drinking and washing and shaving. Army discipline demanded you shaved. And that's not much water; you had to closely ration your drinking, especially in the desert. If you were on the march you were told not to drink until you got an order to, otherwise you tended to finish off your bottle. Then you were spitting sparks. You got used to it and for your own sake you rationed; one mouthful of water is better than none.

One thing we all looked forward to was the mail. I wrote regularly, even when there was nothing much to write about. I never ever said terribly much about the very bad things, but after each big battle I'd be pent up. I'd write and get it off my chest. As for the in-mail, best of all were the food parcels. One time there I got twenty-three parcels in a month — an accumulation of mail from relatives and old friends. I was regarded as one of the most popular men in the army! Shared it all out, of course.

One chap in our platoon never ever got a parcel the whole time we were over there, and I never ever saw him get a letter. No, he never said anything about it. Later on in the war the patriotic association sent parcels, then he got something.

It was wonderful opening up those parcels — cakes, shortbread, tins of fish, and coffee and milk in a tin; that was very popular. What I longed for? Roast dinners, with potatoes and pumpkin, the whole works, and fresh things. If the cook wanted more eggs or fresh veges and fruit, I'd go off to the market and buy them from the locals.

Yes, there were all those officers and soldiers criticising us quartermasters about the food or the clothing or the boots or something else. I remember being in the desert in Libya. There was no natural cover, no trees, shells dropping everywhere. We'd come up from the rear in trucks, bringing in the food. The dust would rise up from the wheels and actually *attract* shellfire as we approached the men. I'll never forget one time that happened; the shellfire approached as we came in with hot food, and some of those men abused me for drawing fire. It was like a kick in the face. That was my reward for doing service; I've never forgotten it.

But you also learned to understand the tension behind some of those actions, and we all joked to cover up danger. Once I was delivering food in the field, a shell exploded and I got a bit of shrapnel in my bottom. It bled and bled; looked quite impressive. Of course, the word got round and there'd be jokes flying when they lined up for meals: "I hear you got hit." "Hit in the bottom Kenny? If you got hit in the bottom you must have been running away."

Me, terrified? Initially, yes. But you became conditioned to shellfire. It was continuous so you just got on with the job. The dive-bombing was another thing altogether. The plane swooped; the bombs screamed down, whistling. You were terrified, wanted to run and get in a hole. Then it was all over. You never got used to it. Even years and years after the war, if a plane went over you'd be tense, just at the sound of it.

But I had my job to do. I just had to shake myself along and in the end I became reconciled to fear; I could cope with it. I became a bit fatalistic — if it's coming, it's coming, that sort of thinking. Then there's another thing I realised. There were shells and bullets flying around everywhere, but an awful lot of stuff was flying around and hitting nothing. If a shell passed you by three foot or three inches, it still hadn't hit you. It was dangerous and close, but a tremendous amount of that stuff was harmless. So I grew to accept the situation. But I don't know how I'd have coped if I hadn't had a responsibility, if I'd had time to think just of myself, like a soldier. I had a duty to get the food out to the men. I'm by no means heroic, but that's how I felt.

Crete was the toughest; the attack was so constant. Germany had complete air supremacy, bombing and machine-gunning us from the air. The tension built up and many men cracked; their nerves gave way. I could tell when it was coming. The tone of a chap's voice changed, changed from a baritone to a screaming soprano. You knew that fellow was near cracking up. I had a mate who couldn't take the pressure so he shot himself — blew part of his hand away to get himself out of the fighting. He got up at night, put his hand over the barrel of his gun and pulled the trigger. Everyone knew. We were there, heard the shot. He was put in hospital then sent back home to New Zealand. In the First World War he'd have probably been shot for cowardice, but there was more humanity in World War II. Yet still there were some looked down their noses at that bloke. I never did. I understood.

He still visits me . . . never lets on. He talks about the war. Says: "I couldn't take it. I was a coward." But he never says: "I shot myself." Quite a lot of men did it — officers as well as soldiers. Others just threw down their rifles and ran. Where to? They just ran away.

Then eventually we retreated. We all marched thirty miles to the beach and the runaways got word of this and headed down to the beach. The British Navy was there to take us away but they couldn't take everyone. Many thousands became prisoners-of-war. I won't forget going off in those boats, zig-zagging to try and avoid the bombs being hurled at us. I began to think, this is it. One plane dropped four bombs; all missed. Another plane dropped one bomb and it went between the rail and the side of our ship as she heeled over. A huge wave came over our boat, then she went on. Everyone cheered and cheered. I remember I had my tin hat on. I threw it in the air with relief and pleasure to see our boat move on. Off we went, to Egypt.

I won't forget that return to Egypt either. Before we'd gone to Crete I was sick to death of Egypt — the heat, the flies, the dried-up land, the Egyptians, the poverty, the long clothes like night-gowns. I was pleased to get out of it. Then when we went back after Crete I was delighted to see it all again. It felt so good to be alive.

Yet it was Crete I really loved; I've been back there three times. The people attract me so much: they're spontaneous, warm, simple-minded. They loved us big, strong New Zealand soldiers. They thought we'd come 10,000 miles to help them fight the Germans.

The truth was we went where we were told; we'd have gone to the Antarctic if we'd been told to. I love that beautiful island, too. I could go back again and again.

Some of us old soldiers went back in 1981, forty years after the battle of Crete. We fell into their arms. I went to a café to ask directions to the military cemetery. I wanted to go and see my old mates. The café owner spoke no English. "New Zealand" was the only word we had in common, but soon as he heard that one word he whipped out two glasses of cognac for us. Some of my mates joined us and soon there was a celebration. The wine flowed; the Cretans fell on our necks. They loved us.

What I really learnt from the war? The overall thing is this: I learnt to put above all other things two qualities in a man — guts and loyalty. I'll forgive the roughest man any sin if he shows those qualities in those conditions.

I also learnt from the war that those two qualities aren't the prerogative of any class of people or any level of education; you find them in the humblest of people. I couldn't have done my job without the courage and loyalty of other people, such as my storeman Jim Brown. He was a very quiet, simple sort of a boy — straight off a farm, no education to speak of. But Jim would take on anything. If I wasn't on the job I knew he'd be there doing it anyway. I'll die in his debt. It was my prime responsibility as a quartermaster to go forward under shellfire and feed the men, but Jim Brown came to me and said: "Let's share this. It's my duty too; I want to be in on it." He didn't have to; he was just a lance-corporal getting less than twenty-five shillings a week. So we went forward on alternate days. He's living still, Jim Brown. He's never married, like me. We're having a reunion this year in Christchurch. He'll be there.

I say it's been a tremendous experience for me, war. If I had my life over again I'd do it again. I believe the cause was right: we helped maintain a liberty. And I'd say New Zealanders today aren't conscious of this freedom we have. We take it for granted. I'm positive World War II was necessary. If Hitler had got his way and brought in the idea of a new Nordic race, we'd now be living in a dark age. His whole belief that the European race is superior . . . it's nonsense. Martin Luther King once said, "Judge people on conduct, not on colour of skin." I agree wholeheartedly.

I have to say this, too: through the experience of the war years I got a big feel for human nature. I'll tell you what was really fascinating. I was thirty-two when I joined the army, whereas a lot of the men were in their early twenties, full of life and laughter — still boys. Then once we'd been into action and they'd seen men die, they changed. Their attitude changed, just like that. They became men instantly, less carefree, more serious. And once you leave youth behind and idealism, that's sad.

But with war . . . yes . . . some of your faith in human nature is lost, some strengthened. I can say honestly, the war years are the proudest years of my life. I didn't know anything when I started out as a quartermaster and I always could see fault in what I did. I felt, "I'm not doing this quite well enough." Then in our last action in Egypt, in the desert at Ruweisat, I felt good about it. We went forward more often with food and water and I thought, we're doing this thing right at last. I knew I'd done well and knew the men appreciated it. One chap had always given me a rough time — he always had something to criticise — but when I went forward to fill his water bottle he said, "Well Kenny, I take back everything I ever said against you." I felt very good. And in the end I got the British Empire medal for doing things the right way.

Mind you, I didn't go to war thinking it would be a picnic, a glorious adventure; I expected to get toughened. I'd had two brothers killed in the First War. I was just a boy of nine when they went. I knew all about their ghastly experiences — the slow dying, and the mud and ice at Flanders. We didn't have those terrible climatic conditions ourselves. The heat in the desert was hard to take, but nothing like the cold and rain of Flanders.

Be another war? I'm afraid there will be. Whether it's a nuclear war or what, I don't know. Some people say we've got to have nuclear weapons, in case the Russians use theirs. Idealistic people say we mustn't have any at all, then the Russians will follow our example. But that leaves us open to attack. And the example of history shows that the powerful are always tempted to impose their power. That's what I'm afraid of. I can't see any reason for the Russians wanting, or needing, to invade countries like they do. It's the temptation of imposing power.

I think myself they'd start off with a conventional war, then one side might be winning and the other side, in desperation, would use the nuclear power. Or else, one side might say, we're going to win come hell or high water, so they'd get in and drop the nuclear. You just don't know, because the whole thing is illogical, isn't it? And it's such a strange thing. The politicians get around the table and talk, talk, talk, yet there's never a strong commitment carried out by both sides. One lot's still always trying to get an advantage over the other side.

I think if we have a coventional war the Russians would run right over us. They spend more money on their army and they have conscription; every fit man has to serve. Nobody seems to know how many men they have in that army, and they're trained to the hilt. The Americans seem softer, and they smoke marijuana and stuff. But if we had a nuclear war we'd be more evenly matched. Only thing is, who'd use it first? Possibly we can learn from what happened in Japan. Two bombs were dropped and the Japs surrendered. Possibly that's all that needs happen again. We can't face what happened in Japan. If the Russians dropped a nuclear bomb on London, I don't think we could fight on. It's hard to imagine because it's so colossal.

What I feel about the peace movement today? That's a very difficult one. I personally think you have to give your life for freedom, but it's not as simple as that. Imagine if New Zealand was surprised by an enemy and they imposed their will on us all — their laws and injustices. A man might want to fight that. But will he risk his wife's and children's lives, too? You can risk your own life, but are you morally justified in risking someone else's? That's a big question. You'd have to be very ruthless to say, "Yes, we'll all die." I doubt if I could do it.

That war should have knocked the romance out of me, but it didn't. I'm incurable. I can be carried away emotionally by music or words; that's the romantic Celtic blood coming out in me. I love the old Scottish songs and poems: Robbie Burns's *Ae Fond Kiss* — Sir Walter Scott says it's the essence of a thousand love songs and it is, isn't it:

Had we never lov'd sae kindly,
Had we never lov'd sae blindly,
Never met . . . or never parted,
We had ne'er been broken-hearted.

This love of Scottish things is almost a passion with me. Robbie Burns brings out the romance in me, and all that Celtic melancholy, too. Yes, no wonder I loved the Greeks.

It's a bit hard being a romantic down here on the Coast. I can't express all of me, down here. I've got wonderful neighbours. The Irish wit bubbles out of them and that attracts me. There's more Irish per head of population here on the Coast than anywhere else in New Zealand, and the Irish are pretty extreme; it's the Celtic blood in them. If you're their friend they'll do anything for you; if you're their enemy they'll blow you up. But West Coasters are mainly very practical, do-it-yourselfers, and all the reading most of them do is about rugby and racing. I'm right out of that. No, I can't often express the emotional Celt that's in me, that spontaneous passion.

But the practical, common sense part of us is valuable, too. After the war I took up some land here and spent the rest of my days milking cows, but I also had to be a midwife for the cows and pigs; you had to turn your hand to anything. It's the same thing today down here on the Coast. Even if there is assistance available you often can't afford it. It's just like living in the pioneer days, down here.

Do you realise it's almost afternoon tea time? We've been talking since first thing in the morning.

I've been living here since 1947, in this house. I know quite a bit about this area. Never say much about my farming years here? It was hard work. The farm was poor. Much of the land was just swamp. I struggled on, milking cows. That's why I get up at half past 6 every morning. It dates from milking cows all those years; I'm awake and ready to get up. Then I went into pigs, and it was the pigs that saved my bacon; yes, literally! I got my head above water a bit. But all the time arthritis was gaining on me. I said, I'll stick it out until I'm sixty-five, but I didn't get there. I got to sixty-three and said to myself, you're just a damn fool, so I got artificial hips put in and my prostate gland done, too. Then the stomach cancer got hold of me. I'd say it started in the war with all that rough food we ate. I'm suspicious of tinned food and preservatives, and we ate so much of it.

Anyhow, they cut out the cancer — took one third of my stomach away. I can't get over how lucky I've been with that. The first three weeks after I came out of the hospital I vomited every day. The stomach was so small there was no room for any food. Now it's stretched a bit and I can eat small meals; that's why I'm always looking forward to morning and afternoon teas and that. I can't eat pickles and sauces, though; I really miss that. And I've cut down on tea. You wouldn't think so, today!

But it all meant I had to give up the farm, over ten years ago. I just kept the house and quarter of an acre. Now there's just me, two cats and two hens. At Christmas time people dump cats and kittens around here; one's still with me. She loves me and no one else; no one can get near her. Then my sisters and brothers die and I inherit *their* cats. But I've got no sisters and brothers left now and only two cats.

I've also adopted plenty of dogs in my day. They sit on the road looking forlorn and I end up putting them on my chain. One was a very special dog — a big, black, curly chap. He was out there on the road for three days, then I brought him in here. He'd go and find my paper. The railcar would throw it out. It'd land in the gorse or the ditch or somewhere. He'd bring it in for me. I cried when he died. He got deaf, could only feel vibrations, so when people came he'd get startled and bite them. I had to have him put down. Yes, I cried. I've always had a dog; I'd love one now. But I won't get one because then I'd die and what'd happen to it?

Same thing with my books; I should have stopped buying books years ago. What'll happen to them all when I die? But I can't stop.

I accept death, but not senility. I can't cope with the thought of being a vegetable, oblivious to my own situation and other people's distress at seeing me like that, not able to respond. When you're young death is a mystery; you haven't thought it out so you're calm about it. But when you're old you've the time to think it out, and I'd say the fear of my old age isn't death but senility. You must remember I've seen a lot of death — the ghastly sights after the bombing raids.

But there's something about death that amazed me. It first struck home in the desert when my friend got killed. The trenches up front weren't getting dive-bombed; us administrative ones in the back lines were getting it. I'd been forward with a meal, came back and my friend, a corporal who'd come back from the front lines with dysentery, came up to ask how they were getting on up there. A group of dive-bombers appeared and we all rushed to the trenches. Five minutes later I was gathering him up to bury him. All his body was mangled, his skull split open. I vomited as we buried him. Yet one side of his face was intact and it was calm and beautiful, as if made of marble. I've never forgotten it.

There's a tendency in people to brush things under the carpet, anything unpleasant, or anything emotional. I don't believe in that. Nor do you. That's what you're doing here, digging up the other side of our history. No one's wanted to hear about that — our feelings, or anything unpleasant about our past. Keep it safe, under the carpet.

Nothing terribly wrong with our past, mind you. Nothing terribly right about today, either! I'd say we were certainly happier back in the old days, with our candles and kerosene lamps and old pianos. We weren't looking, looking, straining for things like people do now. There was the great feeling of neighbourliness and giving a hand. It's not there today, not in the towns at any rate. I don't know how they get on, living in towns. It's just an existence. There should be some other quality in life; mere living isn't enough.

As for any regrets I can talk about . . . . I'd have to say, when I came back from the war I was sick to death of all the army rules and discipline; I'd kicked against it all along. I just wanted to get out and do my own thing. So I got a farm I could afford to pay for, but it was a very second-rate farm, and I struggled all my life to keep it going. What I could have done instead, I could have trained for farming on the rehabilitation scheme, then got a good, viable rehab. farm for a low price. But no, I wanted to do it alone. With a rehab. farm I could have made some money and asked a woman to marry me. But I couldn't ask a woman to share what I had here.

However, I accept responsibility for myself. We've got to be decisive in life, responsible for our own actions. "I am the master of my fate. I am the captain of my soul," that sort of thing. We've got to be moderate, too, in all things. That's the weakness in human nature; we find it difficult to say no. And we're afraid of hurting someone else, or ourselves.

I think we need another cup of tea now. You've really set my brain working. It's easy to let our old memories lie down inside us, dead. That's what us old soldiers do, we keep the old memories going. You know, exactly a year ago today four old soldiers came over from Christchurch to celebrate my birthday. We yarned and talked and drank whisky and had meals. We keep in touch, us old soldiers. It keeps us going.

Things I still want to do? I'd like to go overseas again, but I haven't got the money. I'll save up for a couple of years, then I'll go. I'll go back to Crete and back to Scotland. It's this Celtic impulse that I have. The war should have knocked the romance out of me, but it didn't . . . not when I'm in the company of another Celtic spirit. I could read Robbie Burns to you all day. His love songs are so plain and human:

> . . . *and I will luve thee still, my dear,*
> *Till a' the seas gang dry.*
> *Till a' the seas gang dry, my dear,*
> *And the rocks melt wi' the sun.*
> *O I will luve thee still, my dear,*
> *While the sands of life shall run.*

MARAMA

'Don't take me away from the sea'

Marama lived over the road from the beach at Kaikoura. You could smell the salt, hear the broom pods popping.

She insisted she was a very ordinary old Maori lady. She didn't know much "history". One of her first comments was: "Other ones will tell you a lot, plenty more than me. But there won't be much humour."

As we talked her humour kept coming out. So did the information that she couldn't hold back — poignant details of the struggle to survive in a family of eighteen kids, threatened relentlessly by hunger and the sea.

Those two factors still dominated Marama's personality. Life in a fishing port promised danger and drowning. Marama had experienced and accepted both: "You stand and watch them disappear. Drowned . . . gone. That's how it is in a fishing port."

Life in a family of eighteen children also meant hunger: "When I was a kid I always used to think, if I get married and have children I'll see they never ever go hungry."

At Marama's place it was old-style Maori hospitality: everyone's welcome and there's plenty of kai, the woman cooks and doesn't eat herself until everyone else has been served. Breakfast that morning was two chops, four fried tomatoes, eggs ("Do you want three or four eggs Christine?") and toast, and there was spaghetti bubbling on the stove, just in case. . . .

She was solid and placid, quick to offer a bed and call in the family so we could all talk, happy to wander up the road and introduce me to her friends. As a child she was a tomboy, always down on the wharf or up in the hills, looking for tucker or playing a practical joke on someone. She still loved a joke; the sticker on the car read: "Old fishermen never die. They only smell that way."

But Marama was now old and slow, in her apron and her slippers with pom-poms. She found old age a nuisance: "I like to keep active,

93

but I get tired now. It's my legs. I get very annoyed about that; I used to pride myself on my good strong legs."

Yet Marama still got up at half past 5 every morning, ran the house and lured the grandchildren and nephews and nieces to come and stay. She was calm yet perceptive . . . strong.

And always she watched the sea.

I was born in this street, just over the road there. My Mum was born here and lived all her life here, too. And her Mum and Dad, too, my Toua and Poua. Eighteen kids Mum had. And her brother over the peninsula at South Bay, he had twenty-two kids. So we were forty when we all got together.

I was way down. Let's see, there was Tommy, Leah, Sophie, Annie, King, Mick and Jack, then me. So I was eighth, and ten more followed on after me. My Mum couldn't stop having babies. My Dad was a fisherman, see, and I think there must have been too much rough weather around Kaikoura! She was always bathing new babies. Mind you, my Mum died when she was forty-nine; too many children. And my aunt with the twenty-two kids, she died at thirty-seven; *far* too many children.

But for fifty-three years there was only one death amongst the eighteen of us kids, and that was a baby who died of convulsions. There were seventeen of us living till the year before last. Now we're down to fourteen.

I was always a tomboy, down the wharf or up the hills with the boys, bird's-nesting and that. Don't think I'll ever be a lady. I was brought up with men, just had to leg it with them, but I was always the baggage boy because I was a girl. There's some Maori logic for you. Yes, we acted just like Indians, us kids. Of a weekend we'd tear over the hill to our twenty-two cousins at South Bay. We'd get on top of the hill, they'd see us up there, we'd see them tearing around down below, and they'd yell out: "Here comes they fellows." I always remember that; they never said it properly.

We'd play all day and half the night, then we'd all toss into a couple of beds — six to one mattress was nothing. We'd go from house to house looking for food . . . many a time we never had food in our house. We'd go down the beach with a tin or out round the rocks and that, looking for tucker. We'd find a bit of iron and roast mussels — let them steam in their own juice — or else we'd catch fish off the wharf and fry them over some bits of wood on the beach. Then there were kina; I only ate them raw, straight out of the sea.

Us kids had a saying about finding and cooking up tucker on the beach:

When the tide's out the table's laid,
And when the tide's in the dishes are washed.

We'd spend all day like that, running around and getting tucker. We didn't want to go to the pictures; we just cooked up a feed on the beach.

Then we got an awful lot of bread . . . stole it. Old Charlie would be going down the road with his horse and cart, delivering the bread; we'd be coming home from school. One brother would climb up into the cart. We'd be running behind and he'd throw us down big loaves of bread and the odd bun. We'd have a good hoe in. Got caught, mind you. Got a good hiding for it. We were stealing, but we only ever stole food, not money, and it was because we were hungry. I'll tell you another thing we did, to get bread. We'd stop old Charlie and say: "Mum wants two loaves." Then we'd tear round the corner and eat it. He'd book it up and later on Mum'd get the bill. She wouldn't know what it was all about . . . or else she'd know, but she wouldn't have the money. We'd have to go out and say to Charlie, "Mum's sick," or "Mum's up town."

We had a good vegetable garden, but not enough solid food, the kind that fills you up. When I was a kid I always used to think, if I get married and have children I'll see they never ever go hungry. And I've seen to that.

One thing that helped out, we did a lot of bartering those days; we swapped fish or veges for meat. And when the men weren't out fishing they'd be out on the hills shooting pigs and rabbits, or catching eels down the creek. We'd smoke the eels, then grill or fry them over a fire till they went crunchy. And we had an awful lot of Maori bread, and puha and watercress. We still eat that Maori food and plenty of paua and mussels and fish; fish heads are out on their own, beautiful to eat. But I wouldn't eat some of the old-style Maori food; Mum and Dad sometimes left the kina for two or three days till they went like cream. Same thing with the crayfish tails — they'd leave them in the creek till they went like a jelly, then they'd eat them. And they'd make something we all called rotten corn. They'd leave it to go bad, loved it. At South Bay I always knew who was having rotten corn. I couldn't go in the door for the smell. But the boys would be right into it.

We were very poor, but one thing we always had was a good Christmas. The men would go out fishing all year to earn us a living, but sometimes the fish got condemned in the Christchurch market, because they were crushed or a bit off or something. Then they'd get nothing for the fish, only a bill for the freight. So my father always had to borrow ten pound off the lawyer, for Christmas. Father Christmas would come. We'd get a pair of tennis shoes, a bag of lollies. Not much.

But we always had a real Christmas dinner over at South Bay — a marvellous, big meal. All our family and all our cousins' family; there'd be fifty people and more. The men went out and stole geese and turkeys and the women made the Christmas puddings; there'd always be two or three great big puddings, boiled up in cloths in kerosene tins, they were that big. And there'd be camp ovens going all day, and big boilers. Then my Mum was a great one for cooking up pauas, whole. She cooked them in a batter, with onions; it was just like eating chicken. No fuss. She'd sit there and throw them in the pan.

We had a big old house to live in, but there weren't many rooms; a very big kitchen, three bedrooms and another room for sleeping. Mind you, some kids were going off to work while other babies were being born, and some went to Toua and Poua, that sort of thing. But often we'd be four kids to a bed, top and tail. Then there were always extra people staying at home — cousins and that. And that's how we missed out on the food. Say Mum was cooking up a good Sunday dinner, visitors would call in. They'd get first go at the food; we'd get anything left over. So we'd tear down to the beach to get tucker.

Most of our clothes were given to us — hand-me-downs. People with families would give Dad a sack of clothes. You'd scramble in, trying to get in first. What you grabbed you kept, even if it didn't fit. I got corns on my feet from always wearing shoes that didn't fit. I'd be in agony, going up the road. Or else we'd go barefoot all year. Not just us — other kids also had no shoes. Lucky half of us didn't die, walking up to school in the frost. But the soles of our feet were like leather. We could run on the hard shingle roads, played football with no boots, thought nothing of it.

Then if Dad got a bit of extra money from the fish he'd buy us boots. That was terrible, having to wear boots instead of shoes because they were cheaper and lasted longer. And they were boys' ones, lace-ups. We were so ashamed of them. At line-up time one of the older girls would say, "You have to wear boots," and that'd end up in a fight. Girls fighting girls. Terrible, isn't it? But we had to. When you look back on it, they were probably better than shoes — warmer — but most of the other girls had shoes. We used to cry at home when we were told Dad had bought boots. But we had to wear them . . . or else get up the road a bit and hide them in the long grass!

We were often cold in the winter, but we were on the move the whole time; we didn't really get sick. Those days you were healthy, or you got sick and died. I suppose we were lucky here. The fishermen made friends with all sorts of city people — doctors, lawyers and dentists. They'd come here to Kaikoura on holiday and they'd give their right arm to go out on a fishing boat. Then they'd do us a favour. I remember this dentist who'd come up from Christchurch for the weekend — he'd put all us kids down on the floor and pull out our teeth. No charge. Then he'd do all the neighbours; didn't charge them either. And next day he'd go out fishing; he loved that. There was a barber, too. He'd come up from Christchurch and yell out, "Any you fishermen want a haircut?" You'd sit on the wharf and get your hair cut, free. Then he'd go out fishing.

Then kids today won't believe all this. They'll think I'm making it up. There was no money, simple as that. Only time we ever got anything given to us was Christmas-time. Birthdays didn't mean a thing; we didn't understand what they were; didn't know what a birthday party was like. School was awful, too. I hated going. There were a terrible lot of fights between us Maori kids and the pakehas. Sometimes we'd all be together, playing. Then someone would come up to me at lunch-time — they all knew that sometimes I didn't have any lunch because there was nothing in the house — or a pakeha girl would see my crayfish wrapped in a bit of Maori bread in my kit and she'd yell out: "Look at your Maori dinner." That'd upset everything. We'd be fighting. Our kitchen table at home had a long form along one side. I remember sitting on the form, bawling my eyes out. Mum had made scones for tea and I was bawling out, "I don't like Maori scones." The pakeha kids had had me on at school, and I was thinking, "I don't want any more of our Maori food." I thought no one else had to eat the stuff we had.

Or when we were playing around or having a fight down the back, someone would say, "Go away, nigger." Even if you didn't say something back yourself, there'd be one of your cousins there and he'd say something. Then there'd be a fight. Same thing when the townyites — the kids from up Kaikoura — came down here. They'd call us the wharf rats from down the slums, the scaly end; they'd come down and take over, try and boss us around. But we thought we owned this part down here, so there'd be another fight. . . .

I was often kept away from school to look after the new babies. I was away all the time. I'd be that ashamed to go back, I didn't know anything. Couldn't sit the exams. Left when I was fourteen. I had to go home to look after the babies that kept coming, and the house. Mum kept our house spotless. She was very fussy. We'd have to polish all the floors; drive you mad. That's why I'm not too fussed about housework today. We didn't have many clothes, but they all had to be just so. If I did the washing, hung it out and she saw something not quite to her liking, I had to take the whole lot in and do it again. Not just that one garment — the whole, blooming lot. Washing day was terrible. We had a copper out under the willow trees at the back of the house, two great big wash-tubs and a wash-board. Mum would stand over that wash-board all day. . . . I still use one, too — do all the socks and working trousers on the wash-board; doesn't shrink them like the washing machine does. I'm still a bit old-fashioned. Even now I always do my blankets in the bath, not the machine. I get in, barefoot and stamp them around. Wash the blankets and the feet at the same time!

But you can understand how we had a lot of fun, a great big family like that. We were always in trouble, but we never fought amongst ourselves — too busy! We never had a motorcar, and no money for going out, so we had to stay at home in the evenings. We'd get tea over, do the dishes and then have a "concert". There'd be one of us on the ukelele or guitar, one on the mouth organ, Mum on the piano — she loved music, my Mum — and the rest singing. We sang what our parents were singing, all the real old tunes: *Daisy, Daisy, Knees Up Mother Brown, Letter Edged in Black, There is a Tavern in the Town,* that sort of thing. We had nowhere else to go but home. I remember when we never even had a wireless. Then Mum got the first wireless in the street. That was a big event, getting the wireless. We thought it was beautiful. If there was anything special on, a boxing match or a big football game, our room would be crowded with people.

There were all sorts of characters about Kaikoura those days, and us kids were up to tricks the whole time. Like when one of my brothers and his mate tied a dead shark behind the dinghy and dragged it into the bathing beach where all the tourists were. One of the ladies saw the fin and yelled, "Shark, shark." My brother leaped over the side of the boat, gripping his knife. He thrashed around in the water for a long time, fighting the shark, shouting and stabbing, making a real good show. When he finally "killed" it, this lawyer got up on the rocks and made a big speech about my brother's bravery. Everyone clapped and passed the hat around. Eighteen pound they got, for killing the shark, and a write-up in the paper! It was our entertainment, that sort of thing.

Us kids would be hanging round down there at the wharf, seeing what we could get up to when the fishermen got drunk. Once we found a chap asleep outside the pub, so we cut half his moustache off and tied it around his finger. Then we'd always be teasing the two old men who scrubbed down the wharf after the fishermen came in. There was old Snooky, a wee short man with a long, white beard; he lived in a little shack with sacks for the doors. Us kids would get up the hill behind the shack and roll truck tyres down, hoping they'd go right through the back door, through the house and out the front door into the sea. Old Snooky used to think it was the cows trying to get into his house.

Snook's mate was old Conger Eel Bill. He'd throw a line over the wharf and sit there fishing for cod. A couple of us kids would slip into the water, pull his line slowly in and wrap it around the wharf piles. Conger Eel Bill would yell out, "Help me, boys. I've got a big one, a real big one." We'd pull like mad, till the line broke. Conger Eel Bill would go off home, disgusted. Us "boys" would swim out, get the line and go off fishing!

All sorts of old characters here in Kaikoura, all right. One bloke lost his leg sawmilling, so he'd hack into a bit of wood down the mill and make his own wooden leg. Then when he got drunk he'd drive an axe into his foot. The ladies would scream, or faint. One night he was asleep on the seats outside the pub, so a couple of blokes sawed his leg nearly in two. When he stood up, it fell off.

Then there was old Jack the rabbiter. He'd go to the pub on pension day and get lit up, then he couldn't walk home. Didn't have a home to go to, anyway; he'd sleep under hedges, anywhere. We'd see him stagger out of the pub, and we'd race up with our hand-cart — an old box affair on pram wheels. Barrow boys, that's what we were. We'd wheel Jack from the Blue Pacific to the Pier Hotel, three-quarters of a mile up the shingle road, then we'd tip him out. Five bob he'd pay us; big money for those days. If he had no money we'd grab his watch and he'd have to pay it off bit by bit, to get it back. Lots of those old chaps had no home. There was an old swagger called Mick. He walked everywhere, from one sheep station to another. We'd say, "Where you going to stay tonight Mick?" He'd say, "Oh, at the Star Hotel." That's what he called the cemetery.

Mum's mother and father, my Toua and Poua, were real characters, too. He stole her from Little River. I don't know anything else about that story, only that he stole her and brought her home here to Kaikoura. Home was just a tent for a long time, then they had a little two-roomed bach. I always remember when my Toua and Poua used to go up town to collect their pension. They'd be sitting up in the old gig, yakking away to each other. The horse would be walking slowly up the road and their spaniel trotting along behind.

They'd collect their pension, then go to the pub. And on the way back the scene would be very different. The horse would be going flat out, fast as it could go, the spaniel would be yelling, and Toua and Poua would be standing up in the gig having a fight, the two of them, like men.

Us kids loved watching that happen. But also we knew there'd be all sorts of goodies in the back of their cart, especially the fairy cakes — little biscuits with raspberry jam in them. We used to go over and sit outside the pub, waiting for them to go home. If it was dark when they came out that was very good because Maoris are superstitious, don't like travelling after dark. So Toua and Poua would say to us, take a fairy cake, crumble it and throw it over your head, to keep all the kehuas and spirits off. We'd take the cakes, tear off and scoff them, then go like hell home. Didn't care about the kehuas, we just wanted those cakes. Never got them at home.

One evening Poua got very drunk and was sleeping it off before they headed back, but Toua was very superstitious, very afraid of being out after dark, so she went on home. Wasn't often she left him when he was like that, so when he woke up he thought she might be up to something, she might be back at their whare entertaining another man. He tore off home. She heard someone coming in the dark, didn't know if it was him or not and braced herself against the door. By now he was really suspicious so he took a swipe at the door with his axe and cut her thumb right off! He cut clean through the door, it was that flimsy, and caught her thumb. What happened next? He buried it in the paddock! By the time they got a doctor it was too late to stitch it back on, but he wanted to know where the thumb was. Poua told him. "All that fuss over a bloody old thumb."

But Toua and Poua weren't always that wild, only when they did too much drinking. Other times they were just ordinary fishing village people. We're all country folks down here. We live different to city people. The sea and boats are our life; they're part of us. All my family's been fishing. My Poua worked around here and there in the mills for a while, then he came back here to Kaikoura, to be near the sea again. My father was a fisherman, too. He was just a boy when they were still whaling here at Kaikoura, so he did a bit on the long-boats, early on, then he took up fishing. Been a lot of fishermen drowned here in Kaikoura. You stand and watch them disappear. Drowned. I lost a husband and a father-in-law at sea . . . and a nephew. All drowned. It happens that quick. Gone. High seas and the rocks. That's how it is in a fishing port. My first husband and his father were out crayfishing one night in the dinghy, out past the lighthouse. The wind came up and they never returned. My husband was twenty-four; I was twenty-one. We had one little baby.

Then my second husband lost a hand. Blew it off, blowing up bait out in the bay. But still I don't hate the sea. It's been my life. I was born to it. I don't like to go out on it myself, not way out. But I watch the sea and the weather. I worry, yes, even now. The bad weather comes in, big seas, high winds. My own son can be home, safe, but I still worry about the other boys. And I see the holiday-makers in their wee dinghies; they take too many risks. Won't ask us people who know. We see them on the wharf, the yachties and that. We say you want to be careful. They look at us, "What do you know?" on their faces. They're used to enclosed harbours, and they have white jerseys and yachting caps on. But we know when the wind's coming up and how hard it'll be. You see it, on the water and in the sky. Then the big seas come in. You don't worry so much when there's no boat out; but when anyone's out you go outside, you look around. . . .

Then when anyone's boat gets washed up, everyone turns out to give a hand or to see how it's going. Like what happened this weekend with my son's boat. Those big seas and high winds broke her moorings and she came up on the beach. All of Kaikoura was out today, watching, as the men tried to get her off the beach. Some of them were there all day. They had thermos flasks and beer and that. Some of them went home and brought their tea back. They all stayed until the cranes and bulldozers got her free at high tide. All of Kaikoura was there, even the publicans; the pubs were all empty, they might as well come! It was the entertainment of the year, but also they were concerned. She was one of our boats and they wanted to see her freed.

Sea ... I was born to it. When I was a kid my father would get up at 3 of a morning to go fishing, and I'd get up with him. Then my husband did the same thing. He'd be away for sixteen hours, fishing, get home at 9 or 10 at night, then we'd have to clean the fish, clean the boat down. The women worked alongside their men, those days. I'd be down there when they came in of an evening, frost on the wharf in the winter. I'd be helping with the fish or taking down hot soup and big billies of tea.

One time I remember we were there till 3 next morning. You got used to it over the years. I'd get up at 3; never went back to bed. I'd be out there ironing or something. Even now I get up at half past 5 every morning, winter or summer. Some of the women would knit craypots and splice lines, things like that; some of them even went out fishing all day with the men. One of them from down here used to take the baby out with her, and I'll tell you what: she could work. Had to, to keep the family going. But nowadays the fishermen go out at 6 of a morning, and they're home after lunch. And you wouldn't catch the young wives down there on the wharf. Too much else going for them these days.

Then we took over the fish shop up town for a while, the husband and me. We needed the money because he wanted a boat of his own. Sold wet fish, groper mostly, and fish meals I cooked up in the dining room. All I had to cook on was a petrol stove — a great big pan with two petrol burners under it; the damn things used to flare up on me and I'd drop everything and run outside. But on that one cooker I'd do up fish, chips and eggs — that's what the public wanted. I cooked, one of my cousins helped waitress, and sometimes a sister would help out if we got very busy. We got a lot of convoys going through Kaikoura those days — air force and army and that; thirty or forty men to cope with and only one pan. They'd never warn us either, just turned up.

Then there were the Maoris from the East Coast up North. They came down to help finish off the railway and, boy, they'd eat! Some of them came in three times a day. I felt I was robbing them. They'd come up to pay for their third meal and I'd say: "I'll toss you for this one."

We did all right in the fish shop. Got the boat. So in the end we gave up the shop. I had two small kids, they needed their Mum, and we'd be feeding them only on fish and chips — the meals I cooked up in the shop — not veges and that. They needed my attention, but the shop was a lot of work, me cooking and the husband fishing. We had no car either, so he'd have to cart the fish up from the wharf on his push-bike. He'd put the case of fish on the handlebars and off he'd go, up the rough shingle road. Many a time he nearly ended up in the tide. Most he ever carried on the bike was 240 pound of fish. He broke the handlebars in the end, so he'd push a bit of manuka in; when he saw some kids he'd whip the manuka stick out, pretend it was a gun.

Took us everywhere, those old bikes. Of a Sunday we'd go down to do the washing at Mum's because she had an old washing machine by that stage. He'd carry the two kids, one on the bar, one on the handlebars, and a big bag of washing on his back. I'd be on the other bike. We were just like two old spiders, going up the dirt road. One time I remember, it was raining like billio so we borrowed a car; it was like being on the moon! But it was more trouble than it was worth, that old thing, backfiring and getting wet and stopping.

Been a hard life, all right, but I'd do it again. Plenty of struggling and death. But time heals everything. Yes, anything we wanted we had to earn. We had to think up some way to earn it. The kids would see people stranded over the channel at the seal colony so they'd row over and get them. Charged them threepence. If they were panicking, charged them a bob! We had a struggle to feed our kids, but they never went without. I went short, but not my kids. I always said to my husband I'd steal for my children. I would, too. My second husband came from a family of fourteen. He wanted us to have twelve kids. I said to him, you can get on your bike and go somewhere else. I didn't want that many, not after coming from a family of eighteen and hungry half the time. None of us had big families ourselves.

Mind you, I loved my kids — cuddled and kissed them to death. Love babies. And I'm Aunty Marama to all the Maori kids around here. Seems to me kids today don't get the right sort of love. The mothers are too busy doing other things, going out to work or to meetings, up and down the street visiting their girlfriends. I say, they should be at home. The kids come home from school and Mum's not there. It's a very hard life for the kids — too many pressures. My kids ... they came home, chucked their bags in, you'd hear, "You there Mum?" then you didn't see them again till tea-time. But they knew you were there. My kids lived on the wharf. They had lines and pots for crayfishing, they knew how to row the dinghy; never wanted to go up town, never asked for money. Of a Saturday we'd all go down and sit on the wharf — Dad, me and the kids — and catch bait for the men.

Yes, I think I was born to cook and look after people. But eighteen or twenty kids, that's too many. Those days we knew nothing about sex and birth control and that. We were too frightened to ask our parents, and no such thing as sex education in the schools or books and pamphlets about it. Mum and the aunties would get together and talk. We'd hear little bits and pieces if we were hanging around, then they'd realise we were there so they'd box our ears and send us outside. Today kids just sit and listen to what's going on. So I knew nothing when I got married. Just learnt as I went along. I'd say that the fear of having more and more children made many marriages unhappy in our day. That's what made men and women quarrel. Once the babies were born they were loved, but at the time lots of them weren't really wanted.

My mother had all her eighteen born at home, with her aunty there to see it all went okay. The very old Maori women just used to go out in the bush and have them, on their own. They'd take a clean sack, squat out there and have the babies. No help from anyone. Soon as they were done, back home they'd go. That was their way. Whether it's better or not, I don't know that. What I say is this: as you get older you can sort things out better in your mind. I very rarely panic over things now. Used to, but not now. When you sit and think a lot you can sort of work things out.

And all sorts of things happen in little Kaikoura; we're always in the news. But when you get my age you can sort out what you think about all the excitement. Like that UFO outfit a year or two ago; everyone around here was seeing them. The TV and radio and newspapers were ringing us up all the time. Then we came home from up town one day, there was a white van up the road and people running around setting up cameras. They were from Australia!

What I thought about the UFOs? I was one of the first ones to see them. It was November. I was lying in bed looking out. I could see all the sky because I never have the blinds down. I thought, what's that reddy-orange thing out there? Thought it must be an aeroplane, but it never moved, never moved. A big, round ball, pulsating for a long time. I thought, must be a cloud. I looked and looked at it, woke my husband and got him to have a look. He wasn't very interested. Then it just rose up and disappeared. Then suddenly it was there again. I thought of going over the road to get someone else to have a look at this thing, but I thought they'd think I'd gone bats. So I never mentioned it to anyone. Next thing everyone was seeing things — people around Kaikoura, pilots in planes, everyone was talking about UFOs. I asked: "What are they?" I'd never heard of them before. Then I said I'd seen something, too, but I didn't have a clue what it was. I don't know to this day.

I don't mind admitting I think there's something in it. If a little green man turned up one day I wouldn't worry. If they wanted to harm us they'd have done it long ago. You've got to have a sense of humour about it all, too. But I'm not one for the limelight at all. I couldn't be bothered with the TV and all that carry-on. They came screaming around here and wanted me to talk about it. I stood here with my mouth open. Even if I saw a little green man I wouldn't tell them. I didn't want to talk about it.

Our lives are getting that commercialised now. We're spoiling things. I don't like seeing what's happening to Kaikoura, and especially South Bay. It's meant to be a holiday place, baches, but it's all beautiful homes. They all dress up and entertain, get up early and fuss about their houses and gardens. It's not like the old-style holiday place: chuck everything into the bach and go off fishing. And it's full of strangers who move on, South Bay.

Same thing here in Kaikoura — it's all strangers. In our day it was a little fishing village; you knew everyone. Now it's a holiday resort. Lots of these places up our street are baches. Not so many permanents, like us. And there's only two of us originals left, old ones born in this street and still living here. Up town is commercialised, too; prices going up and traffic everywhere. That's moving with the times, isn't it? I just can't get out of it quick enough.

The city people are supposed to come to a place like this and relax. They don't, you know. I notice it in the shops; they sort of take over. They're rush rush rush, and shoving. You get pushed around in your own shops. We're used to going up there and doing things in a leisurely way, having a chat with the shopkeeper and our friends.

Yes, I'd be happy to see Kaikoura go back to just Kaikoura people. I'm too possessive of this little village, I don't like seeing what's happening to it. You take Christchurch. You live there, you don't know your neighbours, except perhaps the ones on each side of you. You see them every day, you pass them on the streets, but you don't know them. It's an awful way to live, isn't it?

I couldn't go away from the sea for long. We'll go on a holiday later on, to Akaroa! It's lovely there, but still not as nice as here. We've got open sea and also mountains here in Kaikoura. We see the ships going past. It's all right to go to a city, but not for too long. Tell you how far out of Kaikoura I've been: Timaru and Rai Valley. So I've travelled a lot! All I know is Kaikoura.

I like to keep active, but I get tired now. All my life I was never still — got up early and hated going to bed; had to be on the go all the time. Now my legs get tired, but there's so much I want to do. And my legs are aching. I fell asleep this afternoon....

My wish is to work till the day I die, then drop dead. You don't usually get your wish like that. But I don't want to be a sick person in the hospital, a burden to everyone. People say, that's what we have nurses for. I understand that, I really do. But one old lady, she was up there at the hospital for twenty-two years, something like that. She shouldn't have lived that long; she was in a wheelchair all that time. Too long. Another one went completely senile, didn't know what was happening to her. She'd run away every day, trying to get home to her farm. She wanted to go home, but she didn't know how to get there. Most of the others are just sitting, sleeping all day. I'd hate to be like that, but I'm not to know what'll happen, am I? And I don't want to go to any of my family, especially not that. I don't want to be a burden to my family. No.

So if I don't get my wish and just drop dead one day, put me in the Kaikoura hospital. Yes. You can see the sea from up there. And when you think about it, they're darned spoilt — visits here and there, morning and afternoon teas, wandering around and going down town. It's beautiful — mountains one side, sea the other. You can see the boats going in and out. . . .

Don't take me away from the sea.

MAX

'The Paganini of the South'

Max was still in bed when I first called. He yelled, "Wait there a minute," hitched up his trousers with binder twine, shuffled outside and started talking. By mid afternoon we were still at it.

Max was a bachelor, a loner, an individual, perhaps an eccentric. He lived in a tumble-down, unpainted hut in Hokitika. There were sacks on the floor and cardboard in many of the windows. He spent his days playing his violin, bicycling around Hokitika and swimming in the wild West Coast sea.

The locals had labelled Max harshly: he was the hermit, the village fool, the bore of Hokitika. The kids taunted and mimicked him; the adults tut-tutted about his shack and avoided him in the street because they couldn't get away once he started talking. Yet there was a place for Max in Hokitika. He was invited to play his violin in the library and post office each Christmas Eve, and the locals hadn't called in the health inspector to demolish his hut. I soon got to know the other Max: the thoughtful and almost painfully sensitive man. There was no laughing at our sessions. Never.

We did our talking perched on boxes amongst the chaos of junk outside his hut. My dog fossicked through the treasures: old tins and milk bottles, broken bricks and pipes, plastic bags, window frames, rusty tubs and churns and drums and wire and bits of tin, piles of rotting timber, overgrown grass and thistles with the occasional cabbage and potato poking its way through. Inside, the hut looked much the same, and Max preferred us to stay outside. He talked and waved his arms around a lot and strode around in the junk. Then he said: "I'm going to play for you now. I'm a violinist ... you mightn't think so. A chap in Dunedin called me the Paganini of the South." He poised himself in an empty space and started to play. I sat on my box and listened; my dog started howling and dived off to hide under a drum; people going down the road must have thought it was the local drama group practising.

But Max swept on through his pieces, oblivious. He'd obviously once been good, but now he was shaky and rusting, like his surroundings. Occasionally he'd find the old true notes, his eyes would gleam and demand approval.

Other times we sat on the beach and talked. Max loved the sea: "My gills don't work right if I'm not in the sea water every now and again."

Max was colourful, certainly; eccentric, maybe—but definitely no village idiot.

Ten o'clock one morning:

I was a grocer most of my life. Had a little shop in Dunedin at Highgate, a mile from town. You went up the hill in the cable car. I'll dig out a photo of my old grocery shop. I've only got one photo left; and tell you what, it's taken at 10 o'clock in the morning. I'd worked all blooming night and I was still at it. I was running all day and all night in that shop; many a time I worked twenty-three hours a day. One of the bakers came with his bread at midnight, another came at 1, another at 2, another at 4, then I'd deliver the bread to people's back doors—hundreds of loaves of bread, every morning before breakfast. I had a hand basket, a great big one that held about ten loaves. I'd walk all round the district delivering bread. We had about twenty different types of bread in my day. The Vienna loaf was one of the favourites and then there was French bread with half a pound more flour in it, and you broke sections off like a bun; it wasn't a long stick like French bread today. Then there were barracoutas and roly-polys and square pans and raised pans. Now there's more or less just one kind of loaf, and you just call it bread.

Any rate, off I'd go, delivering all these loaves every morning. I'd shut up shop and do a round, open up and serve for a while, then shut up again and do some more delivering—a hell of a big job. And twenty-five bob a week, that's what I earned in the shop. I got three farthings profit on an article. Now we've gone to the other ridiculous extreme: the millionaires are becoming multi-millionaires and the small men are struggling more than ever.

I was a small man in a small shop. I had to work the hours, had to be open when customers were off work. I opened my doors at 7 of a morning, stayed open more or less all day, closed down about 9 or 10 of a night and much later of a Saturday. But I was strong those days, could lift two seventy-pound bags of sugar with one hand—yes, one hand. Today the union wouldn't let anyone do it, and they'd get danger money or heavy money or something.

What I sold? General groceries; fruit, veges, butter. When rationing was on you could give customers only half a pound of butter, and I got that correct at judging half a pound I'd just cut it with a knife; didn't have to weigh it. The church put on a cake-guessing competition. I won it easy. Shows how correct I was. But now with the grams and that, they throw me out a bit. Then I had all sorts of lollies—160 jars of them in my shop. There were penny santé and cinnamon bars and conversation lollies—thin, flat ones, all shapes and all colours. They had all sorts of messages on them: "I love you", that sort of thing; you'd get quite a lot of them for a penny. I sold ice cream, too. When I first took over the shop you could still buy a penny ice cream, then costs went up and penny ice creams went out.

But the kids loved my shop. The bible classes used to come down of a Saturday night. They'd buy a few little bits of lollies and things and then they'd want me to play a tune on my violin. I'd play them *Show Me the Way to Go Home*. Then when the war came on lollies went out, couldn't get them, so I had to change the shop around, go into ordinary things like flour and tea. And another blow to a little man like me came when the schools began to put in their own tuck shops, and the factories set up their own shops. That gave the big man a good run. Not me.

I got no damn money out of my shop, but I got a lot of respect. When I closed down a chap said: "You've got only one fault, Max. You're too good to people." I always gave a present to the blokes going away to the war—a parting gift—and if someone got married I'd give them a couple of saucepans or something. Then I had to turn round and help a lot of customers. There were really poor people who couldn't pay the bills. They'd come back months later to pay and I'd say, "Forget it."

We all had a rough time during the wars and the slump. I knew a family of seven girls in Dunedin. They had only one dress between all of them. They'd have turns wearing it and going out. They had to keep swapping that dress around. Then there were two terrible laws during the slump: one was that no two members of a family could work in the same company; the other was that single men were put last in line for a job, so they were often kept out of work. I remember a notice outside a mill in Dunedin: "Men wanted. No single man need apply." Made me wild. We wanted to work, but they said, "No, you can't, you're single." Nowadays they *won't* work, some of the young, single ones.

How long I had the shop? I don't worry about years. It's the same with age; you never want to think you're old. When I came here to Hokitika? Twenty years ago now. In the end it got tough at the shop. The slump hit us small grocers hard and I had to give it up. You bought a thing for sixpence and sold it to the public for threepence. The tribunal had the prices fixed; nothing you could do about it. Okay for the big man who bought stuff off the merchants; not okay for us small ones. I'll give you an example: I had to pay sixpence for a tin of Nestlé's cream, whereas Wardell's paid twopence halfpenny off the merchant and sold it for threepence halfpenny. So they were still making money and I was losing. The big man gets bigger, the little man littler. That's how tough it was, in the Depression. Then the war was coming on and the bakers had to give up. And on top of all that my father died, my mother was an invalid with arthritis and I had to run backwards and forwards looking after her and working the shop, too. There was that much work my legs went—varicose veins. I had to go to hospital three times a day for five years. In the end the doctor went and cut and tied my veins, but they grew again. So they pulled the veins out in the blooming finish. Having veins out, it's like having a stream in your garden. You take the stream away, the garden's not so good. When you take the veins out you've got no blood, and when you've got no blood you don't heal up well.

Mind you, I was lucky. I wouldn't even have my legs today if the doctors had got their way. They thought they'd cut off my legs. I said you're not taking them off, that's all there is to it. It was just the easy way out for them. But the main trouble wasn't the veins, but the sulphur ointment they put on me; it ripped my skin off. In the end the medical people gave it over the B.B.C. that they'd made a mistake with that ointment; it'd deformed babies, all sorts. Any rate I believe in the sea; I'd go and swim in it. It's the best thing out for healing, the sea. Mind you, it keeps the doctors out of business!

My legs okay today? They're still not perfect, but they're getting there. I've got bandages and things, but I get around all right. I ride my bike if I'm going up town or any distance. I'm not meant to get in the water because this new plaster bandage soaks off, but it doesn't stop me. You can't keep a fish out of water, can you? I started swimming when I was about four and I've been swimming all my life. I'm the only one around here who swims. I've been seven miles out into the Tasman, seven back. Still get out there, but the weather's been a bit rummy lately.

I believe in the sea. But what with my legs and the business going fut with the slump, and the war and the big men, and my mother being an invalid ... I couldn't keep going at the shop. Had to give up. They bulldozed my shop down in the end. Nothing there now, not even another modern sort of a shop.

Oh, you're going now? Come again won't you, I'll be here.

113

Another morning:

I'm a violinist ... you mightn't think so. My teacher turned round and said I could be the best in the world. What I thought about that? I think there's no top. If you get to the top there's only one way to go, backwards. And this world thinks more of money than of people's brains and talents. It's money gets you to the top.

Tell you what though, I've got 10,000 pieces of sheet music in my house there, and I play sixteen positions on the violin. My music's my life; I just can't help it. I played in the Dunedin orchestra for over eight years and there was this chap there, he'd been chief violinist in the Berlin State Orchestra. Well, he always called me the Paganini of the South. Paganini—he was the greatest violinist in the blooming world!

Anyway, the music was in me, that's all there is about it. I used to practise in my shop. People'd come and sit outside and listen to me playing; one bloke'd sit there for four or five hours. I'm going to play to you now. Favourites? I don't have favourite music. There's twenty thousand pieces to pick from, but I think Paganini's still about the top in the world. It's tough, intense. And the Russian composers are up there at the top, too.

Listen to me....

I tell you what's wrong. I haven't got my coat on; I need the pad in the coat to grip the fiddle. I like this one, *The Last Rose of Summer*; it's one to remember me by.

There you are.

I was just unlucky not to make a living out of music. I'm a musician. I don't know whether anyone else thinks so. I think so. I'm a pianist, too. I like Beethoven sonatas, but I can't afford a piano, and I also play the organ. I still play the violin for two or three hours every day. I practise, play studies. I go through three books some mornings and there's forty-two studies in a book. A violin's an awful lot of work—you're always playing studies, not pieces. You've got to play and play. It's something you can't press a button and get, music. It's hard work. But I say work doesn't kill people; money does.

I just play for myself now, and I play in the post office and library and the supermarket at Christmas-time. I play them carols and that. Gives people a bit of a change. You should see the looks on people's belly faces. It's been my life all right, music. When I was about two years old I showed Mum a fiddle in a shop; I wanted it. Wasn't till I was seventeen that I got my first real fiddle. I'd had an old thing I bought in an auction room, but it was no damn good. So I saved up my money from my hobby—sharpening saws—and bought myself a good one. Paid for all my music by sharpening saws. I learnt from my grandfather and was doing it when I was nine years old. I could sharpen a saw in three minutes and give it back to you, perfect. It's a real trade—took me three years to learn it. But the trade's gone nowadays, and I'll tell you why: the big man makes a power saw and turns around and sells it. When it goes bung you just have to go and buy a new chain. My trade's gone. Same thing with knives and scissors and things. They started to go into automatic things that sharpen knives themselves, and the women started to knock off dressmaking. They wanted to go out and work, not stay at home with their scissors and thimbles. So my trade got cut right out.

Then I'd sharpen lawnmowers—spend four hours, lug the thing a mile on my back and get seven and six for it. The big man sells a new lawnmower for $600, and he gets $200 profit. The small man hasn't got a show. I blame the system. The Government can print the money if it wants to, but this crowd won't do it. They think money's some magic thing, but it's man who makes it, not Christ. And if it's a money world, people've got to have money to buy their stuff and do things. Trouble is, some people have lots of it—they go on all these holidays and carry-on; the money disappears. Others have nothing.

Any rate I got a bit of money from sharpening saws when I was a kid. Paid for all my music—had violin lessons for twenty years. The music was in me.

My teacher reckoned I could be top in the world, too. I could have been chief violin teacher in Dunedin, all sorts, but we had to come here to the Coast. Why? Mother was an invalid. She wanted to come here when father died, to be near my brother who was a minister here in Hokitika. I didn't want to leave Dunedin, and last thing mother said when she was dying was, "Biggest mistake we made was leaving Dunedin, Max." I didn't say anything....

Go back there now? No. I've got no home there now. A musician's got to have his own home; he has to practise. My home's here. It mightn't be much, but at least it's mine. And I can practise.

I tell you what, in my life everything seemed to go fut. I always did the wrong thing, or was in the wrong place at the wrong time. My first job when I left school was making taps and things for A & T Burt in Dunedin. I was there three months—got two and five pence a week—then I got laid off because they couldn't keep going, couldn't compete with overseas. Then when they opened up again years later they just took the younger ones on. I missed out again. So I went into tool sharpening after that and worked at the woollen mills in the heavy season. But same thing, no money in that job when I was there. But I kept at it all right. You just couldn't get regular work those days and especially if you were a single man. Then my mother helped me into the grocery shop. I'd have been all right, too, I was coming on well, but they went and put that darned Second World War on and that ruined everything.

I never went to the damn war. I stayed in the grocery shop. Someone had to supply the food, even though there was a war on. I don't regret it, no. But some people gave me a hard time about it.

No, I don't know how they're going to stop the damn wars. It seems to me we can't do without them; man's got to fight. Protection. See your dog there, he doesn't throw away his claws, does he? They're his protection. Same thing today with the nuclear weapons. People say if every country throws away its nuclear weapons it'll be all right. But we haven't got a perfect world, so we can't do that. I say we've got to have the weapons; we've got to be as good as the next joker. I don't say we've got to use them. It's like two bullies: if one thinks the other is tough he won't touch him.

Think we'll have a war soon? I don't think, I know. It's got to happen, a big clean-out. It's coming. But it'll be the end of an age, not the end of the world like some people say. I'm not telling you this so you believe it, I'm just telling you what I know. It'll be a good thing if it brings peace; and peace is something we have to be shocked into. Happen in my lifetime? I wouldn't be surprised if it does. We need a clean-out. When my grandfather died he turned round and said, "What's the world coming to?" When my father died he said, "The world's not worth living in." What I'll say? I say the world's not worth living in today.

I can tell you how the world's changed. In our day you lived by honour. If you went out and did anything wrong you disgraced yourself and the family name too. "To thine own self be true," that was the idea, and I stick to that. You've got to be true to yourself. But today everything's upside down. The question is not how fast you can do a job for someone, like it was in my day. You take me doing a saw in three minutes; but now it's how slow you can do it. You muck around, do it slow and get twice the money. It doesn't fit, does it? Doesn't make sense. You used to take pride in your work. Now it's just how much money you can make. The kids come here and they don't say, what a nice violin or what a nice tune. They ask how much it costs! Money's the root of all evil ... or the *want* of money is the root. If I could do without money I'd burn the damn lot. I had someone want to buy this fiddle here. I said, "What the hell do you want it for?" He wanted to sell it!

I feel sorry for them today. The world's gone bung. I don't know what to say and what to think. I don't like it. There's nothing for the young people to do, no jobs. They can't get money so they steal. I'm not for thieving, but I can see how it happens. When we were kids we worked all the time. We had hedges and dandelions and lawns to mow, knives and forks to polish, everyone's boots to clean. Today the kids wander around the roads swearing. And I pity them. They get a dollar, but you can't buy much with it. We could get all sorts for a penny — a stick of barley sugar or a long chocolate fish, threepence for a big bag of old-fashioned acid drops. I got some the other day — ninety-nine cents for a little bag on special! A whole *kerosene tin* of lollies cost five bob in my day.

And I'll tell you what, in my day you could get yourself a house to live in, and pay it off. My father earned three pound a week. He paid ten shillings down on a house and within two years the house and the land were his. With today's prices you've got to reincarnate and come back a second time to pay the mortgage! And that house of ours was made of five-inch by five-inch heart wood; today they build with five-centimetre cardboard, little bits of wood. Sometimes you can't even *get* the wood to make a house.

The solution? Cut the damn money out. Yes, we'd be better off with bartering; the money system's definitely not working. I get the pension, but you can't do anything with it. Rates were seven pounds when I came here; now they're $300 and I only get half what I used to. They've cut out the gas in Hokitika, that sort of thing. I've cut all my heating out now. It's had to go, even in the winter. If I use it, I'm a gonner. Cold? I get into bed. I vow I won't owe anyone money; I learnt that from the shop.

Cooking? I've got a pressure cooker. I scratch around and get enough to eat. I cook anything that happens to be knocking around — rely a lot on soup and that sort of thing. I buy up knuckles and I used to put in pounds of carrots, but I can't now — they've got too damn dear. I used to buy a big sugar-bag of perfect carrots for five bob in Dunedin. Gone are the days. No, I can't put all the old things in my soup any more. You take celery: it used to be sixpence; now it's one or two dollars a stick. Other than the soup, I get the crumbed sausages, and I make toast and eggs. I used to have three eggs; now it's just one. So that's it: soup, sausages, eggs and bread.

This year I was lucky, I got a couple of Christmas cakes for playing my fiddle in the supermarket. That was a great help. The old ones with relatives living nearby get a hand with veges and cakes and that. Not me. But it's kind of a departed world now, not a family world like it used to be. And everything's expensive for old blokes like me.

When I go to the supermarket I sometimes tell them what prices used to be like in my shop. One pound of peanuts was threepence halfpenny; now, the damn things . . . . The other day they were a dollar forty on special. You'd get a cauliflower the size of a big kettle for threepence. There's not the quality there used to be, either. Costs you seventy dollars for a pair of shoes and they wear out just as fast, or faster. You've got to pay that much for the pleasure of wearing them out. I can tell you this much, I can't manage on my money. I used to go to Beggs in Christchurch and buy my music, enough to last me a couple of years. Last piece I bought was Elgar's violin concerto. Now I can't afford to get to damn Christchurch. They've cut the People's Palace out too, and I can't afford hotels.

I don't know what life is, now. I can't understand things at all. There's only one way to live, and that's the natural way; if we go back to that we'll be right. But now they put powder on the potatoes so they don't sprout, and that means you can't grow them yourself, and they put these sprays around the gardens and the sprays poison the bees, so the fruit doesn't grow. Poisons everything.

No, the simple life's the happiest. Like in that old song, *You in your small corner, and I in mine* — that's a good way to live. You only need a small corner, a wee, small house. If everyone did that there'd be enough to go round. And you've got to stay in your own corner, keep independent and stay out of people's squabbles.

What everyone wants isn't money, it's happiness. Me happy? To a certain extent. But I get a bit lonely. I've only got one nephew left and I haven't heard from him for six months. Loneliness is a big problem. You just can't help it. But I've got my music, I suppose. I'm different, what with my attitude to life and that. I say you only find one or two friends in your lifetime . . . *real* friends. I never got married. Never had the money. You can't do it without money, can't do it just on love. I never ever had enough money to do things right.

You're going again? If I'm not here I'll be on the beach. I sit there and look at the waves.

Six o'clock that evening:

Good, it's you again. I'll just finish my breakfast here. Yes, it's breakfast. I'm different eh? Well, I talked to you all the morning and half the afternoon, then I went to have a look at the sea, and I got in, swam way out. My gills don't work right if I'm not in the sea water every now and again. Time I got back here the day had had it. So I'll just finish my breakfast. I was always thinking of living on love, but I could never find a girl, so now I've got to live on tucker.

I'm good and close to the sea. Let's go and sit on the beach and talk. The fresh air off the sea . . . you'll live another ten years.

That sea is low.

I reckon I've had a very interesting life. I started off with buggies and gas lamps; now I'm seeing people landing on the blooming moon. I reckon myself they'll find a new earth to live on. It's getting too full on this earth. We've mucked the world up, so when things come to an end they'll have to find a new place. I don't like the world at all. This depression now, it's getting bad. It'd be disastrous wasn't for the pensions and the dole and that.

People say to me: "How would you cure the depression, Max?" I say, first thing I'd do would be put the women back into the homes. That'd get the unemployed young people into jobs. Anyone can do most of the jobs today; it's all just press the button. Then when you did that the building trade would pick up; the women would want nicer homes and jobs would be created. Today most of the women don't worry about what their home is like; they just want money.

Where they'll get the money to pay for all this building? I don't know that. But I do know this much: a lot of things have to go backwards before we get a better world. But people don't have my sort of mind. They look at only one side of the story, their own side. Self first, second and last. I never forget what a German teacher told us at school. He said: "There's never only one side of the story. There's always two sides. Get both sides, then take the one that makes most sense." I always remember that. Then there was the notice my brother put on my wall when I was a kid. It said: " 'Can't' is not in the British dictionary. But 'I will not' is." That's a good one, too.

Getting hard sitting on this log, isn't it? I collect wood from the beach here. I saw it up and light a fire now and again. I'm different, just live my own way. Pensioners' flats would drive me mad. Give me a year in one of them and I'd be in a cemetery. I live simple. I've never smoked, didn't drink; didn't need it, I had my music. I've had one glass of beer in my life, when I was in Dunedin. I don't think I got drunk. Tell you the truth, I didn't like it; lemonade's much nicer to drink. Only thing is, it's too dear now. I got some at Christmas and, phew, it's only for special occasions now.

Wasn't for my legs, I've kept healthy. When I was a kid I wanted to swim and play the violin, and I accomplished both. The bloke in charge of lifesaving at St Kilda reckoned I was the best sea swimmer he'd ever seen in his life. I was the only one ever swam there in the winter, out into the ocean. It's no different in winter, only rougher.

Yes I was a swimmer, an athlete, until they put me onto drugs for my legs. The veins sucked the stuff in and it crystallised in my bloodstream. It's like me putting stones in your veins. I knew it was wrong for me. I got an electric heater and sweated the stuff out. Had to use my own brains, otherwise I'd have been in the cemetery. Me, I do things my way. And I still say the sea's the greatest cure in the world.

My doctor here, he's not a swimmer. I'm for it; he's not. He says: "How does the sand get in under your bandages, Max?" I say: "I don't know." It's the getting out of the surf does it. They've gone and tipped concrete in the sea, so when you get out from your swim you step out on concrete, not sand. And you've got to hang on for grim death when the surf's up. I get tipped all over the show, and that's why the blessed sand gets in under the bandages. Makes me mad, seeing people tip things into the sea. They throw all their junk in, yet still the sea stays neutral. Wonderful, isn't it? She heals herself.

Only other trouble out here is you've got to swim with the in-tide. There's a whale of a strong current out there. I've had a lot of them say I'm mad. They think I'll go out to sea. I've seen them run back into the sandhills, afraid they'll have to come and get me. But I'm happy. I go way out past those flags, darn near to the horizon. I like to get three or four miles off the shore and float, have a sleep on the water. It's lovely. Now and again a plane comes along and the pilots get worried; they think I need rescuing. They can't understand it at all. Cold? I never get cold, swimming in the sea. Would do if it was fresh water.

Tide's almost out now, see.

How I feel about my life? I've done my best, that's all I know about it. I look at myself and I reckon I did darn well, I don't care what anyone else says. It's not what you do but who you are that matters, isn't it? People think I'm strange, they call me all sorts and they judge me by what sort of a house I live in. I say, that's my life and that's all there is about it.

And, yes, I could surprise a lot of them. I'm a thinking man. You can see that, can't you? And after all, I *am* the Paganini of the South.

Tom.

TOM

'I've got a simple approach to things and I'm happy'

Tom had spent his eighty-four years on the farm at Bruce Bay, north of Haast. When I turned up he was out the back, castrating and dehorning calves. Tom was proud of his health and usefulness, pleased by his son's insistence that his father could still keep up with the younger men: "Too right, he leaves them for dead."

Eventually, Tom came up the road on his horse. He turned her out into the paddock, chucked down his hat and got a good cup of tea on the table. He was very quick to offer dinner and a bed.

Above all, Tom was friendly and uncomplicated: "I've got a simple approach to things and I'm happy." He had clear blue eyes and lots of white hair. He loved showing me round his animals and veges and flowers. He loved getting up early to make porridge for everyone and bring cups of tea in bed.

The wild, wet West Coast land was Tom's special pride: "The wild space fascinated me, and the air . . . the beautiful green of it."

So was his housekeeper: "Tell you what, I'd be dead long ago, wasn't for my housekeeper." She came for a month, stayed fifteen years; she shared Tom's feeling for the trees and the rain. She also ground wheat for bread, spun and wove wool from the farm and subscribed to Mushroom magazine.

Next day at lunch we ate bread and butter she'd made that morning, and we sampled the new gooseberry jam bubbling on the stove.

I left their place feeling warm and humbled and armed with farm eggs and scones and butter-pats, and also a box of homemade goodies for their friends out on the coast: "Why don't you go and see Albie and Ken at Gillespie's Beach — they're real old characters."

So I did.

I've lived down here at Bruce Bay all my life, in the hills and bush and that. If it wasn't for that trip away to Europe for six months when my wife died, I wouldn't know what the world was like. Then was I pleased to get back and sit down here! Beautiful water, green everywhere. I'll never forget coming back through the pass, back to the green, green West Coast; the beautiful green of it. It's hard to get away from here. It's a big effort.

I was born at Haast in 1899. My mother lived here in Bruce Bay, and when I was due she rode fifty miles to Haast on the old cattle track, up and down the hills and into the bush. Her mother confined her there. All that way, into the bush; wouldn't happen today would it? We stayed at Haast for a while, then my mother took me down to Okuru and we came back here to Bruce Bay in the old barge that brought around the groceries and that. But on the way the sea got up and they had to bolt into Jacksons Bay for shelter. My dad was back at Bruce Bay, very anxious because he knew the boat had put out from Okuru. No way of contacting anyone; no telephone down here until 1909. So it took me a long time to get back to Bruce Bay, but I've been here ever since!

I'm eighty-four now, and very happy to be as good as I am. I can ride my horse way out the back. I come in and have a good bath and I'm right as a bank after it. You see all those old people with arthritis and that — I'd say it's those hills out there kept me fit. I've done an awful lot of hill climbing in my day; and I've never been a great meat eater. It suited me not to. I knew I didn't need it.

Mind you, I've done a terrible lot of hunting in those hills back there. Wasn't very long ago I'd be getting up in the dark and heading out into the hills. I'd be back home with a deer before the rest of the household was out of bed. We needed the meat — yes, to feed the family. But it was also an art, hunting. You had to have a feel for the land and the wind, everything. I watch the young lads today: they walk up the creek beds making a hell of a din, tumbling the stones and even *chatting* as they go along! I say to them: "You're not careful enough. The deer are very sensitive creatures."

Even now I get the old urge to go after the deer and the ducks, but I stick closer in to the house here. I don't walk way out the back; knocked that on the head a couple of years ago. Those hills . . . they're getting higher every year!

But for eighty years or so . . . yes, I ran wild. I know all those hills back there; they kept me alive — Bannock Brae out the back and the Valley of Darkness up near the Paringa River, the Copeland Pass and all over the Landsborough. I liked it in the frost and snow, way back in the hills there. And no such things as sleeping bags in the very early days. I'd just take a big wheat or chaff sack; you could fit right down into it. Cold? Yes, but you kept turning into the fire. You built a darn good fire and kept it going all night, and you kept turning around into it, to warm all sides.

Tell you what, I was really good at making a fire. People'd say: "Tom! He'll make a fire in a damn water hole!" I never failed, never. Way in the back of the hills, in the Valley of Darkness and that — a very cold place where the sun doesn't shine much — you'd have to scrape the snow away from under a tree and make a camp, or get under a rock when it was raining. First thing you'd do was find some dead manuka or rata and get a good fire going, then you'd cook up your tucker, get into your sack and lie down for the night. And that same sack was your pack. In the morning you just walked out of it and threw your gear back in. You dropped a small stone in each corner, put a bit of string around each corner and up around the neck and then just threw it over your back. Could put a terrible big load into those packs, too. That's what I call convenience: a bed and a pack, all in one.

But I was real wild. Dad used to run 500 sheep up there on Bannock Brae. We'd put them up in early October and bring them back down in May before the snows came. I'd go way up there when I was a big lump of a lad, twelve or so. Too steep for horses; I just walked — barefoot! I was fifteen before I wore boots. Yes, I remember getting those boots, all right. Big excitement, my own pair of boots from the bootman in Hokitika. But then I'd only have them on an hour or two and I'd take them off. Too hot! I see these joggers on the roads today and I say to myself, I'd have lasted better than them in the hills. I didn't jog everywhere, I ran. Took us about three days to muster Bannock Brae. It always intrigued me, being on the tops — the wildness and the beautiful, clear air. The sheep loved it up there. They'd come back with bright eyes and lovely, clear white wool.

Yes, it was my delight to go mustering. When I was seven years

125

old I'd get up behind my uncle and ride down to Haast, bareback. Fifty miles, that trip; it'd take us all day. Then the men would go off mustering cattle in the Landsborough and I'd be left to fend for myself in an old house down there. It used to be a store. There were great big biscuit tins with a few biscuits left in. That'd be my tucker till they got home.

After that, for years I helped take cattle through from Okura to Paringa and then out on the open track to the Whataroa saleyards. That'd be 140 miles from Okura, and then a couple of times we went right through to Hokitika. We did that trip once a year, in the autumn. There'd be a big crew of us, four or five different families, and about 1,000 head of cattle when we joined up all our herds.

Took us eleven days, Bruce Bay to Hokitika, five to Whataroa, and then three days back on the horse. Tough on the horse; you had to have the very best. But I really looked forward to those trips. I was young and tough, and plenty of people wanted their stock driven. One time I came home from one trip at night, shod another horse next morning and took off on another drive next day. I remember it was raining hard. I was shoeing the horse up alongside the wall for shelter, then it was back for another eleven days in the saddle. Only once I did that quick turn around. Usually I had weeks or even a month at home before I went for the next lot.

Thought nothing of it. It was my job and the same two dogs would always come with me next trip. One of my dogs in particular, old Ring, he always knew which cattle were mine. He'd pick ours out and leave the others behind. He worked overtime, old Ring. I always thought that was a bit far fetched, when other fellows said their dog knew which cattle were theirs, but I saw old Ring do it many a time . . . .

You come out with me now and have a look at my dogs and fowls and my horse; I'd like you to see my animals. You'll see for yourself how I handle them. I hear about this one and that one who can't catch his horse. Not me. I come out here and call out. The horses yell back.

See that. They come right up to me. Always have. This is my horse, the piebald. I've always had a piebald. They're tough, real tough. You can see how my horses like me, eh Christine? He treats me like a companion. I've always had that. Kindness is a big factor. I never abuse them. You treat them well, they treat you well, that's what I say. The horses have always been a big part of my life down here. I was always busy breaking them in and that.

I'm in the right place, all right, down here, with the animals and the bush and the rain. When I was a kid I'd be crawling round after ducks in the water. My Mum used to say: "You're never dry. You'll suffer from arthritis when you're old." Anyway, I haven't got a sign of arthritis. Just the other day a chap said to me, "If you've ever been stung by bees, you won't get arthritis or rheumatism." Well, I've been stung plenty of times. We'd rob the old schoolhouse and fill up our bath with honey. Mum would be there putting it in little containers and the robber bees would be coming around, after the honey. We'd be stung all over. We were wild and tough, too right!

In winter we'd go up to Bannock Brae and slide down on our bottoms. We'd see the blue streaks from our denim trousers on the snow and we'd follow that line, knew there were no rocks. Fancy going way up there for entertainment — it's 4,500 feet to the top! But we were happy as Larry way up there. First visitors we'd get would be the keas. They'd hear us laughing and come round in mobs. They'd sit on the snow with us. Or we'd go swimming and all that sort of thing in the summer. We never missed the city thing. No films and carry-on way down here at the bay.

We had a school, though, in my day, in a clear patch up the back on the old road. Just a small one-room school, about sixteen kids and one teacher. I remember all my teachers' names, too. There were Mary Ellen, then my aunty Nell, then Alice Cuttance. I remember one of them — I won't say which one — she belted me fourteen times on the hand with a long cane. Left big weals on my hands; they were sore for days. What I'd done? Nothing. The others had done something, not me, but I didn't split. Then later on the teacher asked me to take her up to the neighbours in our horse and cart. I did it, but I wouldn't talk to her.

Instead of liking school, you hated it those days — slates and slate pencils and learning spelling and poems by heart. The teacher would give us stuff to learn at night. Sometimes we wouldn't get it done, so we'd cheat like mad. She'd sit at her desk with her back to us — silly woman — someone would have it all written out and we'd just read it off. We beat her that way.

Yes, I hated being at school. I wanted to be out in the hills. My old grandfather used to keep me home from school to weed the paddocks of horse carrots. He'd sit on a three-legged stool and follow me, to see I did it well. By the end of the day I'd be down on my knees, he'd whack me with his walking stick and say, "You've got lazy in your back Tommy." But I'd still sooner do that weeding carrots than go to school.

Or Grandad would keep me home to wash the sheep dags in the dip. He'd say, "I'll give you a bob for it Tommy." I'd be there all day, and I'm still waiting for those bobs! Yes, we did whatever we could to get out of a day's school, and we dawdled all the way there. In winter the cows would be lying down in the frost. We'd get them up and stand in the warm, dry patch with our bare feet. It was a great gag; we'd all race to get there first. None of us wore shoes, but we never got frostbite. Funny, isn't it? Then in summer we'd be going barefoot over the dry river bed. The big stones got so hot the soil would dry away; you could put your hand down between the stones.

There wasn't the rain those days to cool everything down. There'd be big floods all right, but then it'd dry right out. The rivers were much lower than they are today, and we'd have to drive the cattle up the river a mile or two, for water. Then we'd go out in the hills and just sleep on the ground — no tent, no sleeping bag, just a fire.

Nowadays the land's afloat, water running everywhere. A lot of us old ones think it's wetter nowadays. We never get a week without rain. As a matter of fact, rain's fallen on the last thirty weekends in a row. And the fogs've come right down to the paddocks, too. They used to stay way up in the hills, that's what I reckon.

The weather's changed right around. We've got cooler summers, warmer winters now. No snow down here around the house like we used to get. Last winter we only had two or three light frosts, and you never see ice here any more. When I was a boy, there'd be three or four inches of ice on the ponds. I remember on the way to school we'd gather up the geese, drive them onto the ice and the poor beggars couldn't get off; they'd just slip around, flapping their wings, and we'd find them still there on the way home from school. Yes, cruel, wasn't it? They'd have cold feet all right, and we thought it was a great joke.

But as for school. . . . Soon as I turned fourteen I left and started work on the farm. Been here ever since.

A darn good place for a kid to live, down here. Peaches out in the paddock — as good as any from Central Otago and that — and big, blue plums. I loved cold, stewed plums with thick cream straight from the cow. Then sometimes Mum gave us a treat before bed. She'd let the coals in the fire die down, throw in some onions and cover them up with ashes. Once they were cooked we'd pull off the skins and smear butter all over them . . . wonderful to taste. Another treat on winter nights was hot muscatels; you never see them nowadays do you, those muscatel raisins? Mum would put some in a basin, pour brandy over and set it alight. There'd be a lovely blue glow flowing over the basin, and we'd poke the muscatels out. Never burnt us, don't know why.

I miss some of those old things Mum used to make: doughboys and duff and roly-poly. We loved them. And she'd shoot a pigeon or two and make up pigeon soup and pigeon pie. It was good, I tell you. Or she'd sometimes get a rabbit and make up a good strong rabbit pie — that was a cracker of a meal.

Yes, I've had good, simple food all my life. Every morning I make porridge, made with milk, not water. Had porridge for breakfast all my life. And I'm very lucky with my housekeeper. She grinds the wheat and makes all our own bread. She's the only one around here who still makes the bread. She makes all the butter and jam, goes out with the horses and dogs. She likes it here, likes the rain and the quiet. She came here for a month, and now fifteen years have gone by, just like that. You see, Christine, it's hard to get away from down here. It's a big effort.

My life . . . when you look over it, I've had a wonderful experience. And the younger ones don't know anything about our style of living. In the old days the hard way seemed the right way — that's what my dad always said. Now the easy, quick way seems right. It's much easier to get your whole mob to market in one load, in a truck. Two hours and twenty minutes up to Whataroa, and the cattle don't lose condition. Speed's the answer. Only thing is, everything's gone up in price, too. It's $1,000 now to get our cattle up to market. In my day the only cost was fourpence a head for paddocking at night. Cheap.

I think we've had the best of the days, oh yes. Everything was clear, and clean. This house has no lock on it. We'd go away and leave it. Never lost a bob, never found our tools and that were missing. We knew what was going on in our lives . . . still do, way down here. But it's bad in the towns nowadays, even down here on the Coast. And everything's instant. You just press a button. Computers and things can work out your bill at the shop and even translate from one language to another. The children come around here collecting for this and that or selling poppies. I ask them: "How much for three poppies?" and they don't have a clue. Can't work it out; they have a card with it all written down.

We had to rely on ourselves. We'd head off into the hills with a few loaves of bread, a couple of pounds of butter and a bit of tea and sugar. Billy tea, you can't beat it. Then you relied on your gun, shot your own meat, and that was it. None of the fancy bits and pieces they take into the bush these days. I never even carried a torch. Never. All the boys have them now. They can't go outside the door without a torch. Not me. And I was never ever lost in the hills. I've been all my life in the wilderness and I never lost my way, even in that thick West Coast fog. When you get into that fog you just stand and face into the breeze off the sea. You can't go wrong.

No, I never get lost out here. It was my instinct, the hills. The wild space fascinated me, and the air. Yes, that's it, Christine. Everything makes sense out there. But you put me in a city . . . I'm hopeless, lost all the time.

Never minded being isolated? Oh no. I was in Europe, in the big cities; it's all rush and people drinking. And I'll never forget the first time I was in Canterbury, everything so very hot and dried up. There were taps in the street. You'd turn them on and drink from a cup. I was always going for a drink. I missed the hills and rain and the green bush.

Yes, farming down here in the backblocks was my life. I've got a simple approach to things and I'm happy. As I say, Christine — and you'll understand this — we live in a different world today. The young want fast things, towns and motorbikes. I never did. They want instant things; I like the hills. Their life is more of a . . . what would you call it? . . . a convenience life. Everything's done by power: power saws, power bikes. Our life was healthy. And I'm very pleased I'm healthy. It still gives me a thrill that I'm eighty-four and I can ride the horse and work the cattle, do the castrating and dehorning. My son says I can still do two calves to another man's one. I've had seventy-odd years at it, Christine. I've learnt the little touches. The young fellows, my cousins and nephews and that, they pushed me out of the way at one stage of it. Said, "We'll do it, Tom." I watched them; they had to have two or three tries, and they used two hands. I do it with one cut, with one hand. So my son put me back on, and I still do two to his one.

. . . Christine, I haven't told you the worst. I'm going blind. Cataract. Just these last few months. Sometimes I'm filling the teapot and I miss. It's my shooting eye. Maybe I've strained it over all those years, but the doctor says he won't take the cataract off till it's gone right over my eye. I don't like that. I want him to take it off now. I'm afraid it's going to affect my shooting. I can't change over to the other eye, not at this age. And I've been doing it all my life, shooting. I won't give it up easily, bung eye or not.

You see, Christine, I like it way down here with the animals and bush and rain . . . the beautiful green of it. I've lived in this house since I was six. Look at these gooseberries and old plums. They've been here as long as I have. Here, have this moss rose. It's a real old-fashioned one with a deep, deep smell. I'm at home here, Christine, absolutely. Everything makes sense.

CHARLOTTE

'I didn't see any reason to run with the mob'

Charlotte stood out as spirited, intelligent, professional. She had never felt compelled to conform; she had always formed strong opinions and aired them. As a four-year-old with a broken arm, she'd informed the doctor there was no need to come back next day.

As a young woman she chose to follow a career teaching dancing and later speech and drama, at a time when most "nice girls" stayed at home to cook and sew and keep house, then marry. Charlotte was still teaching speech and drama at the age of sixty-eight. She also chose to marry a Maori, to remarry eventually when he died after six obviously happy years and to cope once again when her second husband died only two years later.

As an 80-year-old she was crippled and battling with poor eyesight, but she was interested in the world, assertive, philosophical. We hibernated for long hours in her cluttered room in a rest home. She sat on the bed propped up against a stack of pillows with a hottie and a shawl over her legs. Then she talked about her early years in the Dunedin district, about her aspirations and griefs and failings, about old people's homes and euthanasia and her fears for the future of the world.

Charlotte loved words above all things. She revelled in their potency, in talking and exchanging ideas: "I've thoroughly enjoyed these days because I've got no one here to talk to, not really. It's all superficial. And I always did love having people listen to me." She'd sit bolt upright on the bed and quote large chunks of Hamlet and Twelfth Night and The Blind Beggerman.

She was prepared to talk not only about her achievements but also about her fears, loves and doubts, willing to sing her old school songs or show me her buckled feet and cancer spots. I came away from our sessions reeling from the creative power still surging in her broken body, yet at the same time humbled by her appreciation of our conversations: "All this talking is doing me a power of good. It's bringing all sorts *of things back. It's like having a plough-up. And it's making me consider things I wouldn't say to anyone else.''*

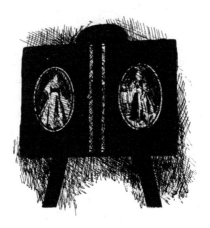

I love talking. The doctor told me: "You've got a lot of problems, Charlotte, but nothing the matter with your tongue and your brain." I always did have a mind of my own, and I was always mad about books and stories . . . words. As a child I was known as a bookworm and that always upset me as I thought of myself as something yellow and corrugated and crawling, something not really nice to know. I think I was blessed with far too strong an imagination, far too strong for my comfort. The family realised it, too. I was never allowed to have "Penny Horribles", the comics of the time, because I'd read about a horned man — everywhere he walked his feet left a burnt print. It affected me dreadfully. I raced to my bedroom, pulled down the blinds and got in under the blankets. It took me years to get over that. I was very nervous, could never be alone. So after that I never got my hands on any of those "Penny Horribles", as much as I wanted them.

Then one day my grandad told me King Edward VII had died, and that shattered me. It was the first time death had entered into my world. Where had the king gone? What had happened to him to make him die? The family all said he'd gone out in the rain and got wet, and that's the worst thing they could have said. After that, if anyone went out in the rain I'd be yelling, "Come in quick. You know what happened to the king." I wish to dickens they hadn't told me he'd gone out and got wet. The truth of the matter was he was just a bit of an old rake, died of old age and dissipation!

Then to get me indoors at night the family would yell out, in awful voices to torment me:

Now the day is over, night is drawing nigh,
Shadows of the evening creep across the sky.

I can still remember the feeling, still see those awful hands coming across the sky. I'd get inside just before they got me. My aunt loved to yell it out and see me tearing in, through the macrocarpa trees, but it always frightened seven years' growth out of me. Same thing with:

Gentle Jesus meek and mild,
Look upon a little child,
Pity my simplicity,
Suffer me to come to thee.

I quite liked Jesus. I thought of him with a long white gown, a crook in one hand and a lamb in the other, but I didn't particularly want to go to him just then . . . far too vivid an imagination.

My grandmother and I used to sit out on the verandah at night, looking at the sky and watching the clouds piling up. We'd tell each other long, involved stories about what we saw. Or we'd sit in front of our open fire — a huge, great thing, took two men to carry the log in — and we'd tell each other what we saw in the flames. I always saw a great deal. It thrilled me and awed me, too. Some people always used to say I had "the sight" to a certain extent. That's what they call it in Scotland — "the sight", a sixth sense. My great-grandmother had it strongly.

Yes, in some ways I was quite bright. My Aunt Sally thought I was a living wonder; she always thought I'd end up a genius, or mad! She more or less brought me up, my Aunt Sally. My mother died when I was born, so my grandmother and grandfather took me in. They already had twelve kids, all a lot older than me, so I was the baker's dozen. They were my family, and Aunt Sally was my special aunt. I remember those early days very clearly. My memory is almost photographic and it's full of colour.

I clearly remember falling off the neighbour's donkey and breaking my arm when I was four. The doctor, one of the very early women doctors in New Zealand, arrived on a grey horse, wearing a divided skirt and riding side-saddle, and she got my two uncles to hold me down on the couch with a yellow rug on it while she set the arm in a splint. I knew something bad was going to happen, and it hurt like hell — no anaesthetics and plasters and things those days. I remember it vividly. I was yelling to high heaven and everyone else was howling, too, except the doctor. She said she'd come back next day and see me, and apparently I said "You don't need to bother." I was quick with words even then, a little horror. After that I got taken to see the doctor once a week, and she'd always have a boiled sweet ready to pop in my mouth to stop me talking!

Another thing I remember about the day of the broken arm, I got asked what I wanted for tea, and I wanted tomatoes. Tomatoes were a very new thing, a new "invention", and someone had to go the half mile down the road to the shop and get me tomatoes. And then nearly everyone who came to see me brought me *books*.

I never ever wanted dolls or other presents for Christmas, only books. One time I remember getting a doll. I threw it up to the ceiling and broke its head!

Primary school I remember perfectly well. I could read and the other kids couldn't, and we played lots of games — hopscotch and hoops and marbles. There were all the different kinds of marbles: Glassies were very clear ones; Agaties were brown with white through them; Stinkies were brown and rough — they looked like they were made of clay; then there were white ones called Milkies and the big one, the Taw. Skipping was also very popular — Double-Dutch, and All in Together This Fine Weather, the Last One to Trip Gets Pepper, and Wash the Dishes, Dry the Dishes, Turn the Dishes Over — and we had all sorts of singing and dancing around games, too, like *Nuts and May*, *The Farmer Wants a Wife*, and *Oranges and Lemons*. Half the time we didn't know what the words meant — like that game where one stood in the circle and everyone danced around and sang:

> *Here's a pretty little girl of mine,*
> *She cost me many a bottle of wine.*
> *A bottle of wine, a guinea or two,*
> *See what my pretty little girl can do.*

Us kids had no idea what all that was about. But if she wasn't a prostitute, I don't know what she was.

At first I was in "the little seats" — we had all the primers and Standard One in the same room, and one teacher did everyone. She taught my father, that teacher, and I laid her out when she died!

We were all book-mad at home. It sounds awful, but I remember meal-times — all of us around the big table and all reading books! It made perfect sense to us. We had to really slog all day milking sixty cows by hand, separating, putting down fresh straw, growing oats and wheat and that. So the only times for reading were at the table or in bed with a candle.

We weren't wild west or murder readers, but we'd read everything else. Everything. I started off with Beatrix Potter and *Alice in Wonderland* — I can still recite all those — and then came Anne books: *Anne of Green Gables*, and all the rest of the series; and I loved the Katy books — *What Katy Did*, *What Katy Did Next*, *What Katy Did at School*. She never measured up to Anne of Green Gables, mind you. But they were like the kids next door. I grew up with all those characters and I'd howl and howl when one of them got killed by a falling tree or something. I didn't ever like books about "good girls", like the Elsie and Daisy books; they gave me a pain in the neck. They were the ones I was supposed to read, but I wasn't interested. I was always like that, knew what I liked. And I can still list all the books I read as a child. Those days you read them again and again; you didn't read them and put them away like you do today.

So, naturally, I was always good at words. But as for arithmetic ... I was never good at figures. They didn't interest me at all. I got the strap every day for talking in arithmetic, but I couldn't care less. And when it came to fractions ... I had no intention at all of learning fractions. I'd be at the top of the class for English and spelling and that sort of thing, at the bottom for arithmetic.

I couldn't see any sense in those blooming questions: how many rolls of paper would it take to paper a wall twelve foot by ten foot? Or how many hours would it take so and so many men to dig a ditch such and such feet long? I always said it depended on whether the men worked hard or not. And as for how many rolls are needed to paper the wall, I said I'd just get the man in to measure up the wall and he'd tell me, and I'd get the man to put the paper up, too. All I'd do was choose the paper. And that's what I've done, all my life. I've never come up against the problem of how many rolls of wallpaper I'd need, and I've never dug ditches either!

I suppose I was a bit precocious, but luckily my maths teacher had a marvellous sense of humour. I think she saw the futility of those questions, too.

Then later in life I did have to use figures, for working out dosages for X-rays and things in hospitals; no charts to do it for you those days. Luckily, I had a friend, a lecturer in science at university; he was a wizard at figures. We both went in to work on the train, and he sorted me out in one trip! I found it was no trouble to do maths when I could see sense in it. I knew why I had to do dosages — it was life or death. You'd burn a patient if you gave him the wrong dosage.

Yes, like I told you, I didn't see any reason at all to run with the mob, and it seemed to pay off. Just after World War I the League of Nations came in and we had to write an essay on it. I remember walking into the classroom and thinking, I don't know a thing about the League of Nations. I hadn't read up about it and I was cornered, a rat in a trap. So I sat down and relied on my wits and my imagination. I wrote pages and pages on the League of Churches. I argued, why were we talking about a League of Nations when the churches were all against one another? I got first prize for that essay and felt terribly guilty about it. I knew why I'd *not* written about the League of Nations, and I didn't tell anyone why. The judge said he'd never seen anyone put so much thought into an essay. I'd thought about it all right — had to!

So I'd get 100 percent in English and French, but for maths all I'd get was 5 percent for neatness!

What I like in books now is hearing people say what they've got out of life. It keeps your mind developing, and it brings back periods of my own life, too. Shakespeare's still way up the top for me, definitely. He always shows what human nature is really like. My favourite play is without doubt *Hamlet:*

> *. . . to thine own self be true;*
> *and it must follow, as the night the day,*
> *thou canst not then be false to any man.*

I also love *Twelfth Night, The Merchant of Venice, Macbeth*. And one thing they've improved on no end, they act Shakespeare much more naturally these days. In our day they used to orate too much. Now they just sit down on a tree stump and say:

> *Life's but a walking shadow, a poor player*
> *that struts and frets his hour upon the stage*
> *and then is heard no more: it is a tale*
> *told by an idiot, full of sound and fury,*
> *signifying nothing.*

It's not elocution but said naturally, as if you were saying it to a friend, and that's a good thing.

Then after Shakespeare comes George Bernard Shaw and Oscar Wilde. They stick to home truths, too. Shaw said the most important things in life are free bowels and easy boots, and I say that's absolutely true. My feet and bowels were always nothing but a darn trouble to me all my life.

I read anything I can get my hands on, anything except wild wests, or those light romances, full of strong, silent, cruel men, and women taking it all. I'd have bashed those heroes; they were all brutes. I like a good who-done-it, but they're not memorable, just time-passers for me.

I'm limited now, though, because I can't walk to the library. I can only get hold of what's on the shelves here or what people like you bring me. I'm liking the Sargeson. He touches on what we are. Nearly every page starts me thinking about old characters I used to know, old situations. It's very good.

I've been very fortunate. I was able to combine my love of books with a career, selecting all the books for the local library for years and years and teaching speech and drama, or elocution as it was called in our day. Unusual for a woman to have "a career"? Yes, when I was a girl the only females who really worked were the poor, who had to, and they worked in the factories. Most women stayed at home. They sewed and cooked and kept house, then they got married. Some went off nursing, a very few learnt typing and shorthand, and if a girl was very bright she went teaching. But it wasn't really the done thing to be a "career woman". As my aunt said, " 'Every man to his taste,' as the old woman said as she kissed the cow."

Anyway, I started teaching when I was twenty-one and taught on and off ... mostly on! ... until I was sixty-eight. As a kid I always wanted to learn speech. I used to listen to the other kids talking about speech lessons and I was so envious, but one of my aunts wouldn't let me learn. She thought I'd be better than my sister who was already going to lessons. She was probably right, too! But Aunt Sally encouraged me and in the end I did go to speech lessons, and I was right in my element. I loved the exams. I was always word perfect at the orals and I adored reciting and writing like mad; I'd be in another world. When I stopped writing it was like suddenly coming up from a deep pit and seeing everyone staring at me, because I was the only one still writing. I suppose I loved the challenge of the exams. ...

I've certainly had some really high peaks for speech and drama — my own successes and my pupils', too. Anyway, I taught until I married Matt when I was twenty-six, then six and a half years later Matt died. He got the flu. It developed into double pneumonia and he just drowned. No antibiotics and things those days. I was devastated. Absolutely. I remember standing there at the graveside and saying to Matt's father, "I wish it was me." "My dear," he said, "we would never have comforted him." And an extraordinary thing happened. I was always a very nervous person, but that left me, after Matt died. I can't explain it, whether I felt the worst had happened, or whether he was with me or what. But it was sure, my word it was sure. The last thing Matt said was, "You'll be all right, Charlotte," and right from the night he died all fear left me.

Anyway, I couldn't stand the round of morning and afternoon teas. I went up to friends in Auckland and one day I marched myself off to the Mater Hospital. I explained everything to the Mother Superior. She said, "You go out and get yourself four smocks," so I nurse-aided there for four months before returning home. It was the best thing out, sitting people on bedpans, giving them enemas. I was kept so busy and tired I kept my mind off my grief. Then eighteen months after Matt died, World War II was declared and I knew I'd be manpowered into essential work because I was a widow. I remember I stood stock still in the Octagon in Dunedin and thought, I'll get in first, before they manpower me, but what kind of work will I do? I thought of being a taxi-driver — I knew a man who ran a motor firm so my chances would have been good there — but then I thought, no, I know how to drive a car, I won't learn anything there. Then I thought, Matt died of pneumonia and I knew nothing about nursing. I could have been more help to him. So off I went to see the superintendent of the Dunedin Hospital — awful darn cheek. She said I was too old and they didn't take married women anyway, but she'd take my phone number. So I just wafted off, a widow, well into my thirties, with a lot of cheek and nothing much else going for me.

Anyhow, later on the superintendent rang me and I ended up nursing for the six years of the war, right up until peace-time. Most of the time I was at a children's long-term and convalescent hospital where they treated TB bones, polio, congenital hips, osteomyelitis and that sort of thing.

I loved the nursing there at the convalescent home. I was a damn good nurse, too; but with all that walking, up and down the stairs and all over the place, my knee started to play up, and then my feet. I had everything — fallen arches, bunions, hammer-toes, you name it. They sent me to a foot specialist, got me special shoes, but it was hopeless — my feet were hell. So in the end they put me in the X-ray therapy department. There wasn't quite so much walking as before, but I had to walk the whole hospital with the radium treatment and, sure enough, my feet started to play up again. My knee was hell, and I had developed arthritis, too.

The sister sent me to the top foot specialist. I was used to doctors looking at my feet and saying, "Oh dear" or "Oh my God", but I remember this specialist's words, "It's wicked. There's not one bone in your feet in the right place." I told him it was like walking around on glass and he said, "My dear, I quite agree with you." He put me under anaesthetic, manipulated my feet and put them in plaster. That was my first experience of the modern anaesthetics, and I became a perfect bore. I couldn't stop talking about how wonderful they were. I'd already had about a dozen of the old anaesthetics and I always thought they were the worst part of the whole blooming operation. You felt like your jaw was being broken and you were being choked at the same time, then afterwards you retched for a fortnight. I always thought I'd rather be operated on without an anaesthetic.

Anyhow, my feet were never right, so that was the end of my nursing. They eventually filleted my toes, took the bones out and off I went back home. A few months later I was walking down the street. A lady stopped me and asked me to teach her daughter elocution. Well, I was over forty by that stage. I hadn't taught since I was twenty-six. I knew if I took it on again I'd have to do lots of revision — the syllabus had changed, techniques had changed, everything. I looked down at the child, saw her beseeching face and that was it. I said yes, I'd start teaching again. I said I wouldn't take more than six pupils, though, and they were to keep it quiet, but that's impossible in a small town like ours. Every mum had either a potential genius or a child that stuttered or was slow at reading or something, and of course in the end I had twenty pupils, then twenty-five. On it went, and I always had a waiting list. Suddenly, there I was, sixty-eight years old and still teaching.

I couldn't begin to count the number of children I've taught; there'd be hundreds. See all these photos around and under the bed? I'm glad they didn't all send me their photos! So many of them still keep in touch, that's the lovely thing, and even some of their parents write quite frequently.

But it's the best move I ever made, taking up speech and drama again. It shook my brain up, kept me in touch with young people.

When I was forty-six I remarried, fourteen years after Matt died. I was loath to get married again. I wasn't desperately in love with George; it was still Matt for me. He was a Maori from just out of Dunedin and something very special, Matt.

Other men wooed me. I was reasonably attractive and a good dancer. I had plenty of marriage proposals from wealthy men, but I had no intentions with them. I was quite prepared to accept their chocolate and ribbons and whatnot, but not to marry them. I didn't love any of them. At one stage I got myself almost engaged to one of the rich ones. We got to the stage of buying the ring, but I wasn't happy. I loved Matt, so one night I rang Matt from a phone box and asked him: "Can a woman change her mind?" Matt's reply was, "If that woman is you, yes."

The reaction when I decided to marry a Maori? It was considered unusual, but then I wasn't a usual sort of a person. I never ever felt any sign of racial prejudice. I'm intolerant all right, intolerant of people's conduct and character, but not of their *colour*. I was never *aware* of their colour — I don't know why. I went to Sunday School with Chinese children and I never even knew they were Chinese until I was an adult, even though they had strange names. I don't know whether I was dumb or what, but it never entered my head. As for now, it just seems pathetic to me that people think they're better that others because of their skin. It's ignorant and pathetic. I remember once going into a shop in the islands. There was a dark woman at the counter waiting to be served, but the shopkeeper came up to serve me. I said, "This woman was here before me." She said, "I'll serve you first." Well. I answered, "In that case I won't be served at all," and walked out.

I had six wonderful years with Matt. I'm still in touch with him. When I was blind and disorientated for four months after my double cataract operation two years ago, he came to me. I got a real thing about the sister; I didn't want her to attend me. I wanted to lock the door so she couldn't get into the room. Then I heard Matt's voice saying: "Don't be so silly, dar. It'll be all right," and I calmed down in seconds. It was his voice all right, and no one else in the world has called me dar, short for darling. Mind you, I didn't tell anyone how he came to me like that. They'd say I was nuttier than ever!

And another thing I learned when I was blind after that operation: you do have "that inward eye". It's very true what Wordsworth said: ". . . that inward eye that is the bliss of solitude". I could remember exactly what people looked like. They'd come in and I'd say "talk", and I could see them more clearly in that inward eye than I could before, seeing them physically. If I shut my eyes now I see you clearly as can be, when you speak. And it's the same with places you've been to, or daffodils. You remember what they look like. But I'd say most people don't really know that inward eye until they're blind.

Another thing I think is this: they say "no man is an island", but I think every man *is* an island. I've discovered that when I've been in a crisis — no one can reach me. Not really. People can try. They can be very kind, but they can't really reach through to you. When my two husbands died I got hundreds of letters and all sorts of thoughtfulness, but none of it can help, not really. It's inevitable that every man *is* an island. Our lives are certainly joined up together, but when it comes to the real depths, no human can help you. All you can try and hold on to is a religious belief. If there's a God, only He can help. But as for God . . . three-quarters of me *has* a faith, but that quarter. . . .

I can't say I'm an agnostic. I'm certainly not an atheist, but with religion I can't say I've ever really grasped things as I'd wanted to. Maybe I'll see it some day. I hope and pray I will. Far more intelligent people than me have seen it. They have faith. Why can't I? The whole thing can't be a colossal accident. There's a pattern. You can't stop the sun rising when it's got to.

Bitter? No, I'm not bitter. Not now. I was for a time, mind you. When Matt died I went up to Auckland for a break and I remember *wanting* war. I hoped war would be declared; I'd listen avidly to the news. Then I realised that other people's misery wouldn't make mine any less, and luckily I got over that bitterness.

All this talking is doing me a power of good; it's making me consider things I wouldn't say to anyone else. You're like me, a person who needs to be told the truth.

Another thing I wonder about a lot and that's euthanasia. I'm a great believer in it. I don't see why we have to live in the one body when the body's intolerable. I can't see why religion should be against it. If the Christians are right, it'll be wonderful. I might have a little while in hell, but then it'll be heaven for me, because I've done nothing dreadfully bad in my life . . . not yet! And I'm certain my friends will be in heaven, and they'll beg for me! I'm quite sure, if the Christians are right, the wonderful thing will be the reunions. And if the atheists are right, it'll be good, too, because it'll be perpetual sleep. And what's more lovely than sleep? So if you're an atheist and believe in sleep, not in an after life, then euthanasia doesn't matter anyway.

We talk about death, some of us here in the old people's home, and everyone I've spoken to believes in euthanasia. We don't want to lose our dignity. Why should we have to go through years of drooling and wetting the bed and not knowing who anyone is, or who we are ourselves? Families feel a duty to come and see us, but mostly they don't really want to, and we get looked after by people who aren't always very compassionate. Why should they be? No, I don't want all of you people to come and see me in a few years' time and find me senile.

Yes, I said to my doctor, "If I have a turn, don't you dare resuscitate me. That's an order." He said nothing. I said: "If you do bring me back, when I eventually get up there to heaven I'll get back at you. I'll come back as an evil spirit and play merry hell in your life." But I say, I've had my share, three score years and ten plus nine. We're so irrational. We say you can't take an old life, yet we spend millions producing weapons to kill the whole race out in a few minutes. It's so irrational.

No, death's nothing to me now. I know we're all under a death sentence, and I firmly believe in life after death. But also I look on death as a great friend, not something to be feared. I've nursed people whom I was frightened to touch, it hurt them so much. It's so lovely to lay them out and know you're not hurting them. Death's a wonderful thing for those people. Our 102-year-old here died last night, and you couldn't be anything but happy. It wasn't her there at the end, only her body. The real Miss Jacobs was gone long ago. Senility. You go back to being a child, and you're happy in that state, and it's not the real you that we've all got to know.

Old age does have its compensations. As long as your mind's clear, you've got all your memories to look at and you don't have to do domestic chores. But in some ways you feel frustrated. You've got to give out to get satisfaction in life. For half a century or so I was constantly giving out through my teaching and nursing, but now all I can do is read to people. And, during my life, if anyone was in trouble or sick they came to me because I was a free body; I had no husband most of the time, no family because of all my operations.

But now I *can't* do anything for people. I can't do anything physically. Can't walk properly — I just get giddy and fall over. Can't see and can't smell. My electric blanket could be on fire for all I know. My joints don't work, either. Seeing me get out of my long winceyette nightie must be hilarious. I have to stand up against the bed so I won't fall over. I can't reach up, can't reach down. As for cutting my toe-nails — I can't bend because I've got a hiatus hernia, so I sit over there on the end of the bed, file a couple of toes, vomit in the basin, file a few more. I get sick cutting my toe-nails! The staff aren't allowed to cut our toe-nails nowadays . . . union regulations . . . and I'm not going to pay a chiropodist eight dollars to do it for me. I object to that. But I dread the day when I can't do my own toe-nails and they call the chiropodist in.

But I'm all for old people's homes. It's an ideal set-up. I've been here ten years and no one can convince me otherwise. I'd reached the end of the road as far as looking after myself completely was concerned. I couldn't reach up to the shelves or under the bed, couldn't sweep the garden path. An old people's home is the place to be now. People say, "I won't let *my* mother go to an old people's home," but they've got the wrong idea about the whole business. Same thing with a lot of the old people who start here. I've noticed they come in very resentful. The cry is, "They don't want me." They resent their daughters or sons or sisters or someone. I say, wait until you settle down into your routine and you'll find you're far more independent than you are living with your daughter or someone.

Sounds mad, but it's true. You can have your friends in when you like. You invite them for afternoon teas and dinners. You go out when you like. You've always got someone to talk to or play scrabble and cards with, or you can sit in the lounge and read. Then if you get fed up you can go to your own room. And everything's done for you — your meals, your linen. You don't have to worry if the drain's blocked or the roof's leaking. I look at it this way, Chris: I might have a stroke or a blackout and be over the hill any day. It's a good place to be if that's going to happen. And we're so forgetful, always losing things. There's always someone to come and help you look for them.

Then there's all the other little things that happen in a rest-home like this. Volunteers come from outside and serve teas and do our hair and nails and that; they look after us. Mind you, I'm not fond of being sung to. I don't like people coming in and singing silly songs or putting on tripey little plays. I could do better myself, but I very rarely perform now. I tell you what, I've seen too many people performing for too long. It's pathetic. People here get up and play the piano or recite poems and it's absolutely pathetic: they were once at the top of their field, and now. . . . They like me to recite, but I've said to myself over and over, don't go on too long, Charlotte. When you start to go downhill, stop.

As for going back and living with your daughter or son or someone, I don't think three generations can live together. The children are always being told, keep quiet for Granny. Granny's in the way when they want to tear around or go off on holiday. Granny can't think, I'll have a bath, or I'll whip up a batch of pikelets, or I'll leave my washing hanging in the kitchen today — it's too cold to hang it outside. You can't do these things freely in someone else's home.

And then again, the way to keep people is to let them go. If you cling to your family, you lose them. I was determined no one was going to say about me staying with them, "Oh well, it won't be for long." I wasn't going to have any mother reassuring her kids that way when they complained about Aunt Charlotte. I think those are the most terrible words — it won't be for very long.

There are problems of course, living here. Superannuation doesn't cover the board — $360 a month. A lot of the old ones worry about that because they have to eat into their capital all the time. You get a feeling you've *got* to die; you can't afford to keep on living! And there's still that stigma about an old people's home, yet they're so different from the old type. I remember there was only one in Dunedin when I was young — the Little Sisters of the Poor, an old building run by nuns and hidden away behind high walls. The nuns used to come round in a horse-drawn cab and collect for Little Sisters of the Poor. But old people's homes are very different now. We're warm and well looked after.

Made friends here? Oh yes. But there's no one here right now I'd call a great friend. They've all died off, my closest friends, the ones who stayed sane to the end and had a sense of humour. They'd come in here and watch TV at night with me, for years. Mind you, I made up my mind when I came in I wouldn't get too emotionally involved with anyone because it wouldn't be for long.

And another thing, you don't suffer so much, emotionally, when you're old. It's blunter. You don't get hurt so much.

Feel the good things so much? I don't know about that. I think you're even more receptive to some good things. You're very grateful to young people, to young people doing things for you, and you appreciate letters and things. But your suffering is definitely lessened because you're more realistic. You know death's not just for others but for you, too. It's just there, waiting, so you're more accepting.

I think you suffer more through someone else's suffering than your own. I've had a tough life in some ways. I've had to cope with having no mother, with the deaths of two husbands, with sicknesses and nearly every operation you can think of, from nasal and abdominal operations to clean-outs inside so that I couldn't have children safely. And now I've got lameness and near-blindness to put up with.

I've had an awful lot of good things, mind you. I've certainly had to suffer, but it's other people's suffering that's been the hardest to accept. I always say — and this is almost heresy — that I'd believe more in the Christian faith if Christ had stood at the foot of the cross and seen his mother crucified. That would have been an even harder thing for him to bear. I think it was worse for his mother than for him.

I'm enjoying this, but I don't envy you your job of trying to make something out of it all. You'll have to be a Philadelphian lawyer to get it all together.

Yes, I've thoroughly enjoyed these days because I've got no one here to talk to, not really. It's all superficial. And I always did love having people listen to me. I was no Victorian, prim and modest. What I said went? I'm not that bad, am I? But I'm afraid I always did have a mind of my own. I wouldn't have my wedding photo taken, that sort of thing. There's not one wedding photo of me and Matt, and I even drove myself to the church . . . as one old lady said, "A most unbridal thing to do".

To a degree I've retained my outspokenness; I've tried to contain it, but I've got a fair bit of it still. I don't suffer fools gladly and I'm a bit bitchy at times. But one thing I have controlled is nagging. I'd like to do it at times, but I've controlled it. I've always had spirit, but I've been lucky. I had friends who liked me as I was, and I'd been teaching dancing since I was fourteen. That gives you self-confidence. Can you imagine, me, dancing? I can't even walk without a stick now. But I was a good teacher of dancing.

We'd have big classes — seventy adults on a Wednesday night, seventy on a Friday night and about sixty children on a Saturday afternoon. I taught dancing for about six years and earned half a crown a week. I kept that money in a little blue box and spent it all on Christmas presents.

But the dances and balls were quite something those days, oh yes. We'd start at 8 at night and go right on until 2 in the morning; you had to be fairly fit! A ball always started with a Grand March, with the most important person and his partner leading off. If it was the Masonic ball it'd be the Grand Master and his wife; if it was the hockey ball it'd be the captain of the team and his partner. The man would bow and say, "May I have the pleasure of this dance Miss Morrison," and you didn't ever say no — that was bad manners. The women always wore evening frocks and both men and women wore white gloves and pumps. You never wore ordinary shoes, and the gloves were a very sensible thing because a man's perspiring hands could stain a girl's dress.

Yes, we had wonderful balls. We'd all decorate the hall, polish the floor and organise the supper. It was always a sit-down supper those days, at tables; none of this buffet business. We'd have all sorts of sandwiches and cakes and then trifle and fruit salad and Spanish cream. No liquor at all was allowed. If anyone left the hall to drink outside, no way would he get in again, not even by paying. Then at 2 in the morning we'd all have beef tea. That was it, but we always had a wonderful night.

And we had a lot of fun at dancing classes, too. The kids loved it, oh yes. They came from the age of six or seven and on until they were in their early teens. You see, those days you didn't really grow up until you were seventeen or eighteen. A girl didn't put her hair up until she was eighteen. No one had short hair, unless they had nits and had to have it cut off. We were always warned not to hang our hats near those kids' hats.

I remember the day my girlfriend and I went down to Dunedin and had all our hair cut off. We arrived home with the modern, short look. Well, we walked in and her husband blew up. He took one look at us, yelled, "You're a pair of fools," marched out and slammed the door. Even next day he looked all round the room, not at us. Me? I gave my packet of hair to Matt, my future husband, and he looked like he was going to weep.

But I had a go at all the new things those days. I was the first female in our family to fly in an aeroplane, around about 1925 at Wigram, which was the only airport in Christchurch at the time. Planes those days were as different from planes today as a Tin Lizzy is from a Rolls Royce. We walked out onto the field and there was this plane, a Bristol fighter from World War I — an old, open affair. They dressed you up in a leather jacket, helmet and goggles. You just got in and sat in the cockpit and they strapped you in. No self-starter — the ground crew had to go out and whirl the propeller, it made a terrible din. Then off we went right around Christchurch. Whenever we turned we were leaning over; looking down on the square and that. I didn't enjoy one minute of it, but I wasn't sick. I was too frightened to be sick! And part of it was just sheer determination, being able to say I'd been up flying. Those days, if a plane went over you ran outside and looked at it. Nowadays half the time you don't even hear them; they don't even register. Yes, you could say I liked the fact I'd been flying, but not the flying.

I was a smoker, too, believe it or not; started when I was twenty-seven. I always had hay fever, and one day when we were playing tennis a doctor handed me a cigarette and said it might stop me sneezing. Those days we didn't know what smoking did to your lungs. But then I gave it up one day when I was about fifty. The stories had begun about lung cancer. I'd seen the cases in the hospital and I said to myself, I'm not going to be a fool. I'll give it up. Then the deciding factor was, my friend said, "If Charlotte says she will, then she will." So I *had* to stop!

I've never drunk alcohol, though. There's no doubt alcohol is bad for your body. You get that glazed, silly look in your eye and go dizzy and fuzzy. I've questioned around this home, and every old person whose brain is good to the end didn't drink.

Matt didn't drink either, not at all. We had lots of friends, we were very social, but we never served alcohol, and everyone loved our parties. Matt saw what drink had done to the Maoris especially — he was *very* anti-alcohol. I'm glad Matt's not alive today; he'd have been ashamed of what's happening to the Maoris. In our day they never got into such trouble with crime. You never heard of a Maori being had up for theft, assault, rape. The only thing they got into was money troubles, buying things and not being able to pay for them.

And Matt always said he could see problems arising for the Maoris. He felt they were beginning to want the best of two worlds: the ones yelling about their Maoritanga still wanted radios, cars and Canterbury underwear! He saw that you couldn't hold down a job and also expect to go off to a tangi for four or five days. His view was tough, but then he was a Maori and entitled to his opinion on those issues.

As for the Treaty of Waitangi, he said there was no doubt about it, the Maoris were treated unfairly. And same thing with Mount Baldy north of Dunedin — I've heard that the whites gave the Maoris a few muskets and blankets and trinkets for all the land they could see from the top of Mount Baldy; they certainly diddled them. But Matt firmly believed there's no use always looking back, harking back and fighting for your rights. All you can do is pick up and start again, build for the future.

We're doing too much talking? Not at all, it's bringing all sorts of things back . . . .

And another thing that's not going well today — you have to lock up your house. When someone dies the solicitor says, don't put the funeral notice in the paper under your own address because the criminals come while the funeral's on and clean the place out. We never ever had a key in our house, not one key. I don't think anyone did. You never thought anyone would come and steal from you. Parcels were put on top of your letter-box; you never dreamt that anyone would touch them. I suppose you could say you had no fear of people those days, no fear of walking down the street or through the parks, no fear of the swaggers or the old characters around town.

There were wrongs, of course — especially the false morals and the starchy modesty. We didn't talk about our natural functions, going to the lavatory and that. I don't think anyone had bladders and bowels! When Matt and I got together we'd be out all afternoon, and I'd come home in agony, bursting to go to the lavatory. We wouldn't have told each other we wanted to go. No, not even me! If you did feel urgent you just slid off in a furtive fashion and hoped no one saw.

But with modesty, nowadays I'd say we'd gone too far the other way. All the romance has gone out of life. This sounds a bit corny, but I think we need a lot of romance. There's all those lovely little things men can do. In our day if a man held your hand you got a kick out of it; now he's got to do a hell of a lot more. They're losing out, I'd say.

As for equality of the sexes, it never ever struck me we weren't equal. We're just two different species. We complement each other, men and women. Muscularly, men are stronger, but not mentally. I always said men were here to do all the things I didn't like doing: cleaning the soot out of the coal range, chopping the wood! I never ever felt inferior in any way. Someone asked me the other day, "What would you do if a man hit you?" I said, "Well, he'd have to sleep some time!" One thing for sure, he'd never hit me twice. No, equality is no new invention to me. Mind you, we've certainly gained in some ways. I'm not one to go back to washing with a copper and a board; I'm all in favour of washing machines and Electroluxes.

As for all the modern transport and communication systems, they are beyond me. But transport has always fascinated me. When I was eight or nine I'd sit outside on the verandah with Aunt Sally and we'd tell each other funny stories about transport in the future. I always imagined you could get into a nice, comfortable, tube-like thing. There'd be a whole lot of buttons, you'd just press the one you wanted and, zoom, you'd be there. You'd just have to go down a ladder and you'd be there, wherever you'd chosen to be. We didn't know about planes and things — it was pure invention. Aunt Sally's idea was a bit different. She thought we could have a space platform right up above the Earth. You'd just go up there and sit, waiting for the Earth to come round. You didn't go to London; you waited for London to go to you. And we've got it now, what Aunt Sally imagined — we've got space shuttles and things docking way up there in space.

As for going to the moon, I think that's an utter waste of time — ridiculous. You might as well go to the middle of the Sahara Desert; it's arid and dead like the moon. Mind you, I think the Earth will soon be like the moon or the Sahara, and very soon. A dead world. We'll destroy ourselves. We will. People say we'll never use the nuclear bomb, but it'll happen, either by accident, or because someone gets up a little hate for five minutes and bang, off we go. We've got all those politicians jumping up and down, but we've also got all those brilliant scientists. I say anyone as brilliant as that is on the verge of insanity anyway. There's that fine line, and who's to say they're not going to slip over it? If we have nuclear weapons we'll have nuclear warfare. It's human failing; if you're going to have a bow and arrow, I'm going to have a bow and arrow. We'll have a war all right unless we work on the Gandhi principle and allow a skinny little man in a loin-cloth to get somewhere by peaceful methods.

But I say we'll knock the place to bits, I'm sure we will. I've got the strongest feeling about it. I look at young children today and I think, you're not going to live. I may be wrong, but I've had the feeling for a long time that this planet's just about had it, in every way. We're wrecking the land and sea; we're spending money on killing, not living; discipline has collapsed and people won't work enough; our standards of morality have completely fallen. In my day a murder was a real shock. Now it's so common you hardly bother remembering it. If there's a God, I think He feels the time has come for a sort-out. Whether it means He'll wipe us out and start again, I don't know, but I think He's pretty disgusted with the way things have turned out.

I do believe there's a force behind living. I don't know if it's a God or what it is, but there must be something; it's all worked out so marvellously well. The jonquils and hyacinths come out;

later on the plum blossoms; later on again the apple blossoms. The sun and tides and seasons are all patterned so perfectly. Haley's Comet will be back in two years' time. It can't all be a colossal accident. Everything created is predictable — everything except man.

I've got very strong views on things. I'm not a bit pussyfooty, and I've always been determined. And I've never really worried about what people thought. If I'd made up my mind and felt good about it, I didn't give a damn.

Mind you, it took me eight years to make up my mind to marry Matt; six to marry George. Matt didn't rush me, but the day we eventually got married someone asked him how he was feeling and he admitted "Very relieved". I've had marriage proposals since George, too, even when I was in my seventies, but those men only wanted someone to do the cooking and wash the blooming shirts, and I had no intention of doing that. I was a rotten housekeeper. I did it but had no love for it at all. I was a good cook and I could clean a house all right, but I got no sense of achievement out of it. I love teaching, not housekeeping. You can tell by my room I'm not the tidy type!

No, no regrets there. I do have one regret: I always wanted to ice-skate, but we didn't have a car to get to any ice to skate on. And I would have liked the chance to get into more acting on the stage myself, instead of just teaching speech and drama. Things I'd still like to do? Hell yes, but they're all impossible!

And as for now . . . it's the same thing. I've got my lameness and my arthritis and my blindness to cope with, but as the doctor told me, nothing wrong with my tongue and my brain. I go down and read to the old ones at 2 o'clock each afternoon — the old ninety-year-olds and the blind ones. They love it, and it's therapy for me, too. We've done all sorts, from *The Strange One* to *The Forsyte Saga* and I'm re-reading Joy Packer to them now. We all sit there and re-live the wars. But mostly we stick to biography and autobiography now; we want real things. As you get older you are not that interested in fiction; you think the heroes and heroines are perfect asses. I couldn't finish *The Thorn Birds*, thought it was a waste of eyesight.

And if I go completely blind myself and can't read books, even with my specs . . . I think I'd rather . . . I don't know . . . listening's not the same. That first time I knew I was losing my sight . . . I picked up *King Lear* and I couldn't read it — couldn't see it. Frustration. I'd have a go at it — determination. Real frustration.

I'd rather die.

ALBIE and KEN

'I can teach you a new way to live, lass'

Albie and Ken lived at Gillespie's Beach, twenty-three kilometres from Fox Glacier. In front of their cottage the Tasman hurled black sand — and sometimes gold — on their beach. Behind, Cook and La Perouse frothed at the sky.

Albie and Ken were brothers, bachelors . . . tall, strong men, both nearly eighty. They were miners for most of those years, as Albie explained: "I've always gone after the minerals, lass. I had a feeling for them."

Twenty-six years ago they "retired" at Gillespie's Beach and built their own cottage, a simple, comfortable place — one long room crammed with their beds, table, wood stove, wireless and television, plus a porch-cum-pantry tacked on the end. They grew practically all their own food: wild-looking sheep on the sand-dunes and old mining tailings; potatoes and nearly every other vegetable you can think of in two huge, thriving gardens. In the evenings they would boil up a big pot of potatoes, then recycle them for fry-ups at breakfast and lunch. There'd be meat and spuds on the table three times a day.

There were all the usual signs of seasoned back country bachelors — pink singlets and checked bush-shirts, trousers hanging on a nail on the door, stale scones in the cupboard. But then there were all those other comfortable details: their geraniums and livingstone daisies; their small but meticulously-kept bowling green, curiously perfect in that wild West Coast setting; their chutneys and pickles and jars of preserved peaches in the pantry.

I was automatically expected to make the tea, bunk down in their hut, play cards and yarn all evening with their mate from the Chatham Islands who'd turned up to shear their sheep. There was no questioning my leaping out of bed at dawn, poking down a plate of fried liver and spuds and thick wads of toast and heading off to help muster their sheep, tearing around the river flats and up the bush and all through the sand-dunes.

Albie always did most of the talking. He was outgoing, sometimes bawdy — the traditional Kiwi practical joker. He also had the West Coasters' tendency to exaggerate. At one stage he stopped and grabbed my arm to point out an important detail of the coast; my dog pounded back to see what was happening. Later I overheard Albie's version of the incident when he "confessed" to his mate: "I went to give her a canoodle and her damn dog attacked me."

Meanwhile, Ken kept well out of the limelight. He tended to retire and get on with it, feeding the dogs and sharpening the tools and washing the spuds.

My lasting impression of Albie and Ken was of deep respect for their way of life and the partnership they'd worked out. Above all, I admired their easy hospitality, their welcoming and feeding of the streams of old friends — and new ones — who bumped down from Fox Glacier and arrived on their beach.

Albie: Look here lass, you're not in the way. As a matter of fact, I think you're quite pleasant. You've got to remember this: you're on the West Coast now; we don't let things bother us too much down here. Mind you, we *can't* let things bother us. We've got this saying on the Coast: if you can see the mountains, it means it's about to start raining. If you can't see the mountains, it *is* raining.

Then there's the sandflies down here; you've got to ignore them. The more you kill, the more crowd around you. They all come to the funeral. But we can take it all. We're a tough lot, us old miners.

Always been keen on the mining? Yes, lass, that's been our life. When we were kids there were goldmines all around us where we lived at Orepuki, way out to the west of Invercargill — miles of tunnels and tailings and horses and cows getting caught in the water races. We'd go out and give Dad a hand with the gold. We had our own boxes and that, thought we were real men. Orepuki was quite a mining town those days — hotels, a school, a band and all. Nothing there now. And there were lots of old Chinamen; I remember them well. They couldn't write English, so when any of them had any legal problems they'd come to our house and Dad'd help them out. The Chinamen were very good to us kids. They'd give us lollies and things, but we used to laugh at their long plaits and their funny English. When they got drunk and the policeman questioned them they'd say: "No, me no drunk, legs no working."

Then there were all sorts of other miners there at Orepuki, like old Jacob — he was a German Pole and he couldn't talk English very well. He milked cows and sold milk and butter to the miners. Jacob always got very upset with another bloke living handy to him because this chap's dog used to go for his cows. Jacob would scream out, "I shoot de dog if he keep runs after de cows." One day he did shoot the dog and got had up before the Orepuki magistrate. The magistrate says, "Did you shoot that dog in self-defence?" "Vat you say?" says Jacob. "Did you shoot that dog in self-defence?" "No," says Jacob, "I shoot him as he go *under* de fence."

You're doing a lot of writing lass.

Yes, I suppose it's no chance we turned out to be miners, me and Ken. Only thing you could do in Orepuki those days. I never had a big education — went out to work when I was fourteen and just had to battle my way from then on. First real job I got was cooking for six men at the mining camp way round from Tuatapere, when I was fourteen. Had to do it; we had no money. My father and Ken were both mining there, working the race fourteen miles into the bush. We just lived in tents and hunted meat from the bush — deer and pigs — or flounders from the beach. Only thing I had to cook in was a camp oven, but I made all the bread; sometimes it was that hard you could bowl it down the scrub like a grindstone. I even made all our own yeast way out there, from hops and potato water and this and that.

Knew how to cook before that? Bloody oath, yes. We were brought up to look after ourselves when we were very young. Sometimes I'd cook up scones for the men; I've got a taste for scones. Got a taste for anything that's good, even women. Trouble is, the only ones I decide are any good are already hitched. No, it'd bugger up my way of life. I do all my own darning and mending anyway. Christ, have to! And anyway, half the women can't sew.

Yes, us two always went after the minerals — hell yes, lass. We worked a big gold claim at Reefton for ten years or so, in the 40s. Did all right, too — we had half a dozen men working for us, and winches and a horse to haul stuff. Waitahu Gold Mining Company, that's what we were called. A whale of a lot of those old blokes from Waitahu are dead now, and the other ones all come and see us here at Gillespie's. They all like to talk about the old Reefton diggings. One of them came out here and started us on the bowling. We set up a damn bowling green out the back of the garden there. Then he didn't come any more; he went and got married. And he died soon after — the strain was too much. You been married? Why?

Me? Married! I'm buggered if I don't know. I wouldn't mind dying that way myself.

Ken: We had a good go at the scheelite mining, too, up at Glenorchy. It's the best part of New Zealand for scheelite, up there behind Lake Wakatipu; it's lying there in reefs in the rocks. Most of it gets exported to England and Germany and that and used for toughening steel or making surgical instruments or filaments for light bulbs, all sorts of things.

We did years and years of scheelite mining, when the price was right. Took in all the gear on horses and lived in little camps, way up there in the snow. Tough country? Hell, yes. Just like us. We'd have to go down 3,000 feet into the forest for timber for the mine props and that and pack it all back up on horses. And we'd string up wire ropes and cable-ways from one mountain to the other, then get stuck in and blast the scheelite out of the rocks with gelignite. Next job was shovelling it all into bags and taking it twelve miles down to the battery where it got treated for export. It got crushed and jigged, then roasted, bagged and sent away by rail to the boat at Kingston. From there it went to Bluff and off to England and that.

Albie: Quite an industry, all right. Everything had to be packed in with horses, even all the tin and wood and gear for our huts. Those huts had to have three skins to keep out the weather. There'd be building paper, then sacks sewn together, then iron. And there'd be a good, solid rock or sod wall around it, to stop the thing blowing away. We'd pack all our tucker in from Glenorchy, and sometimes we'd even have to go way down for water. In winter, no problem; we'd melt snow. But there's no water up there in summer.

We'd be up there eight or nine months a year, only going out to Glenorchy now and again for stores. Lonely? What the hell would I get lonely for? One stage I was up there for one whole season by myself, blasting and shovelling scheelite. What I did in the evenings? I went to bed. I was up there to make money, lass, not friends. And I was running that whole outfit; I had to be there all the time. I always had a good tilly lamp. I'd get papers in now and again, and I had a good, warm hut and any amount of tucker. What I lived on? Same as here — meat and veges and rice — good, plain food, but plenty of it. We never ran short. When you work hard you've got to feed yourself well and sleep well. You've got to make yourself a damn good camp near to your work; you're wasting good time walking to work.

Yes, a bloke had to fend for himself up there in the hills; who the hell else was going to? I didn't mind being alone, not at all. I've never really worked for a boss; I'm not that type. Independent, that's me. We all liked the life way up there in the snow, looking down on the lake. And we got that fit; we bloody near turned somersaults, we felt that good. I'd come down to Glenorchy. I'd be striding around with a big beard and a brown face. One time someone said, "My God, he's back." He thought I was Jesus!

But I've always gone after the minerals, lass — even had a go at the opals at Lightning Ridge in Aussie. A real experience, that.

I was only there five minutes, but I did well, got a lot of opals. Lost a lot of money too, buying and selling. It's like going to the races every day, opal mining; I loved it. But my interest was back here in this country. So we came down here to Gillespie's, me and Ken. Why here? I could tell this was a good spot. I came down here to put in a report on the gold dredge up Five Mile Creek, about five mile up the coast from here. So I had a good look around and I found gold on the beach here, in the black sand. Right then and there I decided that when we retired from the working racket, me and Ken, this is where we'd come. It's twenty-six year ago we came here. We both retired when we were around half a century old and it's home here now, Gillespie's.

A good choice? Hell, yes. You know if there's gold there when you've been at it as long as we have. You know all right. You look at it, and you know. It's secret. And we've worked the beach for twenty-six years — not constant, but when there's gold there. Gold comes and goes in the black sand — the sea throws some up on the beach, then there's nothing. It might be here only twice a year, for a couple of months each time. In between you don't even take a shovel down on the beach. One time there we had ten months, got nothing. But she provides plenty for us two.

Ken: There's gold there, all right. The early miners had already worked it, in the 1860s. Gold was discovered at Gillespie's and pretty soon there were well over 1,000 miners working the beach. Straight out the window there, that's where the town was: eleven stores, two bakeries, two butcheries, a couple of pubs. Up to 2,000 people here at Gillespie's at one stage, so they say; whether you can believe it or not, that I don't know. But they weeded themselves out pretty quick; only a few families stayed on till 1910.

Later on another lot came with a dredge and had another go at Gillespie's, in the 1930s and 40s. They brought in the electric power, well-established houses, pubs and a church. But they never ever got a great deal of gold, and the whole outfit was gone and done with by the time us two arrived. Nothing here but gorse. There were still dredge tailings everywhere — still are, but they're covered up with gorse so you'd never know. Too right, we had to start off from scratch. We even had to build bridges across the Black creek, to get out to the Fox, and we brought in all the soil for the gardens in lorry loads, from the other side of Fox's township. Everyone thought we'd gone mad.

Albie: But we've got a good place to live here, lass. Hell's teeth, yes. Nice and quiet and out of the wind. Nice and flat. I've had enough of the hills, hell yes. I came here and I said bugger the glaciers and all that rot. I've seen enough snow in my life. We came here for the gold, not the glaciers. Then people say, why do you stop here? I say, you've got to stop somewhere and here's as good as the next place.

But I tell you what, lass; we've had problems ever since we got here. Had to cut a track through the gorse to get the truck down to the beach. Then the condensation got to the truck and she wouldn't work. But we got onto the gold straight away. We worked the beach for six weeks with pumps and boxes, and that was it, we wanted to stay here. So we decided to take over the whole shooting box: buy the land, build a house and garden. Now we've got all that, and a bowling green too!

Mind you, took us years and years of trying to get the damn papers through, trying to get this place freehold. It's worse than Russia — all these papers every time you do a deal in this country. And they won't say yes, you can buy it. They say the place is still national park land. When we die all this goes to the Crown.

Yet we've come in very handy down here. Thousands of visitors come and they get stranded at night-time or stuck in their motorcars. We do a good P.R. for the park. But when we die they'll all be in like hawks. And the park board's taken over the land we've always used for grazing a few sheep for tucker — the river flats and drowned forests and that. But we've got the grazing rights. I say to them, we're old now, getting on for eighty. Pretty soon you won't have to worry about us. Leave us alone. We've paid our rates from the first day we came here and started chopping out the gorse, and they won't give us the freehold title to the place, so what do they want? We're not squatters. We've a right to be here and we're looking after the place.

Hell's teeth, you're quick at writing, lass. If you're as quick at everything else, hell. . . .

Ken: We've done all right here. That black sand's got gold in it — all fine gold, mind you; no nuggets. Plenty there still? Enough.

Albie: You never tell anyone how much you're getting, bugger that.
Still get a kick out of seeing the gold? No. People say it's a fever, this goldmining, but it's not. It's just a thing you get used to. It's my job and I do it.

Ken: I like getting gold because it's valuable. It's not any damn fever. Mining's just what we're used to; it comes second nature and we don't take any notice of it. So when the gold's there, we mine it. Last time I used the boxes? A couple of months ago. In between I carry on with the garden and the sheep. I'm the sheep man; I like them. Only got a couple of hundred. They roam all around and now and again we sell some wool or give them away.

Then sometimes I might do a bit of fishing, when the sea's right; I go surf-casting for sharks. Good eating, shark. We used to get plenty of all sorts on the beach here — snapper and gurnard, red cod, conger eels. Not now. All you get out there's sand-flies and the odd shark, nowadays. The big trawlers, the Russians and Japs, and our boats, too — they're catching all the fish that used to come in here. They're cleaning up the breeding grounds for the flat fish; they just scoop them all up. They'll wake up when it's too late. Won't listen to the fishing inspector here when he says they're trawling in too close. He can't do anything; they don't listen.

Albie: Tell you what, lass: it's the same thing with the bush here. The trees are dying. There's not enough birds around to keep the grubs down. So the grubs have run wild. They get all the tender regrowth and they've also got stuck into the mature trees. Stoats are the culprits. They've got all the parakeets and kakas around here. They're all gone. We'll find that out in a hundred years' time, when all the trees have gone. See, we've lived in the trees all our lives, lass. We've seen it happen. And until they clean the stoats out they won't help save the birds. But the people in offices here, the parks board and that, they don't listen to me. And they're told what to do from Wellington. But they all hate the truth, that lot. They argue the point that the stoats kill the rats, and therefore there's a balance. That's nonsense. The stoats are everywhere — they climb trees and get the birds' nests, they swim rivers. The birds haven't got a chance.

What should happen now? These parks people, if they're bird lovers, they should wipe the stoats out. Otherwise that's the end of the birds, and the trees, too. The balance of nature is gone in the bush.

The environmentalists? They're all right as long as they don't stop industry altogether. Minerals make the world tick; when the value of minerals goes down we have depression, and it's the minerals that opened this coast up, got in the roads and the electricity. Otherwise we'd only be opening up now. But you take the Haast road — if it was going to be put in today it wouldn't be allowed; the environmentalists would all be waving their arms about. Yet wasn't for the minerals and that road, the West Coast'd still be like Fiordland: just deer and tourism.

But no matter what us West Coasters do, there's someone up in arms. . . .

Felling too many trees? No, lass. I don't want to see the trees ruined, but I don't want to see the trees die and no use made of them. Any land useful for trees should be used and replanted, or left to regenerate, or used for agriculture. We're not that big a country. We've got to use what we can.

Ken: We're self-supporting here, us two. Made all these buildings. Just picked up carpentry and plastering and that, got the house done, and later on we added the little baches for people like you to stay in. Then we live on what we grow: plain, home-grown food, meat and spuds, duck eggs and veges. But we're not damn hippies. I suppose they'd be all right; I don't know much about them.

We both do the cooking, me and Albie, whoever's in first. We do right up to scones and things and great big pikelets, damn near a foot long.

Albie: I do all our own preserves, too — chutneys and pickles and tomato sauce, and bottled fruit. Do a deal with people in Central — I give them a sheep or two; they give me apricots and peaches. I like those old ways. Mind you, wasn't long ago it was the only way you *could* live, bartering. And we do it all the time out here. Someone gives me a cake; I give them sacks of veges and mutton or some new spuds and a lettuce or two.

Ken: The garden ... it's a part of life, isn't it? We don't go for the tinned stuff, except in emergencies. We grow rows and rows of fresh stuff: cabbages and caulis, lettuce, silverbeet, red beet, spuds, carrots, parsnips, corn, beans, onions, shallots, everything. We like good tucker — hell yes, the best. A bloke doesn't live long; might as well have the best.

Albie: Yes, I can teach you a new way to live, lass, here at Gillespie's Beach. Clean and quiet. All sorts of people come and call on us, bring us cakes and jam; you brought us eggs and butter and things. We've always got something on the go here.

Last Christmas we all got together, thirty of us from around here. We thought it'd be good to have a big Christmas dinner at Gillespie's Beach. We had roast goose and ham, plenty of fowls and all sorts of other stuff — cole-slaw and rice, fruit salad and trifle and plenty of whisky. Any amount of tucker for everyone. We had a Christmas tree all lit up with electricity and presents for everyone. I asked the old bloke up the river. He lives on bread and jam and he's fine, old Sid. But he wouldn't come up. He's a loner, didn't want to have to mix with the kids and that. I went down and asked him again. He had tears in his eyes, but he wouldn't come. Then the ladies went down and gave him some meat and trifle and that, and a gift — a shoehorn with a horse's head on it. Sid was pleased as punch. He told me later on, "That's the first gift I've ever had." I told him he could use it as a back scratcher or something.

What I got? Let's see — a cake, shortbread, a big box of tea, boxes of chocolates, all sorts of things.

Get tired? Yeah. Lots to do, being self-supporting. I'm just lying here to keep you happy and answer questions. Good on you, lass, you've made a cup of tea. Hell's teeth, three tea leaves out and three in; we like it strong as hell, me and Ken.

No, you wouldn't get better than our way of living, lass — simple and honest. And that's what's wrong with the world today: people are too selfish. They're taught all sorts of fancy things, but there isn't a good foundation to work on. The only foundation we've got to work on is religion, and it's not good soil. Religion hasn't brought stability. It's only brought comfort. And a lot of wars. . . .

What soil we should have? Truth. Honesty. That's the only religion there is. I tell them all that — the priests, anyone who comes here. I tell them there's only one religion and that's honesty.

Other people honest? No, dead right there lass. They're not all honest; they'll rob and do anything they like, yeah. But that's their way of living and I leave them to it. I don't interfere. But our way's simple and honest. You can call it what you like, our way; maybe it's a religion. The religion of trees . . . no other branches in New Zealand! That's why no one else has heard about it.

Most people's religion is only fear of dying. Me? Afraid of dying? No. When my time comes it'll be all right. I've been very near death a couple of times, like when the mine roof fell in on me when we were 200 foot in. The timber started cracking like a shotgun, then she all swooped in on us. Damn lucky to get out of that one alive. Then another time I was in a plane crash. I remember after it happened. The pilot bloke made this joke. He says: "I'm bloody sorry I made such a poor landing." Sorry! The plane was a write-off and we were a hell of a lucky to crawl out of it.

But I've got no damn thought of the hereafter. No damn way. I don't mind if they bury me in the garden like a dog. It's now that I think about.

You're a bit different from most people, aren't you? People tell you things. You listen, and you've got an open face or something.

No, I don't worry about time. I had a watch, but I gave it away, to a young chap who was working the beach with us. He lost the watch his father had given him. He got really upset about it so I gave him mine. Haven't had one ever since. I just live one day at a time nowadays.

But I do say this, lass: everything's got a fear. Animals fear thunder and earthquakes. And there's that tribe they discovered in the Philippines — they'd never been in contact with other people and they had only one fear: thunder.

My fear? Same as dogs. Things I don't understand. Death? Well ...

I'd like to finish my days here, too right. I haven't got that long to do, now. And what's wrong with it? Ken's out doing the wood and the spuds. When I get rid of you, lass, I'll get a bit of work done, too! We're going mustering tomorrow — me, Ken, you and that dog of yours. Up Cooks River and into the bush. How many sheep? Oh, not many — about forty.

Ken: Oh, about five or six up there I'd say.

Albie: Come on lass, it's grazing time. We like good tucker and good air. The towns, they're polluted with petrol and diesel fumes, and there's aeroplanes shooting it down on you, and everyone's spraying plants. We don't use the commercial sprays at all. No damn fear. For the white butterflies we boil up rhubarb leaves and spray that on. Works well. We get kelp from the beach, throw it in a drum with some rainwater from the roof, leave it for a while and there's your Maxicrop. And we dig dead possums or a dead sheep or two under the tomatoes and grapes — good blood and bone. That garden's got thousands of possums under it. We'd put you in it, too, if you snuffed. I'd put you under a peach tree.

We keep healthy, all right. I used to smoke, but gave that up thirty odd years ago. No bloody use lighting a fire at the back of your head. I was getting short of breath carrying loads in the hills, so I gave up. I was going up the track one night, and finish, I says. Had a couple of packets of tobacco in my pocket, gave them away. Finish.

Done a lot of drinking? Hell no, that's as dumb as smoking, letting it all run through you. Better ways of spending dough than that. I've saved a lot of money. I'll never spend it even if I live to 150. I'll give it away. If you want my opinion, the financial system's had it in the Western world. Once they went away from the gold standard they made a backward step. There's a lot won't agree with me, mind you. Otherwise, the world's bloody marvellous. It's the age of science, and science's a great thing. It'll eventually explain creation. People say it's a damn waste of money, sending satellites all around space and putting people on the moon and that. I'm bloody sure it's not a waste of money. I don't mind my taxes going on space travel.

I'm all for science. It's the only thing that'll teach us a bit of sense. Religion doesn't. You'll see them all next year, the religious ones, when Haley's Comet comes. They'll all be having conventions and heading for the desert and predicting the end of the world.

No, all these new inventions are a good thing. It's progress. You can't stand still.

Yes, that's a tricky point, lass; we're living away out here, worlds away from progress. But the thing is, I believe in *scientific* progress. But I don't ever want to be part of the social progress, in the towns and that.

Come on, lass, we'll all have a game of cards. You can't write a story about the West Coast and not mention Forty-fives. And you're not a real West Coaster if you can't play Forty-fives. This game originated in Kumara, and now they come from Australia and Wellington, all over, to play in the Forty-fives championship at Greymouth once a year. And all the old ex-Coasters come back to play it. What it is? Euchre back to front. It's a complicated game. You gamble on it, too right. You've got to play it and lose money to learn it. We'll make a real West Coaster of you yet, lass. You can say you got initiated at Gillespie's Beach.

Yip, I want the rest of my years here at Gillespie's. It's not lonely. People are always coming here, from all round the country. And they ask me back to their places, but I don't like going to airports and that. Filling out forms and getting passes and buggering around airports and that, hell. . . .

Bugger the towns. What the hell would I want to live in a town for. It's all irritation. Bugger old people's homes, too. If they try and put me in one of those, I'd like someone to get his gun out and shoot me.

Mind you lass, us old miners don't die. We just blow away, like gold dust. . . .

KITTY

'Wounds plugged up with cartwheel grease'

Kitty's most striking feature was her smile, a century deep. She was rounded, fresh and fit, at peace with the world — the kind of old lady who welcomes you into her kitchen and, whatever the hour, produces a pot of tea and "a little eat". Her kitchen reflected her homely character: there were flowers stashed between the family photographs and ornaments and A & P show cups on the mantlepiece, and a big pot of soup brewing on the stove.

Kitty's greatest virtue was her kindliness, yet pain was there, too. It showed in her eyes and in the lines of living etched on her creased face. It came out constantly in her tales of caring for people as she remembered back over her life in Golden Bay. As a nurse she had worked seven days a week and had sometimes given up her own bed for a patient. On the baker's van she had made a point of remembering who liked barracouta loaves better than long johns, who preferred rainbow cake to currant buns. And always she found time for the old characters around town — the tailor and the print-setter and the lonely old remittance man who played hymns on the organ when he'd been on the whisky.

There's no longer a newspaper in Takaka, and no tailor's shop or bakehouse. You buy your bread sliced and wrapped in cellophane at the supermarket . . . .

Me? I'm old, but I can still look after myself — too right I can. The vicar came up to me the other day when I was going to Senior Citizens', and "Kitty," he said, "you're far too young for *that!*"

Mind you, I've always had a busy sort of a life. I was just a bit of a kid when I started nursing here in Takaka. There's this old house still standing in the main street, but if you ask me, even the locals wouldn't know that it used to be a hospital early on this century. Only hospital we've ever had over here in Golden Bay, except for the maternity home down the road. Mind you, I had no training to be a nurse, no fear. I'd say you can't really learn to be one; you can't learn out of a text-book. No, it just came automatic, working as a nurse aid at the old hospital.

All us staff lived-in there — the doctor, the sister-in-charge, a man gardener who provided all the veges and flowers for the hospital, and me. I'll tell you what, though, I didn't always have a bed to sleep in at night. We could take as many as nine patients at a time in that old house, but that meant you gave up your own bed!

Right from the start it was a seven-day-a-week job. If we were busy we never thought of having time off. Nurses today! They don't know they're alive. I was up at the Nelson hospital the other day and one of the nurses was *walking* around. I said to her, "You don't see anyone run like we used to run." We'd get up at 6 of a morning, and it'd be round about half past 10 by the time we'd finished up of a night. Never thought anything of it. Worked all week, then Saturday night we'd go to the dance up the hall. Stayed there till about midnight, came home and got up at 6 to start working again. Made no difference if we had nine patients or two, we still had to get up early.

Get exhausted? We just went on. We didn't think about being exhausted. And tell you something else, our wages were no more than twelve and six a week, but that was big money those days, in the 20s and 30s.

We had this system, me and the sister: we both washed the patients first thing of a morning, and they all got washed in the beds those days — no showers and this and that; never heard of them. They just weren't allowed up those days, not even for a bath. Take an appendicitis patient — he had to stay in bed for ten days before he was allowed up at all, and then only for half an hour in the chair. But now! Operated on today, up tomorrow.

After the bed-making the sister got the breakfast and I took the trays around, then we had breakfast ourselves, collected the patients' trays and did the dishes. Next came cleaning out the surgery and doing out all the rooms, upstairs and down, while sister got the midday dinner ready. And in between there'd be baking and starching and ironing — there was always starching and ironing to be done — and sister would be busy mending or doing jams and sauces and that. We never sat down in the day.

At night we'd have a light meal, and time we'd washed up it'd be around 8 o'clock. So we'd have an hour or so off, then it was supper-time for the patients; it'd be around half past 10 by the time we'd finished up of a night. But it was just a way of life to us, the nursing at the old house. Mind you, it was a cold show, freezing in the winter. You didn't shut doors winter or summer; the front door was never closed unless the rain was coming in that way. I can remember only one night when the upstairs doors were closed in the four years I was there.

And as for the nursing, I loved it. I'd wear a green frock, sister'd wear white, and we'd both have a white veil on all the time; sister's was flowing, mine was tucked in at the back. And I just did everything that had to be done in the nursing line — the dressings and helping out in the theatre, handing instruments and doing swabs and that. The doctor had everything in that theatre, X-rays and all.

A traveller would come over to Takaka once a month and we'd stock up with medicines and stuff. We always kept a good supply because we could get completely cut off over here; the hill could be out at any time with slips and that. Anything could happen while we were shut off on the other side of the hill. And even if the road and the weather were good, if there was a serious case we had to depend on the ambulance from way over at Collingwood. That meant bumping around for eighty-odd miles over to Nelson; anything could happen on the way.

Then, of course, in the very early days there wasn't even the road over the hill. You had to send the serious cases out by boat — a trip of six hours or more over to Nelson, rolling around on the waves. You had to rely on the tides as well as the rough seas. Often ships couldn't get into Waitap because of bad weather, so the doctor knew he could be completely isolated at any time. And that's where he came into his own, that doctor. He learnt to rely on his own imagination and initiative; he became a real genius at inventing things. If he had a problem he'd lie on the floor by the fire and play patience for an hour or so. Then he'd yell out, "I've got it." He'd been thinking it over, all along.

I'll give you an instance. One stage there he had to empty my stomach and give me a fresh start — 1941 that was — so he sat on my bed and explained his invention. He had two bottles connected with rubber tubes and going through my stomach. He had some fluid in one bottle, a vacuum in the other, and that vacuum gradually pulled everything through my stomach. It worked very well, too. And it was exactly the same principle that I saw in milking sheds around Nelson years and years later. Everyone was talking about this great new invention they'd got, and I said, "I've had that done on me, by the old doctor in Takaka."

Yes, there's a lot gone on in this little valley that people know nothing about. You take the very good work he did on my husband. He took out his appendix and it went wrong on him. Well, he'd seen something done in Scotland during his studies — a very tricky, new thing to do with an appendix — so he tried it out on my husband. It was either try that or see him die. And he fixed it all right, but then it took him a heck of a long time to get the wound healed up, it was that big. And he actually healed that wound with cartwheel grease in the end! There was no ointment around thick enough to do the job, so he just plugged up the hole in my husband's side with thick, hard cartwheel grease. At first he'd tried holding the wound the normal way, with stitches, but they just tore away. So he had to think up something to stop the acids coming out of the stomach and through the hole he'd made for the tubes. Normal ointment was no good. It had to be something very thick so that fluids couldn't penetrate or dissolve it. And that was entirely his own idea — good old cartwheel grease. Worked very well, too.

Another time the doctor had a very serious maternity case. The woman had haemorrhaged badly, so he just inserted his hand and stopped the bleeding with his fingers. They both had to stay like that for about three hours until help was sent over from Nelson, a supply of blood and someone to transfuse it. That woman's alive today, and the child, too.

Yes he had to do all sorts at the old hospital — tonsils, amputations, the lot. And he was everything, the old doctor: medical doctor, social worker, psychologist, dentist.

Then one night about midnight he got a call from a chap in East Takaka — an urgent case, he said. The doctor did a growl, but he got into his little motorcar and off he went. When he got way

172

up there he asked the chap, "Is it the wife?" and the chap said: "No, come with me." He picked up the hurricane lamp and took him out the back to the patient: a little sow pig! She'd got into a fight and torn off half her ear, so he had to sew it back on again. The doctor was the vet, too, those days!

He had all sorts of innovative ideas about medicine, that doctor. He was way before his time. He'd always be telling us that our health problems today have their basis in the primitive. He'd say, look at blood pressure. It's a curse today, but in the old days you had to have it or you wouldn't have escaped from the tiger. It was essential for survival. But it also meant you got rid of all the excess pressure, whereas in our civilised life today there's no running to climb the tree, no need to escape from the tiger. So we live at the high pitch all the time, instead of having it for reserve. The blood pressure builds up and up and it's often fatal. Well, the old doctor was always thinking about those sorts of things.

Any rate, I worked there with him for four years, then later on in the war years I worked in the Takaka bakehouse. First of all I was on the bread run for about three years. I had this little van and I'd go over to Onekaka two days a week, out to Tarakohe two days a week. What I sold? Everything — bread, cakes, buns, pies. Beautiful bread those days, baked on the bricks at the sole of the oven; you couldn't get anything nicer. Great big white or brown loaves and proper wholemeal bread those days, not the junk you get nowadays. People ask me why I complain about the bread these days, but they've never seen bakery bread kneaded by hand like I have. There was a machine to mix up the dough, but that was it — the rest was done by hand. Nobody's interested in baking these days, though; you can't get an apprentice baker. It's on account of the hours. You're working at night when everyone else's out enjoying themselves.

But people loved it when I came round in my van. I'd have all sorts inside: long loaves with a raised top — tin loaves we called them; barracoutas, which they seem to call milk loaves today; cottage loaves — round ones with a little fellow on top — you poked your finger into the top and made a hole; long johns — I think they call them baby sandwiches now; and great big square loaves. Then there were always lots of currant loaves, Boston buns and currant buns, and if people wanted cut bread we'd do it at the shop, with the bacon cutter. Before that we just had to do it all by hand, but it took a darn long time. For dances and that you'd be standing there for blooming hours cutting up the great big four-pound loaves.

Cost sixpence halfpenny for a two-pound loaf those days, and that was delivered to the door. Then when the price went up everyone squealed, but it was still very cheap food. And as for the amount of bread people wasted, chucked out to the fowls — whole barracoutas; you could feed another family on it. Pies were fourpence each, small cakes a shilling a dozen, cream cakes one and six a dozen. People bought plenty, too right they did. Yes, you just ate whatever you fancied those days; you didn't worry about size. People are diet-conscious nowadays, aren't they? They all want to look like a blooming yard of pump-water. And there's all these fads — don't drink coffee, don't eat butter, don't eat white bread. But I tell you what, I don't like this Molenberg bread with the bits and pieces in it. Okay for you, you've got your own teeth, but it's hell on us old ones.

No, I don't worry about the fancy stuff and all the fads. I just have a good meal and be done with it. None of this lettuce and stuff all the time. We're used to good, solid food, us old-timers, plenty of bread and cakes and vegetables and things. And I can tell you I liked being the bread van lady because people liked seeing me come up the road. I remember Friday was always a big day on the bread van because Saturday was half-day closing for the shops, and people always wanted me to pick up a pound of butter or a string of sausages or a bag of flour or something; they'd ring up the shop and ask me to drop it out in the van. Then they always thanked me in a special way. They'd say to themselves, Kitty hasn't got the time for a vege garden, and I'd come home with a basket of carrots and beans, or pumpkins or one thing or another. But I'd say to them: "You'd be surprised what I can do of a Sunday." I'd get up every Sunday at 6 o'clock, same as any other day of the week.

Then they'd all want me to stop for a cuppa, but I said no, I'd never get through my rounds if I kept stopping all over the show. Only place I ever drank tea was with a woman down Motupipi. She'd see me stop up the road and she'd rush inside and get the tea into the cup well before I got to her gate. She knew I couldn't wait around letting it get cold, so she'd have it just right to drink by the time I got there. I'd drink it while she got her bread, then that was it, off I went.

Later on I came off the van and went into the bakehouse. I did all sorts there — icing and decorating, making sponges and things; and none of this three egg business either — five pounds of eggs at a time for sponges! You'd mix it all up by hand, too. I'd be up to the top of my arms in the egg mixture. You couldn't use our old beater in all that goo — had to put your whole hand in.

In my day we even had our own tailor here in Takaka. Old Gillanders, that was his name — he made suits and trousers, anything you wanted. He had a shop in town, just a wee place with a counter covered with bolts of material and a big mirror on the wall, and out behind the counter were more bolts of material, all piled up together. You'd see old Gillanders there in the doorway, stitching away, tacking canvas into the front of a coat or stuffing padding into the shoulders.

Too right he got business. He was recognised as a first-class tailor; everyone wanted one of old Gillie's suits. You'd pick out your material, then he'd measure you up and cut the right length off, then and there. He'd put your name on it and store it away out the back, then next time you saw it, it was all made up, finished. Mind you, if you wanted a suit made in a hurry you had to be in old Gillie's good books or you'd wait three months.

But by and large he was a generous old chap. I remember he'd always give away his scrap pieces of serge to anyone with a small boy, to make pants. He just gave it away. Clothes generally were good and cheap those days, though — five guineas for one of Gillie's navy serge suits with a spare pair of trousers or a waistcoat. If you wanted a double-breasted suit, you got a spare pair of trousers; if you wanted a single-breasted one you got a waistcoat as well as a spare pair of trousers. No matter what, it only cost you five guineas.

Then there were flannel suits — they were even cheaper than the serge. But navy serge was the fashion in our day, and patent leather shoes — we'd polish them up with vaseline. Then there were wire twist shirts for three and eleven — two different colours of grey, light or dark — and there'd be black Italian shirts for best; they had a satiny sort of a finish to them. And there were dungarees for three and six a pair, or four bob for double-breasted and double-kneed ones; they call them denims today don't they?

Us women had our fashions, too, for the A & P show and the floral fête. We'd get all dressed up in little tight hobble skirts — you couldn't ride a pushbike in them; couldn't get up on the things! And we'd have great big hats with long ostrich feathers in them; then ostrich hats went out of fashion and they'd be all squashed up in the cupboard because the next thing was on its way in.

But then, you take a look at the old photographs of our fathers and mothers. It's very similar to what they're getting about in today — stovepipe pants with cuffs on them, just like today, and jackets and ties with great big knots. But in our day the men's pants never went down over the tops of the boots; you'd see a couple of inches of sock. Then at the other end they'd be pulled up near the chest.

Old Gillie made all these things, in his wee shop. He was a little, short, bald-headed, very stout old fellow, just like one of those characters out of Charles Dickens. You'd have sworn he came out of *Pickwick Papers*. He was there in Takaka for years and years. He was one of those jokers who seem so old they're nearly dead when you're a child, and then they just keep on going. He's buried down there at Rototai. . . .

Then there was another old chap same vintage as Gillie, old Bob Sousted. He used to set the print at the Golden Bay Times office. They were the two old characters about the place, Gillie and Bob; they were both old bachelor remittance men and they both loved their drink. But they were two very different types to look at: Gillie was a little, short, fat fellow, but old Bob was very tall and thin as a drainpipe. I can still see him, shuffling down the street in his navy-blue coat down to his ankles, hands jammed in his pockets. He had something wrong with his feet, old Bob; he always shuffled along. But he was a very educated bloke, very well brought up. He could talk about Fleet Street in London — that's where he learnt his trade. But alcohol got the better of him, just like old Gillie.

He was a nice old chap, though. He'd talk away, and it was wonderful to watch him working, setting all the type by hand and printing it. The *Golden Bay Times* came out once a week those days — no pictures, just news, stories and local advertisements. It was a good little district newspaper, though; got thrown out at the gate and cost about threepence. But one of the local wags always used to throw off about Bob's paper. He'd come into town and say: "My word it's a great little paper, best in the country. You can go up there and get it, light a pipe and read the paper, all with the same match."

Yes, Bob Sousted was there for years and years, just like old Gillie. He used to live in a little bach down the paddock. But his newspaper didn't really go very long. It lasted a few years and then went bung. We all said his office was too close to the pub. People went up to pay him and then spent their money on whisky!

Yes, there were any amount of special old characters around the place those days. The likes of Tommy Wilkins, he was a real story-teller. He just lived by himself in an old whare over the creek and he was always saying he had this wonderful garden over there, whopping big lettuces and cabbages. He had an old horse called Nora, and Tom said he quite often couldn't find Nora. She'd be standing behind one of his cabbages and he couldn't see her! Then one day he was telling us all about his wonderful beans, "You don't need a basket or a damn bucket to carry *my* beans," old Tom says. "You just throw them across your arm like a sheaf of corn, they're that damn long." He had marvellous poultry over there, too. He always said his roosters would eat their wheat off the mantlepiece, they were that big, and when he went down the path they'd be standing there looking over the fence at him. His hens were marvels, too. If he ever wanted a couple of eggs for breakfast he'd just go and hold a bowl under one of them and she'd drop them in, just like that!

Tommy was always inventing these stories, just for the pleasure of telling them.

Tell you what, I haven't thought about old Tom for donkey's years. And that's what you're doing to us here — you're ploughing up our old memories, getting a bit of air into them. You start me talking, and then all sorts of things slowly come back to life again — all those old-timer things we used to do: plugging up wounds with a lump of cartwheel grease, filling up the bath from kerosene tins heated up on the range. Primitive, wasn't it? Kids today would think it's the end of the world. We didn't mind a scrap; we were happy. Very contented. We didn't think life was hard. You set the range in the morning and put the kerosene tins on to heat up the water and away you went.

Today . . . I don't know . . . they're clamouring after something. They don't know what they want, but they're clamouring. And we get pulled into it, too, us old ones. Doris down the road got herself one of those electric sewing machines, but it goes so fast you've got to watch it the whole time. Far as I'm concerned, the old treadle was better.

Ever felt cut off way out here? No, because we had the wireless. And we were all in a group, not scattered. Everyone close. We could call out to each other.

You see, I was born here in the bay. I married here and I'll die here, too. I don't want to be in one of those old people's homes, away from here with strange people. I'd be tied down in a home. All that routine and strict times for doing this and that — it'd put me out. I like to get up when I feel like it, have a wash, make a cup of tea and go back to bed if I feel like it. Can't do that in a home. You've got to do what you're told to do. No, I hope I'm taken before I get to that stage.

We'll have another cup of tea now, and an eat. Go on, have some more. And come again, whenever you want to. Time's my own now, and it's something I can tell you about, my life. I'm darn ordinary, as far as life goes, but I reckon I did okay.

I'll tell you what, though, I never thought I'd end up in a blooming book.

CYRIL

'I've missed a lot of waves in my life'

Cyril was a cheerful man, yet uneasy. He seemed a loner, forced to be in a group because he was ninety years old and handicapped.

We sat talking in his room, in a rest home overlooking the sea on the outskirts of Christchurch. Cyril wanted to talk. His thoughts darted haphazardly from one topic to another, and as the hours went by he talked faster and faster. It seemed he had never found enough audience for his lively mind. He needed contact and release. He had philosophies that needed airing. And always Cyril's pain was being exposed: his suffering from being born lame and becoming a stutterer and a loner, and the acceptance that pain had taught him: "If you don't accept hurt, people can't hurt you."

Cyril had a certain wisdom as well as pain. He spoke for all handicapped and lonely people: "You know those people who go out surfing? They sit out there on their boards, waiting. But every now and again they miss a wave; they're stuck. Well, I've missed a lot of waves in my life because I was born lame."

I've been thinking about things and I've come to the conclusion, the more invisible a thing is, the stronger it is. You take magnetic force, or the wind, or thought, love, pain . . . .

When they get old and look back on the important things that happened to them, most people talk about their lives, but before I was born was the most important part of my life. When my mother was carrying me, my father's brother came to stay. My mother already had three girls. I was the first boy in a family of six, and the extra work put too much strain on my mother, and I was born lame. Instead of coming out as I should have, head first, I came out feet first. Before children are born, a woman should be well looked after. If my mother had been cared for better I'd be okay, not lame.

I feel I wasn't treated kindly in life. I was rejected by society in general, but also by my family, and especially by my mother, because of my lameness. I couldn't get around much or play football and things when I was a boy, so I was often on my own. Then when I was hanging around the street, people kept away, too, so I got a bit isolated, different from the rest. A woman started dancing classes. I said I'd like to go, but my mother said to me, "You can't go . . . " because I was lame. I *felt* that I wanted to go. I liked girls; I wanted to be able to dance. Dancing's one of the most natural things you can get. Then I used to stutter, and that's a sure sign of being unconfident, scared. My mother used to say it'd hold me up even more. She'd say: "You'll never do any good. All you'll be fit for is digging drains."

What I felt when people said those things? I didn't have a hate attitude towards them. I wondered why, why do they do it to me? Same thing at school — there were just two teachers, a lady and my father, and the lady teacher treated me very badly. I was good at drawing and that, but I wasn't good at figures. I didn't learn well at school. The teacher would pick on me, mock me for not knowing my sums. She didn't know how to handle me. I was a thoughtful one, sensitive. She'd make me stand up or sit well away from the others. She was isolating me, more and more. I got so fed up I ran out of school and hid in a tank at the back of the school. Everyone hunted; couldn't find me.

Then when I went up to a higher class I got my father for a teacher, and I got harshly treated there, too. No favouritism. Many years later I met an old school mate and he said to me, "We often thought how hard you were treated by your father." Children *observe* how people are treated.

I've been different, kept apart. Yes ... you know those people who go out surfing, they sit out there on their boards, waiting. But every now and again they miss a wave, they're stuck. Well, I've missed a lot of waves in my life, because I was born lame. It's like hens and chickens. If any are born lame or deformed they're thrown out of the nest. And the calves in the paddock ... if one's no good, the cow leaves it to die. It's nature; only the strong survive. And the strong shouldn't suffer in order to preserve the weak. Today we're saving rubbish, but you can't say that to people.

I've been most of my life on my own and yet not alone. You're only alone when you're away from yourself. You've got to be a friend to yourself. When you're an enemy to yourself, you're alone. Everyone has a thread, a spark of goodness in them. If you look for that, in other people and also in yourself, you're okay. Once you stop people living the good in their lives, there's no freedom. And, see, that's the trouble with living in an old people's home, or in a city; people live too close together. If you were in the sands of the desert and someone came along, you'd welcome them. But in Christchurch or Wellington, someone comes along and you take no notice.

You know the best way to make people appreciate what they've got? It's easy, in my opinion. Withdraw it from them. Then they realise what they've lost. But always leave the door open for them to come back. Don't close the door on them; that's very important. It's all give and take ... like listening. To be a good listener you've also got to be a good talker. Like me, I ask you questions now and again, ask you what you think about things.

After school I went to technical college for a year or so. It was like heaven after my state school years. I learnt all sorts — art, carpentry, tinsmithing, chemistry, all manual stuff. Then I went into a private surveyor's office. Shouldn't have done that. I was good at drawing but no good at figures, and I was too locked up in that office. I was like you — liked moving about, seeing new things, doing things.

I stayed in that office a few years, a square peg in a round hole, then when World War I was on I got transferred to a drafting job. I could have had Wellington or Hokitika. Chose Hokitika because I've always had a love of hills. When I was a boy I'd see Ben Nevis and Gordon's Knob out the back of the school; I had to go up them. Same thing when I got down to the West Coast and saw Cook and Tasman; I wanted to go up there. I was on the move straight away. In the first month I biked from Hokitika to Franz Josef Glacier, ninety-odd miles. I left at 6 after work that evening, biked all night, got there at 11. Travelling all night, and on your own, you see things because you have to be more careful. You see the sun going down and the moon coming up, and for a short time they're in balance, both up there in the sky. There's so much life to see. I've always liked animals, birds, any life, and often as not I slept out, under bridges and under the stars. I could bike all night and all day, with just a bit of a rest during the day. There's an art in resting. You don't have to take eight hours, or nine or six or something. Resting's mostly in the mind. If you've got a peaceful mind, you sleep and rest well. See my forehead — no wrinkles. Know why? I didn't frown. But once you get into careers and tricky business deals and that, then the wrinkles come all right.

I stayed in that drafting job at Hokitika for a time, then left and worked in the Forestry department with maps and stuff. But the slump came along and upset things, so I went up to Wellington. Worked in all sorts of jobs — on farms, on the roads, odds and ends. But more than anything else I did a lot of photography work. I always had an eye for a photo; it was the creative side of me coming out. Worked with Kodak for some years, taking photos, then on my own, and that was the best thing about my working life — being independent, doing what I wanted to.

But I have to say this: my life's been in bits and pieces, broken up. It's been a frustration, not being strong enough for some things because of my lame leg. I've had a lot of bumps in my life, but I've learnt from them. I've learnt to accept. And I see the funny side of things . . . sometimes. I wasn't ever great. I was ordinary. Which is the most important brick in a building, bottom one or top one? Yes. Most people say the top but it's the bottom one, isn't it? The support. Same with people — the ordinary people are the support. I'm extraordinary, 100 percent individual, yet my life's been ordinary.

But a lot happened in my life. Being lame made me weaker than I might have been, but I've been around New Zealand on a bike, I've climbed Egmont twice, climbed over the Copeland Pass and back, up Franz Josef glacier and down the Tasman. It was a matter of mind over flesh. Perseverance. I remember when I was on Graham

Saddle on the Main Divide, I looked up at Cook and Tasman and thought to myself: I can move, the mountains can't, therefore I'm greater than them. Even though I'm lame. That had a great effect on my life. It made me realise all the little things in life, the barnacles, are unimportant. If you have a little nuisance, a grain of sand in your eye, you get crabby. People won't accept a little hurt, yet they put up with the big things — that's what amazes me. But if you don't accept hurt, people can't hurt you. I realised all that from the hills. People are handicapped, physically or mentally, through their minds, through not being greater than they could be. And there are all sorts of handicaps: a bad attitude to life, hatred of yourself, hatred of others. They're just as big a handicap as lameness. You give out an aura. Animals feel it. So do some people. If you give out hate they feel it, keep out of your way. Yes, it's back to that same thing — the more invisible a thing is, the stronger it is.

That "how to go about approaching people" is one of the most important things we can learn in life. We teach people how to be an apprentice to work, but not how to be an apprentice to *life*. If you don't know how to live you get into trouble. You can't talk decently to people and sort things out, then a fight starts, then a war. You don't find animals having wars, killing each other and making the unborn pay for it.

The human race . . . we're different. We're taught to obey, to obey society. We're not taught to understand why things are done and how to like ourselves and other people, how to approach them and live with them. If I was teaching people, especially children, that's what I'd teach them first. And I'd show them how to hear and see and think. What did they teach you at school about looking after your mind and body and soul? How to look after your body, how to use it and work it? Your body is like a home — you've got to look after it. If you don't clean the windows of your house, you don't see clearly. And then you've got to learn how to look after your mind, how to take defeat, success, criticism. You've got to learn, then you can go off on your own.

And another thing, all good sermons are short!

In our lifetime we very seldom have a good talk to one another. We're afraid to be ourselves. We go to a meeting, come home and say I wish I'd said such and such. We're afraid people will laugh at us if we make a mistake. I've lived a long time now. Know how old I am? I was going to school last century. Born 1894 . . . started school 1899. Over those years I've done some thinking about things, and I'd say the old people today should tell the young people the truth about their lives. Especially, they should tell them the *mistakes* they've made, so the young ones can learn how to avoid them. They should leave a note of what they think of things, so people can read it.

Me? What I'd tell . . . . You've got to learn how to live with people, and that includes everyone — Chinese, Hindus, or people who don't like you. And the first thing you've got to do is learn how to live with yourself. If you don't like yourself you can't like anyone else, because you're *apart*. Life is like sport. Many times you win when you lose. I've done a lot of losing? I didn't really lose, but I often didn't get what I worked for. I was defeated, by mountains and things. But then I wasn't really defeated because it was an experience, and I'd have another go at it, later on. Or I might even climb higher. You might have to give up, but never give in, that's what I say. We can't all get to the top of specific things . . . there's not enough room for everyone at the top of Mt Cook. But there's plenty of room at the top of life; there's plenty of things you can go for. You've got to do the best that's in you, and then try to do a little bit better.

I'd say our grandfathers and grandmothers were stunted by society. They were *told* what to think — about religion, politics, morals, everything. But we're all extraordinary, we're all 100 percent individual. I'd say you've got to do what you know yourself you can do best, not what your grandfather or your father or anyone else says you should. And then if you've got a creative mind and others haven't, or if they have one but aren't using it, then you're apart. Like me.

And another thing I'd want to pass on: people shouldn't be afraid of death. And why are they afraid? Fear has been put into them by the churches. If you have a god of fear, you have a terrible life. When I was young my mother used to take us to the gospel hall. The preacher stood up the front. He'd have a big picture of King Solomon's temple and hellfire and he'd say, "If you don't believe in God, you'll go to hell," and he'd wave his stick at the picture. Everyone believed it, because *he* said it. Even then, I didn't believe it. I thought, he's just putting fear into people to make them believe what *he* believes. If you fear, you lose eventually. And if you use fear to influence people, they pay for it in the end — and you do too.

I think we worry too much about dying. We should worry about how we live. Dying will look after itself. Life looked after itself before I came along. It'll do the same when I die.

Some of the old people up here say, "I've done all I want to do, the world's changing and I'm fed up with it. I want to go." But I don't agree. Life continues — there's reincarnation, immortality of the soul. When you get amongst mountains and big things you begin to think about those ideas. Mystery is a very important thing in life. Uncertainties. If we knew everything that was going to happen tomorrow it wouldn't be interesting at all. And you've got to accept. It's like friends — you lose some, a few die, new ones come along. Friends are like a garden. If you don't replace it with seeds it's going to be bare later on. But a lot of old people lose sight of mystery; it's worn out of them. They have to have rigidity around them, certainties. But what's certain?

The Greeks used to say, "Those whom the gods love die young." That explained for them why some young, very talented people died young, and why it wasn't a tragedy. But the meaning I take from it is this: if you're a friend of the gods you never get old. You stay young. If I die tomorrow I'm not an old man, am I? Age has nothing to do with death. Another way of saying it is this: it's not how long you live that's important, it's what you've wanted to do, and done.

I'm not going to be buried. They're going to cremate me and throw my ashes up in the air. I don't want people to mourn over my body in a coffin. It's old and worn-out already; it needs to be got rid of. I don't believe in tombstones. Who's going to remember me anyway, fifty years after I'm gone? And I want people to remember me for what I've done. There's going to be no one remembering my work, my photography and that, but the important things that will contribute something to the world were the good deeds I've done — and done for the sake of doing them, not for gain.

I remember one time when I was a kid of ten or so: it was Christmas and I was off to church. An old tramp came up. He was dirty and rusty — he looked at the end of his tether. Most of the people there wouldn't talk to him. I talked to him. I wished him Merry Christmas and gave him a book I'd bought the night before, *The Greatest Thing In The World* by Henry Drummond. No one told me to do it; I just did it. I knew a lot of people who went to church, prayed, then came outside and weren't kind to people, weren't kind to me. And that being kind to the old tramp . . . I've felt the effect of that all my life.

I'll tell you another thing that happened to me when I had a photography shop in Hokitika. A girl came to see me, wanted a job. I knew her past. She'd let her other boss down, but I said to her, "You can come here on one condition: you treat me well, I'll treat you well." I knew if I gave her a chance to work I'd help her along in life, even though I knew she'd done wrong in the past. You don't push people down. You pull them out — give them a wash, you might say. Always help a lame dog over a stile.

A lot of people haven't got the art of being kind. They think kindness is weakness. I've experienced that. You do someone a good turn; they think you're soft and then they walk all over you. But I take it as experience. I learn not to do it myself. Kindness is not weakness, but I'll tell you what, jealousy is. It means you want protection, but it ends up you drive everyone away.

I'm going to tell you something now that's very important. I was often on my own. I've been ill-treated and I've had to stick up for myself all the time. But I'm one of those people who've never really felt fear. I've never really seen it, or had it happen to me. Why? I've learnt an acceptance. And I can think very quickly. What happens ... what's always happened ... if I see danger around, I think, how can I get out of it? I was always quick in my mind, maybe to make up for being lame in my body.

It might seem I'm lonely, but I'm not. I've found out books are good friends. They teach you what other people don't, or won't. You take *Emerson's Essays.* I've read them and I've become a friend of his. People are lonely only because they don't like themselves, or don't know how to look after themselves. Then they start hating. They put themselves in little boxes, and they don't know how to get out. It's a very big struggle.

A lot depends on the age of your soul. Some people are old souls when they're born; they already know a lot. And some people never get old, in learning. They never get developed, because they're afraid to change their mind. I'd change my mind tomorrow if I saw something better. Life is movement, like a train, backwards and forwards. If you get on and you're meant to go 100 miles, you can still get off at a small station before you get there. Then if it's not a good station you can get on again, and you can go more than 100 miles. I judge people not by where they're from but where they're moving — which direction they're going and why.

I've been on the move all my life, lived in about thirty different houses and all sorts of huts, hotels, boarding houses. I've been a wanderer. My life's been very broken up, but it means I've had a good idea what life's really like — sleeping under bridges, under trees. I didn't stay on a narrow road. I got off into the wide, open spaces. I think a lot about things. I'm waiting now for Haley's Comet to come again. I saw it in 1910, and it's coming again in a few years' time. I'll be here? I might be up there, looking down on it!

WINNIE

'Dad's building a thing like a bird'

Winnie's life had been tough, but it had kept her very sane. She'd learnt to be practical and adaptable. Her mum knew which plants and leaves would cure which ailments; her father invented an aeroplane of sorts, "way back in 1912 or something, when they'd only just started building aeroplanes all over the world".

Winnie had inherited her parents' common sense. She'd done nothing outstanding in her life, yet she'd made a good home, raised a good family, dug the carrots and pulled in many a kerosene tin of whitebait. She'd also established herself as a very real identity in the Takaka district, with her crinkly grin and her vivid anecdotes.

The atmosphere was relaxed at Winnie's place. There were vines and pumpkins crawling over the back porch and up the walls, there were tools and chooks all over the yard, and the Tasman sea slapped the back fence. Winnie was always happy to stop and put her feet up. She flowed, like the vines and the tides.

She'd bring the kettle on the pot-belly to the boil for a good pot of tea, then the soup went back on. And all the time Winnie chatted away: small, homely details, from a very calm and earthy old lady.

I was born at home in our old house on the rocks just past the milk factory. There were three babies born in Takaka that day — two at the very same hour, 9 o'clock. No such thing as a hospital or even a doctor in Golden Bay those days. There was just this old nurse, Mrs Hawkins — a tall, thin woman who rode around side-saddle on a horse and delivered babies. She delivered everyone around this district.

Anyhow, she confined Tommy Presland's mother up the back road, then she rode down to Mum and I'd already come by myself. Mum did it all. She was trying to bath me when the midwife got there. And from then on everyone called me Hawkins, because Mrs Hawkins was supposed to be my nurse but she missed out!

Mum had nine of us kids in the end . . . just had them all at home, except for the last two. Nothing handed out on a plate those days. I know for a fact my mum never had a stove in our old house on the rocks, only an open fire. She cooked up everything on that fire, in a camp oven and a couple of great big iron pots. I remember that every time you cooked up something you had to dish it up right away, otherwise the potatoes and corned beef and that would go all black, on account of the iron in those old pots.

We were hard up all right, but we always had plenty of meat. It was quite cheap those days . . . about threepence a pound. The lady at the butcher's was very good to us. She knew we were a big family. When the butcher boy called there'd always be a free shin of beef tucked in his basket.

No water in the house, either. Mum had to pump all our water herself, way out the back, then lug it over to the house in buckets or anything else she could lay her hands on. She had to do all the washing in a couple of kerosene tins; didn't even have a copper for years and years. There were a couple of pieces of iron and a few bricks out the back. She'd build up a fire under the bricks and pop the kerosene tins on top. Then she'd give the clothes a good boil-up; she always believed in that. She'd be standing there all day, scrubbing and rubbing at the damn stuff.

She also did a terrible lot of starching of the clothes. We always had to wear calico singlets — shirts we called them those days — and Mum used to put starched lace around the necks ... I can see it yet ... it scratched our necks, that darn lace. I feel I want to tear it out whenever I see lace. We had bloomers made out of calico, too. They'd go right down to below the knees, with lacy frills. They'd be starched up to glory, too; they scratched your legs. Yes, Mum always starched everything up to billio, as thick as ever she could do it. Then she'd heat up the old Mrs Potts iron on a piece of flat metal on the open fire ... half the time you'd get a bit of black streak on the clothes from those old irons. I always thought that was a laugh. There'd be more dirt on the clothes when they'd been ironed than before they'd been washed! And we wore special leather boots — dairy boots we called them — laced up to the top of the ankle. Everyone had them.

But often I went to school barefoot because we couldn't afford the boots. I remember there were two of us at our school who had no shoes at all, winter and summer: me and my sister. Our feet got terribly cold. Tell you what we'd do: we'd be walking to school, and if we saw a cow pee on the side of the road we'd race over and put our feet in it, to warm them up. We'd always be on the watch for that. There'd be two or three of us fighting to get there first and have warm feet for a few minutes.

These are little things you never ever hear about in the history books. My grandchildren don't even believe them. But I'll never forget them. I hear them all these days, groaning and moaning about this and that, but you've only got to turn the tap and there's hot and cold water and press a button and there's light. It's too easy today. The kids are bored with themselves and they're smoking drugs and that. In my day any woman seen smoking tobacco was cowed down, she couldn't go around in jeans and things. Half the girls dress like men these days. But I remember one woman, Amy Bock — she was more or less classed as a criminal because she dressed in trousers; she was taken to court for it. Poor old Amy. I think she did a term in jail. And you weren't allowed to do anything manual on Sundays. You could get taken to court for that, too.

Yes, there was a terrible lot of talk about respectability those days. It wasn't accepted at all for a girl to become an unmarried mother; she got completely shunned.

Another thing that sticks out in my mind about the old days, we got all sorts of strange brews and cures. If we stuck a nail in our foot, Mum used to burn an old woollen sock on the embers of the fire and hold our foot over it until the foot went a browny colour, like cigarette smoke on your fingers. That was meant to take the poison out. And it did, too. We never ever got poisoned feet.

Then if we had sores she'd give us boiled leaves — lamb's tongue or comfrey leaves dipped in boiling water, laid on the sore and bandaged up. They drew all the matter out. Comfrey's wonderful for sick animals, too. You just give them some leaves and they eat them, like a sick cat eats grass. And if we had toothache, Mum stuck milkweed in our mouth. You'd be spitting for all you were worth. That weed was worse than the darn toothache — made the old nerves go like one thing, but in the end it did knock the pain.

Then once a year Mum gave us flax root. She'd cut the root up, boil it up in water and we'd have to take a tablespoon of the liquid twice a day, to purify the blood ... that's what she said. Horrible taste, but it works — makes you go to the lavatory properly. Then in the spring we'd also get a dose of sulphur and treacle; that was another brew she used for purifying the blood and stopping pimples and boils and things. A teaspoonful of the stuff every other night for a week. It didn't matter if you made a fuss about it or kept out of the way until bedtime, you still got it. And then we weren't allowed to get cold and wet after Mum gave us that brew. She reckoned it opened up the pores and you'd catch a cold easily, so we had to keep out of the creeks for a day.

Dock roots for boils — that was another one of Mum's old brews. She'd cut the root up fine, boil it and we'd have to drink the liquid. It's very, very bitter. We always said the cure was worse than the complaint, but it did the trick all right. There was this chap came back from the first war with a terrific lot of boils. He got all sorts of stuff from the doctor and the chemist — it did no damn good. But my mum's brew worked ... cured all his boils and he never ever got another one.

There's all sorts of growing things you can use for medicine or for eating, if you know where to look. We'd tear off into the bush and get gigis, off those vines sprawling all over the trees. They come out with four fingers and a white flower in the centre. We'd leave them until winter when the tender inner white leaves had become winter pods — that's what we called them. They were lovely green pods as big as a fair-sized sausage, with seeds all along them. Beautiful to eat — something like a Chinese gooseberry taste. We just scraped the seeds off and ate the middle bit. Kids today wouldn't know what to do with them.

Then there's another thing that makes me smile: I see these people get up on the telly and run cooking programmes. They say there isn't any typical New Zealand food. What about the nikau palm? That's typical; you can make beautiful pickle out of the big bulbs.

You peel them down, chop them and make your pickle. I've made hundreds of pots of it. Don't ask me for a recipe; it's just in my head. But I remember six or eight years ago half a dozen nikaus fell down in a storm out Wainui Bay, and I made twenty-five bottles of pickle. The old chap out there went crazy over it. He hadn't tasted nikau pickle since his old mother died.

Yes, I tell you, us kids were like monkeys. We swung up in the trees and stripped the berries off the supplejacks . . . just ate them raw. They're nice; taste like cooked kumara. Then there were the konini berries everywhere, and passionfruit — they're all good, typical New Zealand foods for those people on the telly.

We were tough and healthy those days, too right. We never seemed to have anything the matter with us. Mind you, I think some of those old cures of Mum's would be quite handy today. You've only got to have a sore toe these days and you run to the doctor; he has all sorts of things he can give you. And no one had any money in our day. We couldn't pay a doctor anyway.

Some families had only one basin. You bathed the baby and made the bread in the same basin. Then we'd have curtains and bloomers and things made out of flour bags, with "A1 Flour" written across them in big red letters. Mum always tried to get the letters off — she'd rub dripping on and leave it for a few days, then wash it out with washing soda and water. We'd save the sugar bags, too, for making aprons, and the men would get a big chaff or oat sack to work in. They'd cut a hole in the top, two holes for the arms, and the women would hem around the edges. It's surprising the amount of rain those old sacks kept off. Then there were Dad's grey striped shirts; when he'd worn out the shoulders Mum'd make pinafores for us kids out of the tails. I remember the first day I wore a grey shirt pinafore to school. The kids said, "I've seen your father wearing that." I hid behind the door and wouldn't go back in to school.

You just had to scrape around the best you could — a bob here and a bob there. When I was a baby my mum used to wheel me down to the river in the pram and spend the morning whitebaiting. You'd see continuous runs those days; they'd keep coming solidly for two hours or more. Then she'd wheel kerosene tins of the whitebait around town in the pram and sell them for a penny a pint. Much later on the price rose to threepence. We thought that was terribly dear, then up and up it went.

But we needed those few pence. You could say we had nothing, our family, but we got along. My mum always found the time to come outside and play with us kids — I always remember that. You didn't see all the bickering and divorces like today, either.

And you take my dad: he didn't have a big education, but he went and built himself an aeroplane, way back in 1912 or something when they'd only just started building aeroplanes all over the world. My dad was just trying himself out, to see if he could do it. He was quite old, too, by that stage, but he just thought it out in his head and found a mate to help him out with the building.

I can remember all that very well, when Dad made the aeroplane. Sometimes he used to work all night on it. He did all the planning and structure in an old house near our place, and all the canvas work and that, then he took it outside and assembled it. But us kids weren't allowed to talk about it when he was making the thing. It was all very secret. We weren't even allowed to go over there and see Dad.

Then I remember I had to go and give him a message from Mum. I had a good look at what was going on, then I tore back and told my brothers and sisters, "Dad's building a thing like a bird." I was trying to tell them what the wings were like. I didn't know it was a plane; never seen one before. Never *heard* of one.

The others just listened. They thought I'd gone mad.

No, even then my parents didn't tell us it was a plane. They just said, don't talk about what Dad's doing over in the shed.

But then *we all saw it*, when Dad took the bird out of the old house. He got it all assembled and took it to a great, long paddock down Motupipi. It had no engine, that plane. I suppose it was just sort of a glider affair. They had a couple of horses down there and they hooked them up to the plane. The horses had to gallop along, pulling, then the bloke driving would pull the trip wire, and the wind they got was meant to lift her up in the air.

Well, Dad's mate got in the plane, another bloke drove the horses and Dad just stood and watched. He was too old to be really in the thing. And everyone from round here was watching it go up.

It went up, too, that plane of Dad's. They let the string go and she went up fifty foot. But she had nothing to keep her going. The wind from the horses wasn't strong enough to keep her up. She just came down again — bang! They tried her two or three times, took her over to the Nelson A & P show and all, but she never stayed up long. I think five minutes was the longest they ever managed. Couldn't ever get the wind they wanted. Today gliders get taken up by another aeroplane, don't they?

And I remember my mum was expecting my sister at the time, but she had to go without this and that so Dad could make the plane. She didn't have any real baby gowns and that for my sister.

My dad was going bankrupt anyway . . . and then World War I came along and he dropped the plane idea.

But he was a very clever man, my dad. He was one of those men always forecasting this and that. He used to tell us, "The day will come, you see if it doesn't, when we'll see carts going along the road without horses." Everyone used to laugh at him. Then I remember the day when I first saw that happen: a motorcar coming down the road! I was five years old at the time, and I'm up in my eighties now, but I can still see me and my sister running down the lane and Billy Gibbs puffing past the bridge. We didn't know what it was, that thing moving him along. Something going down the road with a noise like a traction engine, a real old-timer motorcar with Billy Gibbs sitting up top, driving it along the road. We all talked about it for years.

Then my dad always used to say that one day we'd hear our own voices coming back to us in the air and we'd see pictures coming out of the sky. We just used to laugh at him. But we see that now, don't we. It's here, just like my old dad said.

We've always had interesting types of people over here in the bay. You take the old butchers who drove around the district. Jack Flowers was one of the famous ones, the wag of the district. He was tall and thin and six foot three of humour. He had a very deep, very unusual voice; it came from way down in his belly somewhere. I can still hear the old joker telling me he'd been out the coast and he was darn pleased to get back. There was too much damn wind out there for his liking. "Phew, it blows damn hard out there," says Jack. "You're out spotlighting in the bush, and that damn wind blows the torch beam clean over your shoulder."

His Tamworth pigs were wonders, too. He reckoned they were very tall specimens with extra-long legs. They were that long in the nose they'd be rooting for cockles in two foot of water and they wouldn't get their eyebrows wet!

Old Jack Flowers always had a quick answer. Some blokes were talking away in the pub one night about droving cattle. Jack was very good at his droving, so he told these blokes how he'd driven a mob of cattle from North Cape to Bluff. "My word," says one of the blokes, "how did you get them over Cook Strait?" "Oh," said Jack, "I went round the other way."

As a matter of fact, I reckon we've got more eccentric people around here than anywhere else. You've got to be a bit mad to live here in the bay! This chap, a psychologist type, moved over to the bay and he just loved it; he felt at home! He reckoned we're all blooming crackers over here, or else running away from financial problems or wives or something. You've got to have a problem to come here in the first place. The joke is, everyone thinks they're getting away from their problems, but they get into a heck of a lot more trouble once they land in a place like this!

You take one lot: we always had to go down to their place to get the milk, and it always tasted of soap because they never rinsed out the buckets and that. There'd be fowls on the table and goats wandering all over the house. The old girl'd be wandering around, too, without her teeth in and there were hordes of kids everywhere. Their house got twelve loaves of bread at a time. They were the baker's best customer — had a bigger bread account than the local pub. No glass in the front door, only sacks. When the plates started rattling, that was the sign. The fowls all rushed in to get the crumbs, and the goat'd barge in to see what he could get. The story went round that one stage there the dogs heard the rattling and leaped through the window. Bang! That was the end of the glass.

One of their neighbours was a strange one, too. She used to put her teeth in overdrive. She'd talk and talk and then run out of words; there'd just be her teeth going click, click. In the end she'd realise what was happening, so she'd take a deep breath, her teeth would rattle and then out would come the next lot of talk.

Another lot down that way were kleptomaniacs. All the males in the family couldn't resist pinching things. Whatever you had, they had about six of: six axes, six saws, six anvils. But then they were very good about it. If you went down to borrow something they'd lend you your own battery to start your car! And they'd never steal money, only tools and sheep and things — especially tools; they couldn't resist them. Or light bulbs — they'd clean out milking sheds and any empty houses; couldn't resist it. They'd take their lunch to work in a sugar bag — an ordinary tucker bag wasn't big enough — and come home with a couple of dozen light bulbs bulging out of it. No, they just couldn't help themselves. The wife once told us her husband often couldn't sleep, especially on wet nights! "He often has to get up and go for a stroll," she'd say, "and he'll come back hours later. He goes off even on wet, windy nights." The next morning you'd find some of your sheep missing. Then to cap it all off, one of them swapped his wife for a car! He came into the pub one night with a big grin on his face and announced: "I've done myself a good deal, chaps. I've swapped Ivy for a V8. Come and have a look at her. She's a little beaut." He was celebrating the deal, you see.

They were extremes, all right, that lot. I told you we were different over here in the bay! But we all knew we had to live with the situation. You can't cure kleptomaniacs. Old Dick down the road was another of that type. He was always thieving things, but you could never catch him at it. If there was a fishing boat in, next thing you'd see him selling fish. He could sell eggs, but he only had two fowls. He could sell veges, but he had no garden.

And yes, then there was a fellow with a family of four great big boys, all six footers and very solemn — they didn't laugh. Everyone called them The Silent Nights. Every Friday night they liked to go to the pub, but they never ever went together and never to the same bar. One'd have to wait until the other went out, or one'd go round to the lounge bar or something. Each of them had a great big motorcar — a Holden or a Chrysler or something — and you'd see them going slowly down the road, one by one. None of the four married; they just stayed at home and the old man fed them until they went away, or died. The old man was mad on politics, and the story went round that he was listening to Parliament on the wireless one day and he didn't like what the politician was saying, so he picked up the wireless set and smashed it. The boys? They didn't take much interest in politics. Didn't take much interest in *anything*. The highlight of the week for The Silent Nights was the pub on Friday.

It's all coming back to me, all this old stuff. We were a mad lot out here, but we were quite happy. There weren't too many of us, you see. There were hardly any houses between Waitap and town. You'd walk in to town — might take you half a day to get there because all the people'd come out to have a talk if they weren't busy. If they just waved you knew they were busy at something. Yes, it was lovely those days. It's lovely now, but you just go from A to B; you just drive from here to town and don't see the neighbours. People were more generous, too. If you had a good crop of spuds or pumpkins you'd give some away, or you'd swap them for someone else's cabbages or apples or whatnot. Nowadays, you'd sell yours and I'd sell mine.

Today money's the god; that's all there is to it. Money for possessions, money for entertainment. In our day entertainment was a different sort of a thing altogether. Of an evening you'd get out your pocket knife and whittle away at a bit of wood, or you'd chuck an onion on the fire and then eat it. Good days. And what with motorcars and TV and chemicals and drugs, they're upsetting the whole apple-cart nowadays. They're polluting everything to death — the land and the sea and the air. I'll give you an instance: I went up to Wellington and I couldn't get a decent drink of water. I said, what sort of a show is this? It was swamp water or something. I wouldn't give it to my stock, anyhow. I said, as a matter of fact, if we had water like this where I come from, the council wouldn't be allowed to carry on. But Wellington ... it's too big. You've got no control of things like the water you drink. The mayor gets a million dollars to make a new town hall, but you can't get a good drink of water when you want it!

We're polluting the place to death all right. So maybe we won't have to worry about what it'll all lead to in fifty years' time. I'd say they could blow the universe to bits any day; they've got the gear and the know-how. I don't know what we're going to see next. But I'd say this; we've seen all these changes, my generation. We've seen motorcars, electric lights, aeroplanes, computers. We've seen more changes than any generation of people has seen. And I'd say we've seen the best times, too. I don't envy them with their new refrigerators and their electric this and that and their homes that don't smell like homes.

I can't do much myself these days. I can't get about, but I intend to keep pottering all the time. People come and see me — people I went to school with, all sorts. They pull up to say gidday, and then away we go. We have a darn good yarn, digging up all the years we had together. But by Joves, my generation, we're moving on now. We're dying out. You could say I'm one of the old identities around the place. I'm sneaking up among them now. We all used to meet up town, when we could still walk. We liked to remember back to the old days. One passed on, then someone else joined in the group. We enjoyed the part of being an old identity of the bay.

I can remember things all right. I suppose there's lots I don't remember. I don't know. . . .

But come and see me again. You needn't make an appointment because I'll be here . . . as long as the priest doesn't get me first! You know, it's a funny thing, but I was thinking only the other day, I'd like to go back down the Waitap again, whitebaiting. I'd head down the paddocks with my nets and tins. I'd pull in the whitebait. . . .

But it's only my thinking. I'd like to, but I suppose I'll never do it again.

HARRY

'We had the first school bus in Waiau: our old horse, Emma'

Harry was ninety-five, a bachelor, living in Waiau with his sister Flo, who'd looked after him since 1942. Then there was his sister Mary, and strings of nephews and nieces down the road and all round the North Canterbury district.

Physically, he was failing. He still had plenty of white hair, but he had no appetite and found it hard to get around or concentrate for long. Yet mentally and emotionally he was positive, geared for the years to come. He talked confidently of his plans for the house and the vege garden: "I'm going to change that window sill. I'll take it out and put a concrete one in." Do it himself? "I'll do it all right."

At each of our sessions Harry would perk up a little more, his eyes would light up and he'd try to get things out faster and faster. Then he'd get tongue-tied and stop altogether, exhausted. But later on he'd get me out inspecting his veges or poking around amongst his old treasures in the shed: "See that old cream and green stove? Take a good look at her. I didn't want to fling her away to the dump." There was always fondness in Harry's memories of people and things — old Ashleigh Lewis, the biggest character in North Canterbury; the old gear from his carpentry camps; "I like the old camp oven; scones, by Joves. . . ."

The exception was his memory of his four years' service in World War I: "I learnt nothing good from the war. It was just a bad experience."

Flo and Mary were amazed Harry talked as much as he did about the war. They heard things they'd never heard before themselves. They all insisted I stay in their spare room so I could sit with Harry whenever he felt strong and make the most of his outpourings.

Our last session was interrupted by a family gathering for Flo's birthday dinner. We ate vegetables Harry had grown; one root of his new potatoes fed eight of us. Then Harry made a little speech: "Well Chris, I wish you good luck for this book. And I'll tell you what: it's an important

201

*thing, what you're doing. The young ones don't know about these things
unless us old ones talk about them."*

You're right, Harry.

Mr Dalkie! You call me Harry and we'll get along much better.

I was born here in Waiau, 7 July 1888. And I liked it here so I never moved far away. I worked around Waiau for over eighty years. We're long doers, our family. I'm one year older than my grandad; he got up to ninety-four. Grandad was one of the real old settlers. He came out from Scotland with his parents and settled in Nelson, at the time of the Maori land wars. When he was a boy of twelve or thirteen a Maori lady put him into a canoe, covered him up with a flax mat and pushed him out into a lagoon, to save him from the fighting that day. She gave him some water, told him not to lift the mat and to stay out there till dark. Grandad's family had given her people timber and stuff. That was her way of showing gratitude. And that's why I'm here!

Grandad used to talk to us for hours and hours about those days. My mother was a nurse — she was always away delivering babies all over the district — and Grandmother died before I was born. So Grandad came to look after us, and that's why I know so much about his early days. Grandad clearly remembered the Maori slaughters, remembered one warrior chief being taken prisoner and the Nelson Maoris discussing how they were going to kill him. They waited till there was a gale blowing offshore, then they tied him up, cut both his ears off, put him in a canoe with no oars and pushed him right out to sea. No food, no water . . . flies crawling all over him from the wounded ears. They said he'd go raving mad and throw himself overboard in three or four days' time.

Grandad also remembers the whites defending themselves against the Maoris. They put all the women and children into the church. The women would be loading up the muzzle loaders and handing them to their men defending the hill.

I can remember way back to all that, what Grandad said about the wars. But I can't remember what day it is, or where I left the spade. Silly, isn't it? Grandad and his two uncles started up a sawmill in Nelson. He couldn't read or write much, but by God he could reckon up the timber all right — lengths and widths and breadths in his head, no trouble. They got the mill going well, cutting timber with circular saws, water-driven, and sending it to the North Island. But then when the wars came on, the ships got used for carting troops, not timber. They couldn't sell the timber, couldn't do anything, so the mill futted out and they lost all they had. They sold up everything they owned to pay off their debts, then Grandad put a swag on his back and walked down here to Waiau — walked down the West Coast, in to Hanmer and on over to Waiau. No other way to come. He set to work bullock driving in the bush, dragging logs out of the hills back there. Then a couple of times a year he'd take the bullock team down to Christchurch, carting wool to Saltwater Creek and Lyttelton and bringing back stores. He remembered what Christchurch looked like those days: flax swamp, tussock and bog. Our Grandad could have owned Cathedral Square; he could have bought it as a paddock for his bullocks, for ten pounds. But he thought that was a waste of time; he wouldn't have it: "No thanks," he said. "It's nothing but flax and swamp." So he'd just let his bullocks free to roam, with bells around their necks so he could find them in the morning. Then he'd pitch a tent for himself on any dry spot he could find.

On one of those trips he met my grandmother. They got married, and in the end, in 1861, he brought Grandmother and my mother, a six-week-old baby, up here to Waiau, and we've been here ever since.

Grandad was a handyman; he could do most things. He settled his family at Highfield station in Waiau and worked at all sorts — droving bullocks, making bricks, building and thatching cob cottages, pressing wool for Highfield and Leslie Hills and other stations round about. Stayed there till his wife died, when she was fifty-four, and instead of retiring there himself when he was sixty Grandad went up to the sawmills at Kaikoura, back to the bush. He had to get back to the bush. He said he was brought up in the trees and the outbacks; he just had to get back there again. Stayed up there till he was ninety-four, working all that time.

In the end we went up there and got him from his hut in the bush, brought him back to Waiau for his last months. I remember that very well, going up to get Grandad. We went up on a Tuesday in Derrett's coach with five horses, stayed the night at a hotel, got Grandad and the mail and came back to Waiau Wednesday.

Grandad was a great old chap, with his white whiskers and his black tobacco. Now and again he'd cut a bit off and chew it. It stank like hell — old, black stuff. He was a hard doer, all right, but he wasn't an exception. You did all sorts those days . . . had to; had to make everything yourself. Grandad and his mates would go into the bush and shape their own axe- and saw-handles.

They'd make their own lamps too; thought nothing of it. They'd get long manuka sticks — good, hard wood that didn't burn away — wrap an old jumper or something around it, wire it on, dip it in fat or kerosene and light it. Sluice lamps they called them; they'd last for hours, down the creek eeling and that. Or they'd get a big bottle, pour in water and a bit of soil, then fat from a sheep's intestine. Next you poked down a wick and set it alight. Those ones were called slash lamps; they burned for hours and hours, but they stank like hell. Of an evening Grandad would take a slash lamp and sit around the camp fire near his hut. He'd have a pile of silver pine blocks one or two feet long and six inches wide. He'd be sitting there splitting them with a shingle knife and a wooden mallet to make shingles for roofing.

They made use of everything, the old settlers. They'd cut down beer bottles to make jam jars, and kerosene tins were used for *everything*. Cut down lengthways they made meat-roasting dishes; Mum had one for most of her life. Then you could take the other part of the tin, solder down the hole where the funnel went for pumping out the kerosene, pull it all in a bit and make a lid for your roasting dish. Good as any modern one — keeps the steam in. Or you could hammer out all the corners and make a darn good bucket, for water or milk. They'd also make use of the big barrels from the whaling ships, the old ones with lids. They'd three-parts cook wood pigeons, ducks or wild pigs in these big barrels and put them down in their own fat.

Even in my day we had to make most things ourselves. My mother used to make the butter and that, and when I was a little kid I'd have to take it up to the ploughmen's camp. The station supplied jam and golden syrup, but not milk and butter, so Dad would send me up with billies of milk and parcels of butter. Never charged them for it. I remember one of the ploughmen asked me, "Hey Harry, what's your age?" and I said, "I'm half past four." I'd heard people talk about the time — half past twelve, half past six — and from then on, that was my name, Half Past Four.

One thing though, we were never cheeky those days. If we answered back, we got it. Father would wait till we got to bed, then he'd lay into our bare skin with a belt, sometimes the buckled end. Too right, we had to be polite to everybody, call them Mr or Mrs. so and so. No such thing as saying, "I don't want to do such and such." By hang, no. Father was very kind to outsiders, tough on us. "The Apostle of the North," that's what they called him. He'd take the blankets off his own bed and give them to the swaggers.

The odd one would take the blankets down to the pub, sell them and spend the money on booze. Father was kinder to them than he was to us ten kids.

I was like my father and his father. Did a bit of everything at the start, mustering and that. Then I got into carpentry and I stayed with it till I was eighty-four. I wouldn't retire, just like my Grandad.

I was the cook as well as the carpenter half the time, working out in the country, round Hanmer and Cheviot and Oxford and that. We'd just pitch tents and camp out, cooking up a good feed each night in a couple of billies and a camp oven over the open fire. Meat. There'd be eight or ten men on the job and I'd say to them, "I'll get the meat on and peel the vegetables. You get in the wood and wash up and that." I'd get them to help out, then I could spend time making tastier meals for them. What the men liked about my cooking: I'd make up a big Irish stew. I'd get a neck and breast of mutton, put it in a kerosene tin with a wooden lid over the top, heave in a bit of cabbage and onion and a parsnip and carrot or two, any dashed thing, and I'd cook it overnight. We'd eat the boiled mutton one day and I'd make Irish stew from the stock and meat and veges the next day.

Now and again I'd go down the creek and get a few silver belly eels, or a couple of rabbits or ducks. We managed all right. If we were short of bread I made soda bread in the camp oven, or scones — two or three inches high, by Joves. You put them in a hot camp oven, held the lid over the flame so it was darn near red hot, put the lid on and piled hot coals on top. The hot lid pulled those darn scones way up high. Then I'd make suet dumplings whenever we were having stew or boiled meat. Suet ones were out on their own, compared with the dripping or butter ones. I'd get a little heap of cut-up suet, flour, water, pepper and salt, I'd roll it up into a round dumpling and pop it into the boiling water. Secret is, you don't lift the lid or touch the dumpling till you're ready to dish up, then you cut it into squares and tuck in. Joves, it tastes good.

I'll tell you the funniest thing I ever saw out there at the camps. One wet day I decided I'd make a golden syrup duff. All I had on hand was a bit of suet and butter, flour and spice and golden syrup, but I mixed up a duff and cooked it in a big billy. Came a few hours later. I said, "Righto boys, let's have a look at a good duff." I lifted the lid and there was the cloth floating around in the water, going round and round in circles, and my duff bobbing around on top. And I'd invited them to see this wonderful pudding! I didn't have any binder twine to tie up the cloth when I put the duff in, so I'd used my bootlace. But it'd perished in the hot water!

Well, I was lucky it was still all in one piece, so I grabbed a couple of meat forks, got one each side of the duff and hoisted her out onto a tray. We pushed her back onto the cloth and one old bloke there, Charlie, a real old-timer in camping, says, "Look here Harry, I'll get you some flax for that duff." So we tied her up again with flax and threw her back in. I said, "She won't be any good, boys." "Just won't she now?" says Charlie.

We ate the lot. She was beautiful — a great big duff, bigger than a pumpkin. "By God," says the boys, "make some more duff, Harry."

They used to think I was just it, with the cooking. And the boss used to say, "Harry holds the mob together." He reckoned it was my cooking kept them all working well and happy. Of a morning I'd get their breakfast — porridge, chops, bacon and eggs, tea and toast — a darn good feed. Then I'd do the veges and put the meat in the camp oven; let it simmer away while we went off to work. Now and again I'd dump tools, dash off and have a look in the camp oven, and there'd be dinner ready for midday. We'd have meat three times a day, too right.

Just slept out in tents — good calico ones with an open fire at one end and an awning made of sacks, cut down the sides, opened out and sewed up, to keep out the sun and rain. Made our own canvas stretchers to sleep on, too. We'd get bits of timber and make a frame — three-inch by two-inch legs, three-inch by two-inch crosspieces and a bit of three by two at each end. Tack the canvas over the frame and there's your stretcher, and quite good too.

Before stretchers came in we'd just get a sack or two, push in some straw, sew them up with twine and there's your mattress. A couple of blankets, you were right. If it was very cold we'd lie newspapers on top of the blankets; that kept the heat in. What we didn't know about camping in the hills. . . .

If you got caught out you cut a bit of tussock. It's dry and brittle, very good to sleep on. Or if your mattress was too narrow for your bunk you'd fill in the sides and back with tussock — or your clean washing; that aired your pants and shirts and kept them dry.

Baths? In the creek. You'd get in and have a wash. Sometimes there'd be a waterfall in the creek, and by God, it's better than all these showers. Tell you what we'd do in the winter: we had this canvas bath, long as this table, but you could roll it up and carry it anywhere, on your back or on the pack saddle. She was hard on your bottom, but she held water, that old bath.

Yes, I've roughed it all right. You had to be a jack of all trades those days, and all hard work; no such thing as concrete mixers. I made this house in my spare time before and after work; just three rooms it was at first. Then I put on a passage and a sunporch, and when Flo lost her husband I added on an extra bedroom and she moved in. Nineteen forty-two — over forty years we've been together and we've got along well. Later on I put in the sitting room and then the bathroom and toilet. It's a real house now.

Now I do nothing, just the vege garden and a few repairs around the place. I'm not altogether fighting fit — damn long way from it — but I'm still active.

Why I lived so long? I don't know. But I'll tell you this: I used to do a lot of physical culture — physical jerks they call it in the army, press-ups. I could do them thirty times, until a few years ago, and turn cartwheels and backwards somersaults. People'd say, "Come on Harry," and I'd do a few more. I did the press-ups at my nephew's wedding last year . . . but only one. . . .

Then I've always lived a good, simple life. Never abused myself. Didn't drink a terrible lot. Plenty of good, plain, wholesome food — bread and dripping. I still love that. Only thing is, I'm not hungry these days. Eat too many pills. Tell you what, I'd like to eat more. Can't though. I've just had double pneumonia and I've got chronic bronchitis — had it for years — and arthritis to cap it all off. You feel this arm. It's much bigger than the other. Arthritis. And I can't play bowls now — can't spread my fingers any more. I've used my hands too much these ninety-five years, in carpentry and that. I've also got pleurisy; the change of weather brings that on. No, I'm not altogether fighting fit.

But I've had a good time. I haven't regretted things in my life. Had a few knocks. . . .

In the Depression three blokes owed me money for carpentry jobs, owed me 400 pound between them. But then the Government said it was so hard for farmers to keep going in the slump, so their debts got wiped. All three of them went out and bought motorcars!

If I'd got that money they owed me I could have bought materials, kept going during the slump. But I had to give it all up and just do odd jobs, anything I could get, rabbiting and that. Once the slump was over and things picked up, back I went into the carpentry. But by God, it held me back.

Then there was the war, the first one. I learnt nothing good from the war. All bad. War created a rotten atmosphere, that's what I've always said. Just a bad experience.

Not many of us left now either, from World War I. I started off training in the mounted rifles at Trentham. I was used to horses — learnt to ride when I was six or seven. It was our only transport, and I'd also worked them on the farms around Waiau. But at Trentham a horse kicked out and rolled on me, knocked me about quite badly so they sent me home. When I got better they put me in the infantry, in the ninth reinforcement. They wouldn't take me back into the mounted rifles because of my accident. So off we went to Egypt and I finished my training there. Three years and 225 days I had, overseas.

My first impressions? Everything seemed about-face. The sun and the moon were in the wrong places. I lost all sense of direction, and everything was dried up and strange. Then they called for volunteers for France, so off we went, me and my younger brother. Set sail from the Suez Canal at night, sailed up to Marseilles and then took the train up to a place in the north, twenty-five miles from Armentières. A long trip. We just sat, got a drink of tea now and again. Couldn't talk to anyone because we couldn't speak French. Then it was straight into the fighting, shifting up and down the lines at Armentières and up into Belgium. I had a rifle, a trenching tool for digging, a tin hat and a gas mask, a bayonet and a water bottle, and there I was, fighting the war. . . .

Saw a lot of bad things, at the first and second Somme, the Messines and Passchendaele/Ypres. . . .

Passchendaele was the worst I saw. Slaughter. Five thousand killed in half an hour. We failed to take our position, couldn't do anything. Mud everywhere, down under a ridge. The wheels of the artillery just sank into the mud. The artillery got out of alignment and didn't shoot well. There were shells slinging everywhere; they killed some of our own men, I think. The Germans were up on the ridge on dry ground, in concrete pill-boxes. Hopeless. They just wiped us out. I was in the first wave. We got within about fifty yards of the Germans and nearly everyone got wiped out. The fighting only lasted half an hour. Terrible. We pulled back 1,000 yards and tried to dig in. Hopeless again. You couldn't dig in, the ground was that sodden and churned up with the shells.

We just lay on the ground that night. Next day we had an armistice, to bring out all the dead and wounded. Floundering around, mud half-way up to your knees. Men lying spread out, turning black, stiff. Terrible stench. There's lots of things I can't talk about. I don't like bringing it up.

In that slush it took six men to carry out a wounded man on a stretcher. Then we had to bury everyone, the Germans too, so disease didn't spread, typhoid and that. Our own men got taken to the nearest military cemetery; the Germans . . . we'd hook our shovels into their belts, drag them to the nearest shell hole and cover them up. No wonder the soldiers got callous, yanking the ID discs from around the soldiers' necks, and anything they could get away with. But it used to make us think, all those dead Germans. They'd never done us any harm. And those people who started the war, the kings and queens and heads of government, let them finish it. Send them out and let them fight it. Hopeless.

Some of the men cracked up, couldn't take it. Too much dying . . . killing and half killing. But I was surprised we stood it as well as we did. Fear kept us right, drove us on . . . forced us to get stuck in and do things we wouldn't have done normally. We were desperate. A lot of those VC men did things in desperation. Me? I hated the trenches. You could do nothing there. A shell comes, you're trapped like an animal. It shakes you right up. And some of the chaps never thought what they were saying. They'd yell out, "That was close," or, "They're getting closer." That really got to your nerves.

When you were out attacking, that was better; you were doing something. But you never got used to the fighting. Those blasted shells . . . the ground shaking. You didn't know what to do . . . couldn't do anything. And all those close shaves — my life came up before me several times. I saw all my past life, thought, "I wish I hadn't done this." It's just a case of your conscience pricking you when you think your time's up. That's how it appeared to me.

Like when I was at Passchendaele, we'd captured a German trench, had fifty yards to go to the pill-boxes. I didn't get hit in that attack, but one of our platoon did — a bloke we called Hedgehog, I don't know why. Hedgehog screamed out, "I got hit." "Where?" I yelled. "In the guts." He rolled into the trench. No room for me, too, so I lay down, made out I was dead so he could stay in the trench. It was raining like the devil and cold too, but I stayed there from shortly after daylight until dark that night. I just lay there, still, with bullets going over the top of me and all around. Wasn't really scared. I knew it was the war, expected to die. Hardest part was, I was a heavy smoker at the time, but I couldn't light up. Then the Germans would know I wasn't dead and they'd shoot me.

Hedgehog died that night, before they could get him out. But I'd made it better for him, at the end there. . . .

I don't know . . . you get over these things. There's any amount did braver things than me in that war.

Then I got wounded in the neck at Messines — caught a bit of shell near the jugular vein. I went out to the medical headquarters, got a stab with a needle to stop infection and they took out some of the shell, but couldn't get it all; it was too close to the jugular vein. They put a bandage around my neck and said, "You go back now." Back I went to the lines; but pain, I couldn't put up with it. Next day I got sent out to the nearest village where we stayed in tents or old shelled houses, but it was all a big muddle out there behind the lines and too many lead swingers, shirkers, trying to get jobs behind the lines. We were working; they weren't doing their share. I said to the medical orderly, "I'm getting back up to my mates." My neck was still sore. A little piece of it's still there, nearly seventy years later, but I went back to my mates in the lines.

Sometimes we'd be there ten or twelve days in the front line, then back to supports, then back to the front again. When you were on guard you'd be two hours on, four off. The army said four hours' sleep in the trenches was any amount, so we never got enough sleep. Then some nights you had to stand all night, so no sleep, and no sleep all next day. I've gone to sleep standing up, in the trenches. You fall back, hit the back of the trench and that wakes you up quickly. It was a crime to be caught asleep at your post; at one stage early on they'd shoot you for it. So we'd watch one another. When we saw someone moving, falling backwards or forwards, we'd try and keep them awake.

In the end the doctor said he wouldn't be responsible for the health of us men if we didn't get more sleep. And it was damn filthy in those trenches. Now and again you'd get a bath, two or three times a year! Then when the war had been going a few years they built places where you could heat up water with coal and get a hot shower, but still only a couple of times a year. You'd leave all your clothes there and get new ones, we got that filthy. Frightful. Got all sorts of boils and things, and skin diseases and lice. We'd be itchy the whole time.

Lice! They felt damn awful. All around your neck and in your damn hair. But the body lice were the worst of the lot — they were fairly big, like a ladybird but longer. Tell you what we'd do with those body lice: when we were out of the trenches we'd get some wooden matches, take our trousers off, run a lit match along the seams and burn the lice and the eggs, too. They'd go pop, pop as they burnt.

Everyone was lousy because we hardly ever got undressed, and we'd cut the clothes off dead men and use them. Had to. Then a lot of us got trench fever. They said it was caused by the lice bites getting into your marrow bones. Some of the men died of it. I had trench fever very badly — had a temperature of 104.8°F for nearly a month. They put me under canvas in a field hospital for six weeks until I was better.

In hospitals those days they hung your chart over the bed and I could see my temperature: up and down, up and down, just like the teeth of a saw. And you'd get dreadful pains in your legs and feet with the trench fever; they'd put a cradle affair over your legs to keep the heat and the weight of the blankets off your legs. At night I'd black out. I was completely unconscious all night. And I ate nothing but Glaxo for six weeks. All right for bonny babies, but no use for soldiers. I was eleven stone seven before I got the trench fever; went down to under nine stone in those few weeks. I was very weak.

"Finish of the war for you, mate," they said. They were going to send me back to New Zealand. But then the Germans broke through in March and I volunteered to go back to the lines, back to my mates. I tell you what, though, at the time I didn't care if the cow calved or broke its neck, didn't care if I died or not. I suppose everyone likes to hang on to life as long as possible, though, when they're conscious. That's what I'm doing now, at ninety-five years of age.

Then there were rats in those trenches — great big fat fellows. They ran over your face at night. You got used to it. Every now and again we'd have a rat hunt. We'd arm ourselves with sticks and go for them. But mostly they came out at night, so it was difficult catching them. In the day-time you didn't see them much; they'd be burrowed in. Then after a few years they cleared out and I reckoned it was the poison gas the Germans started using. We had gas masks, but even so some of the men got gassed. Cleaned out the rats, anyhow.

Cold? By God yes. In northern Belgium the ground was sometimes frozen two foot down. It was just like ice. And I tell you what I've seen, when we were having a spell back behind the lines: you'd be washing yourself and if some drops of water fell on your trousers they'd be frozen before you could dry your face. Little lumps, on your trousers.

And all that mud and water ... we'd make duck walks in the trenches to walk on and try and keep a bit drier. Too wet to sleep on all the time. We'd put down old pieces of trench timber, anything at all, and lie a sheet of corrugated iron on top, so you were up off the sodden ground a bit. You had to get your hip bone in the corrugation, otherwise you couldn't sleep on your side. And all you had for warmth was one blanket and all your clothes. We used to say, first thing we'd have when we went on leave was a decent bed. But then we felt strange in a bed with a good mattress. We couldn't sleep for a night or two — only on corrugated iron or concrete floors!

What else I longed for? Most of the time you were too damn tired to long for this and that. It was just an endless thing: the Germans lobbing shells and things at you, not enough sleep, not enough food. We were hungry a good lot of the time. In the trenches you got a small loaf of bread that had to do three men for a day and a night, a little bit of margarine and a tin of jam, and now and again a fair lump of cheese. At night there'd be hot stew and tea; we used to call that stew "soup de bouillon" — one onion and two buckets of water. In the morning we'd sometimes get cold bacon. Sometimes it was just bread and margarine. Most of the time you had none of your bread ration left for breakfast, so you had to eat army biscuits. They were extra and there was always plenty of them. Dog biscuits we called them. They were hard as a rock and not nice to eat; no one went for them much.

By God yes, we were often hungry and thirsty. You'd drink every bit of water you could find. We'd even save a bit of cold tea and shave in that; we wasted nothing. Then one thing we really looked forward to was the rum issue in the winter-time. It kept us going, kicked us inside. But we were never as hard up for food as the Germans; you'd see great lumps cut off the dead horses' and mules' rumps, the Germans were that short of meat. We never came to that; the British army wouldn't allow it. We got watery stew and dog biscuits instead!

I tell you what, though: there was the canteen, just an outfit made out of sacking, where you could buy stuff at cost price. One time in Egypt there were eight of us in a tent, and one chap went up to the canteen and bought a big cake in a round tin. Funny part was, we were all having a piece of the cake and someone found a little essence of lemon bottle in the tin with a half gold sovereign and a note inside. It was a message to *him*, wishing him a happy birthday! Families at home in New Zealand were sending parcels over to us soldiers, but the quartermasters were doing a bit of dirty business, selling some of the parcels. And this chap bought his own birthday cake!

We had a few laughs in the war, yes. But when you think it was nearly four years of my life, not nearly enough laughs. Just a bad experience. Yet I only ever saw one man deserting from the trenches. Poor devil was driven to it. He had a German name and the chaps teased him all the time. They'd say, "Oh, you bloody Hun." Got on his nerves in the end, and he deserted to the enemy. He just ran, knew how to get through the barbed wire. But our chaps in the trenches wouldn't shoot at him. The officer did — fired his revolver, but he never hit him.

I tell you what: all that killing in the war made a terrible lot of returned soldiers turn into free thinkers, atheists. They didn't believe in God or anything, after what they saw. Why did God allow it? Made me an atheist, too, for a while. I've got over it now.

Got back to Waiau and been here ever since; I liked the people here, and I'll tell you why. People helped one another. If there was any sickness in a house we'd all take turns doing a day's work for them. If a woman was giving birth to a child, someone went along to help her out — didn't ask for sixpence. Today it's everyone for himself. People pass you in the street and won't look at you. Politeness is gone . . . and helping one another.

In our day we were all friends, here in Waiau. Sociable. Every year we'd have a school treat, a good afternoon of sports in the school grounds, playing cricket and football and running races. Then there'd be the prize giving. They'd go around beforehand with a hat and people would put in a bob or half a crown. Some of the big sheep stations put in a pound, and one station always gave a cricket bat for the boys and a sewing basket for the girls. Then we'd have refreshments, a real good tuck in. There'd be ham sandwiches and cakes, tea for the mothers and fathers, milk or water for us kids. And there'd be a dance at night to finish off with. We were all like a big family in Waiau township.

But I didn't like school. Didn't start till I was eight or nine and left when I turned fourteen; wanted to get away. I was too big a dunce, always getting into trouble. The master had a good long strap about two foot long, two or three inches wide, and phew, he knew how to use it. Lots of us kids were frightened to go to school. We'd be having spelling and we'd be so scared of making a mistake we'd put an extra letter in, and whack with the strap. Now they've turned round the other way; they're too lax. But in our day . . . phew! I remember once being thrashed by my father. I still don't know what I did wrong!

We lived three miles from the school, so if it was raining hard we didn't go. And often as not I was late because I was birds'-nesting, for thrushes' and blackbirds' and sparrows' eggs. The master didn't know that, mind you. He thought we'd been held up with jobs at home. Every morning I'd be pulled out of bed at 6 o'clock to go and find Father's horse and the cows, in the thirty acres of flax swamp out the back. I'd bring them up to the house, Father would throw on his swag, jump on the horse and go out rabbiting. Mother or one of the boys would milk the cows, I'd chop firewood and that, then we'd go three miles down the road to school.

We had the first school bus in Waiau: our old horse, Emma. She belonged to Grandfather and got handed down to us. Emma took all us kids to school over the years. I'd get a bit wild, though. I was second in the family, so often I had to walk while the biggest brother rode, with the little ones up front or behind. Then when we got to the Mason River we'd all get up. Sometimes there'd be seven of us hanging on to old Emma; one seemed to hold the other on. Some would be half-way up the neck and the last one right back on the tail. When we got to the other side of the river us big ones would slide off and walk on to school — yes, or dive into the bushes and go birds'-nesting.

But we looked after our horses very well. They were our only transport those days. And best bloke I ever knew for working with horses was an old bloke who lived around Waiau for years and years — a very dark old Indian gentleman called Ashleigh Lewis. He worked as a musterer, shepherd, shearer and rabbiter on Highfield and other stations around here and also trained racehorses for a while.

Ash lived here till he was nearly 100. I learnt all sorts from Ashleigh Lewis. He always fed his dogs on rabbit, cooked up a bit on the hot coals of the open fire, and I did the same in the end; I found out they worked much better on rabbit than any other meat.

A real hard doer, old Ashleigh. He was a chap you could never beat in the morning. If you said you were going to start work at 6 in the morning, he'd be there at 5, just to fool you. We'd try and head him off, but he'd be there on his horse, grinning away. He'd go to bed at 7 of a night, with a sock over his head because he was a bit bald. After he'd been out on the hills all day he'd feed the dogs and cook up a feed for himself, then it was time to go to bed. And he'd be up early every day — 4 o'clock was nothing for Ashleigh.

Right to near the end he was very fit, could walk in the hills all day. On his ninetieth birthday he walked three miles down to Waiau to buy a bottle of brandy. He drank that, bought another bottle and walked back home. Ashleigh never had any teeth, but he could chew away on bones, anything. Must have had gums on him like iron bars. He could eat anything, drink anything, get up next morning and away he'd go, a box of birds.

Home was an old shack — bits of iron and sack, dark inside, smoke everywhere, sacks on the walls and the floor. Where there weren't sacks there were pages from the *Auckland Weekly*. Ash always said it was the best wallpaper out because you could plaster up the walls and look at the pictures, too. He had a wee pot-belly stove to cook on and keep the hut warm. You'd go and see him of an evening and you could hardly sit with him, it was that warm. Could hardly see him either, for smoke!

He had an old bath sitting out in the open in front of the hut. Later on we built him a roof to go over it; he was tickled pink with that. Then a few of us got together and bought him a new hut. There was one coming up for sale down in Waiau so we all put in and bought it. The boss paid ten pound; the rest of us put in five pound each and took it up on the tractor. Old Ash was pleased as punch. I got some timber and built a little lean-to for him to cook in, and we bought a wee cream and green enamel wood range. I put that up high on a table, with legs and a sheet of iron underneath, so he could cook easier. Old Ash thought he had a palace: a new hut and stove and a proper bathroom, too!

Then one of the pet lambs went and lived down there at the hut with him. He fed her bread and stuff and she wouldn't leave him in the end. We weighed her after shearing one year — thirteen stone! She was half as big again as Ashleigh was. She'd bunt him, stand there and give him a shove along. We were afraid she'd knock him over in the end there.

Then he had Bill the duck waddling around the hut, and his vege garden out the front. He was always giving away the first veges of the season — carrots and lettuces and potatoes. He always had new potatoes before anyone else did. He loved his few strawberry plants, too. He was always giving strawberries to the kids, and he had special little patches of mushrooms growing all over the paddocks; he knew where they all were. He'd get kerosene tins of water and run around watering them. We told him that was cheating.

Ashleigh never talked about himself much. He only once told us he'd been married and the wife had died, or left. He had a son, too, but we never heard where that son was or anything about him. And he only ever once spoke about his episode in the rowing boat. When he was only twenty-eight, Ashleigh saved the lives of his two companions and himself. He held a heavy, eighteen-foot rowing boat on course for nearly three days without let-up, in heavy seas. His hands and feet were skinned raw and bleeding from all that rowing and rubbing against the rough wooden floor, but he hung on, because there was nothing to do but hang on. Ashleigh didn't talk about his stamina and courage. He only once told us exactly what happened. Treated it as a bit of a joke. "Just one of those things" was how he put it, "It was all unavoidable so it had to be accepted." But the scars on his feet tell the story.

A real tough old bloke, Ashleigh Lewis — a great constitution. When he was well up in his nineties some chap in Waiau had a ten-pound bet with him that he'd get to 100 years old. Ash took him on. He reckoned: "If I live to a hundred it'll be all right. He'll have to pay me. And if I die I can't pay it, so that'll be all right, too." In the end he missed by three years. And the chap he'd had the bet with died before he did!

Ash was never sick, until the end. Bronchitis was getting the better of him. He was nearly blind and he couldn't look after himself, so the doctor sent up an ambulance to take him away to an old people's home in Christchurch. But old Ash wouldn't get into it, not until they went up and got his family, the ones he always had Christmas dinner with. He wasn't going away without seeing them. Ninety-three he was when they took him away. His hut's still there. . . .

But he didn't like being in the old people's home, not at all. They wouldn't let him smoke his pipe in bed, and he'd done that all his life. A pipe in bed and cigarettes during the day — good strong Four Square tobacco; he was the only one in the district smoked it and if he couldn't get Four Square he wouldn't smoke anything. But no smoking in bed at the old people's home. We'd go and see him and he'd say, "I don't like it here, I want you to get me home. Any empty houses there now, up Waiau?"

He'd been up here at Waiau most of his life, old Ashleigh Lewis. Born 1873, old when I first knew him and ninety-seven when he died. We got him back here to Waiau, too. We all put in, the bosses and us workers, and buried him here. Got him a little plaque and all. He's down there at the cemetery.

Joves, I'll be getting up to ninety-seven, too, in a year and a bit. And we'll have another cup of tea now, my girl. I've talked more this last day or two than I've talked for a hell of a long time.

PERCY

'Built for speed, not for comfort'

Our first words were straight to the point.
"Hell's teeth, you're different from what I expected."
"What'd you expect?"
"A middle-aged spinster with specs."

Percy had always been direct. As a ten-year-old, yelled at for crying when he was pushed into an orphanage, he vowed he'd never let his feelings show again. When things got tough he'd turn his cheek, grit his teeth and scorn sympathy: "Don't pity me as I gave as good as I got. Other inmates suffered in silence. I refused to be cowed under."

As an old man, Percy dedicated his time to his family, his garden and his special project: helping the old and the intellectually handicapped, people worse off than himself. He admitted this devotion probably stemmed from his traumatic days in Whakarewa orphanage in Motueka. The effects of those three years carved deeply into Percy, hewing his approach to life. They left him a fiercely stubborn and resilient, often cynical old man.

But then there was Percy's sense of humour. He loved to see someone else laughing, loved practical jokes and the feeling he was saying something slightly wicked.

And always flowing beneath the bitterness and the humour was Percy's love for growing things: children and plants; and for vulnerable things: the old and the handicapped.

I visited Percy and his wife at their home in Nelson. Percy would order tea and then start talking. It was hard to leave . . . and hard to get away without a basket of fresh vegetables from the garden, or jars of jams and pickles he'd made himself. Percy was used to getting his own way: "You take these tomatoes and don't argue. We've got to look after our writers and that."

A very stubborn and very generous man.

I became Stumpy the Orphan when I was ten years old. All the other orphans called me Stumpy because I was very small, like a midget. When I was sent from home in Westport and put into St Andrew's orphanage in Nelson, when my small cane hamper with all my belongings was taken from me and I realised this place was to be my new home, I cried my eyes out. But I was told, "Shut up and don't be a baby." So I vowed I would never let my feelings show again. Never. Then on, I turned my cheek whenever things got bad. I enjoyed pitting my wits against someone else or trying to cause trouble. I always had a shanghai or a pea-shooter with me and I'd let fly.

When I turned eleven, in 1915, I got sent off to Whakarewa orphanage in Motueka. It was a big, fierce-looking place for Maori and Pakeha orphans. After you were ten you were too big for the women at St Andrew's to handle, so you got turned over to "The Manager" at Whakarewa. Three years I was there. Hungry the whole time. We milked fifteen cows and made butter, but I never once saw butter on my bread, the whole time I was there ... nor eggs on my plate, and we had fowls and ducks galore. All those sorts of good things got sold to the grocers in Motueka.

We had to get up at 6 every morning, us orphans. Some cleaned the dormitories; some lit the wood and coal ranges, peeled the spuds and things for dinner and made the porridge or the bread and dripping for breakfast. You cut big slices of bread, dipped them in swags of fat melted in two big baking dishes, sprinkled salt and pepper over and shoved them in the oven — beautiful. Then there was the porridge ... that was a story on its own. Runaway Dick, that's what we called it — just water with little balls of oatmeal floating around in it. The pot was brought in, shoved on a board on the table and a woman held up each enamel plate and ladled some out. No such thing as sprinkle your own sugar and milk on top — the assistant did that, in case you took too much. Yes, just like Charles Dickens's days. Then each plate got passed down to the end boys; there'd be twenty-seven of us boys at the big table, twelve girls at the other table, and the farm boys' one next to it.

There were always two farm boys — older orphans who'd finished at the school but stayed on to work the crops and animals — and there was also Reg, who looked after the pigs. I remember one morning Reg complained there wasn't enough seasoning on the bread and dripping. I was always one for a joke, so next time I got a thick piece of bread, cut the middle out, piled salt and pepper in and replaced the hole. Reg fell for it. Well, he got me by the lapels and thumped me up and down on the table. Said nothing. Just acted. But he never complained about the bread again.

Me? That's the whole point of the story. I just gritted my teeth. Wasn't going to let on he was upsetting me.

Dinner at midday would be mostly stew or sometimes boiled mutton. We ran sheep and grew veges on the place, so it was always mutton with potatoes and sometimes cabbage or horse carrots, mashed. It's quite nice. There'd be pudding, too — rice or tapioca; Sheep's Eyes we called it. That pudding was always Runaway Dick, too, more liquid than anything else.

Tea at night would be bread and scrape: bread and jam, no butter. There'd be five plates of it, set out at intervals down the table. When they were empty, that was it, so the ones who ate the quickest got the most. What we'd do was eat the centre out and leave the crusts so we could wolf down another bread and scrape from the plate. Then when the plates were empty we'd get stuck into our crusts — the "grain store" we called it.

That was it at night — bread and scrape and enamel mugs of tea. We were all hungry, all the time. We were growing kids and working hard on the farm as well. We had to do an hour in the morning before school, milking the cows, making butter, working the horses, harrowing and rolling and discing. Then after school we'd be into our old clothes and straight out to the farm duties again until tea-time, 5 o'clock. There'd be harvesting, or making great twenty-three ton oat stacks — no, I won't forget those stacks. I was the midget so I'd always be up at the top of the stack pitching for the stack-maker. And he never gave me a spell; he'd crack me around the shins with the fork handle if I let up. There'd be blood flowing from the blisters on my hands.

Then in summer we'd have to go out again after tea and do more farm work. That stew and bread scrape wasn't nearly enough fuel to work on, not even when we had duties in the kitchen and could sneak a bit of bread. All the cupboards with the jam and that were kept locked up. We couldn't get at anything solid to fill us up, so we'd duck out into the paddocks and grab swedes and turnips, or we'd get out at night, slip down from the upstairs dormitories on ropes and steal apples. Wasn't as if I was a bludger . . . privileged to be there at Whakarewa. My mother paid my board, twelve and six a week, yet we had to do all that work and got starved as well!

But Sunday was a good day. It was the only day of the week we got a bit of spare time, so we'd flog eggs from the fowlhouse and tear up into the hills. We'd make a fire and cook up the eggs, in jam tins with wires poked through for handles. Or we'd catch crawlies in the creek, catch them with a worm and a pin, then cook them up in the jam tins. They were lovely, those crawlies. If we were lucky we'd flog a bit of bread, too — poke it under our jackets and off we'd sneak, into the hills. I always took the chance when I saw it; made every post a winning post.

Then when Reg was cooking up the pig tucker in the copper we'd race over and fish out the spuds. He'd have it all boiling away together, spuds and grain and pigs' innards. We'd grab out the spuds and wolf them down. Didn't matter . . . we were hungry. We'd sit on Reg, pin him down, walk over him; when your belly's that hungry you go right in, do all sorts of things. I've seen us eat raw wheat when we were doing the threshing and that out in the paddocks; we got a liking for it. Then if Reg wasn't there we'd get raw spuds and put them in the hot ashes, underneath the pig tucker. That was beautiful.

We talked about food the whole time, at the orphanage . . . lay awake and dreamt about it at night. The few times we went up to Motueka to go to the Standard Six school we'd see all the lovely things in the shops, the sweets and fruit and tins of biscuits. We could never forget them. And we'd see other kids eating meat pies and cakes in front of us; that brought the hunger to the top. Always the hunger.

Walking back from church on hot days, two miles on the hard gravel, we'd be faint with hunger. We'd duck into the paddocks and grab some swedes or windfall apples. The farmers didn't mind; they felt sorry for us. But if the manager caught us stealing, we'd get a thrashing. He'd yell, "Bathroom!" Up you'd go. There was a great big bath that held four kids at a time, to get the bathing over and done with quickly. You'd have to drop your pants, bend over the bath and he belted you with the britchen strap off the horse harness. Too right, you got at least half a dozen lashes. Depended on his temper which end you got, buckled or unbuckled; I always got the buckled end. Never ever got used to that pain. You were sitting there in fear the whole time, wondering what you were doing wrong. But with me, the fear got to a stage where I was getting my own back. Even if he was hurting me, I would cause him even more later on. I hated that man. Yes, I guarantee it was mutual.

One Sunday I saw things floating around in the stew. Maggots. "Eat your dinner," yelled the manager. "No. I can't." "Get to the Bathroom," he bawled. Well, I wasn't going to be punished for that. On the way I cut a bit of manuka, and when he came through the bathroom door I hit him between the eyes. Down he dropped. I thought I'd killed him. Really speaking, I hit him harder than I should have. I just froze, and that gave him a chance to grab my legs and hold me, otherwise I'd be out the door. I knew I was in for it then — got the biggest thrashing anyone ever got. My back was all cut up, the skin was broken all over, wherever he got me, and in between it was all blue. Couldn't lie on my back for three weeks. A woman at Whakarewa used to sneak up and put olive oil on my back, to try and help it heal.

Fish out the maggots again? I didn't let on. There were always some, so I'd take my chance when no one was looking, and slip them from my spoon into my pocket. The others? They just ate them. Too frightened to complain, or too hungry. Sometimes we didn't know what we could do to stop feeling so faint.

Hop-picking was a bad time for that. School holidays started when the hop season started those days, and us orphans had to help pick — even the little five-year-olds. We'd each be given a bin and we'd pick from 8.30 to 12, go back for dinner, then work on from 1 to half past 5 — all day in the summer sun. No shade and no refreshment except a bucket of oatmeal and water. We were stood over and hurried along the whole time, and at the end of the day us orphans were always left till last, for tallying up. Everyone said the money we earned was ours. No way . . . it went to the Church.

So hop-picking was a terrible time for us kids — hard work all day in the blazing sun, then back for a couple of slices of bread and scrape for tea. No turnips or carrots to flog out in the hop gardens; our stomachs would be sagging with hunger. And worst thing was, the other pickers all had their smokos: pies and cakes and things. We'd sit there, watching. . . .

Offer us any? Hell no, the orphanage would erupt. Only time we ever had a real cake at Whakarewa was when I stole the matron's birthday cake. Like I said, I was always looking for ways to cause trouble. And that cake . . . some of us boys had been sent to bed without tea. We were sitting up in the dormitory wondering how we could get hold of some food. One boy said, "What about the matron's cake in the pantry?" I was the smallest, so I went down the rope and crept into the pantry. There it was — a cake. So I shoved it up my jumper and ran upstairs. Well, we tore bits off and shared it all around. Tasted wonderful, but not enough — only a mouthful. And phew, hell to pay for that one. . . .

That was the only time I ever really thieved. The rest was sheer survival. And we knew the matron and the manager always got very different food from us orphans — roasts and puddings and things. We could smell them and sometimes see them going into the oven.

Then one other time we had a sort of a cake, a potato cake. An elderly couple came for a while to help out at Whakarewa. The old chap was a Cornishman or something. He had a lingo all his own — used strange words to get the horses to stop, or go left and right. Anyhow, this old chap saw the old-style brick baker's oven in the kitchen and he thought, by Jove, any potatoes left over I'll make up a potato cake for the kids. He set to work one day with potatoes and bits and pieces — how he made it I don't know — real old-English style cooking. We were all standing around, mouths wide open, waiting for it to cook. Tasted marvellous, that potato cake. Mind you, if it'd been Christmas cake with cartgrease on it, we'd have eaten it. But the manager pretty soon put a stop to that potato cake business. He saw we were enjoying it so much.

If you ask me, they should've given us little bits and pieces like that. We'd have been happier and worked better for them. I'd always break my neck to help people and work hard, if they gave me a bit of kindness. And as for cake. . . .

It was always my ambition to leave Whakarewa, get some money and go out and buy the biggest feed of cake anyone could buy. I'd dream about it at night. And that's exactly what I did. Soon as I left the orphanage I started work at the post office and at dinner-time that first morning I went and bought a cup of tea and a whole cake, the size of a big roasting pan — an ordinary sponge sort of a cake, just plain, no icing. My stomach was bolting for this cake. I cut it into three bits and wolfed the lot. It was wonderful. The lady in the shop kept staring at me, then she said, "Why are you so fond of cake, boy?" I said I was an orphan boy, we didn't ever get cake. She said, "You poor little devil. I'm not going to charge you a penny for it." And she didn't, either.

An evil place, Whakarewa. Most of my hate was for the manager. I was always trying to get back at him. My best way of infuriating him was to drop things on him, from a door. I'd balance a heavy boot on the ledge above the door and it'd hit the first person who pushed the door open. We'd do something to catch the manager's attention. He'd leap out to grab us and get it, on the head if we aimed it right. One time there I hoisted up a kerosene tin full of stones and he got that on his head. Didn't improve his brains! I got thrashed, too right, but it was worth it. It became my nature. I was "the King of the Stirrers" at a very early age. Wasn't a day went by I didn't get a hiding either from the manager or from the schoolmaster. You wouldn't believe it, the things I'd dream up. But I always owned up. Silly, isn't it?

And us older boys always stuck up for the younger ones, the littler orphans. Whenever we could we covered up for them, said, "It was me" and took their punishment. We knew what they'd get, knew what it felt like. Say someone was caught talking in the dormitories at night, the manager would bawl out, "Who's that?" Then he'd make you bend over your bed and he'd thrash you with the britchen strap. Time and time again I said it was me, too right. You could see the gratitude in the little kids. They cobbered up to you, wouldn't let you out of their sight.

A wicked show, Whakarewa. But don't pity me — I gave as good as I got. I refused to be cowed under and richly deserved the severe punishment I got. But the other inmates suffered in silence. One of my younger brothers came to Whakarewa, too, and one day the manager whipped him with a carriage whip. The matron — the one I called the Jailer as she always had a bunch of keys fastened to her waist, dangling and jangling — she held him down while he thrashed him. Cut his leg to bits because the plait had come undone on the whip and the wires were all sticking out. My brother's legs went all septic and festered. Some time later I was giving him a lift on a horse and the sweat from the horse made his leg sore. He was crying as he got off. I said, "What's the matter with your leg, Ernie?" He said, "I'm not saying. I'll get another thrashing." Nothing you could do about it.

Plenty of fights amongst us boys, too. I remember at St Andrew's orphanage we always had to take a billy or two up to the boys' college in the morning and collect any leftovers. Stew it was, mostly. If it was pudding we'd scoff it on the way home. Then the bigger boys said they'd thrash us if we brought stew back again. We all hated the stew because our orphanage would heat it up again and it'd burn on the bottom; it tasted foul. So next time the college gave us stew I tipped it under the hedge and put the empty billy on our kitchen sink. Only thing was, I didn't clean it out. So when the staff came in and saw what had happened, I got a whale of a thrashing.

Mind you, one good thing the manager did, he did try to stop unnecessary hammering between the boys. After dinner of a Saturday he'd take us out the paddock and give us two sets of boxing gloves. If you had an argument with a boy you had it out, man to man.

We had all sorts of initiation rites, too, us Whakarewa kids. If you were going to be an orphan you had to get introduced to it. We made sure all the new kids knew the rules of running with the pack. Catching the Canary, that's what we called one of those rites. You dug a round hole and filled it with cow muck, the sloppier the better, and put a hat over the top. The new boy was blindfolded and his hands were placed around the hole. He was told there was a canary down there, under the hat, and when the hat was lifted he could grab for the bird. If he got it, he could keep it. Course he got shoved down into the hole . . . always he got at least his hands and chin pushed in.

Me? They didn't get my face in. I fought like hell; knew there was a catch to this canary business.

Another initiation rite was King of the Rusty Sword. The new orphan was put in the middle of a ring of kids and shown a slab of wood. He was told he'd be blindfolded and he could make a swipe at anyone in the circle. No one could move or complain. Then while they were blindfolding him, someone would drag the length of wood through a cow muck, so when he grabbed it he got his hands thoroughly smeared.

But once these silly games were over, us orphans had a great sense of loyalty towards each other. We had a very strict code of honour; you had to keep a steady tongue and own up if you did something. Then if you committed the worst sin possible and pimped on one of the others, you got the Duck-pond Treatment. We'd get two long horse reins, join them together and tie them around the offender's waist, so one rein went one way, the other the opposite way. Then we'd throw him in the duck-pond and drag him one way, then the other, through all the slime and muck. It never failed, that Duck-pond Treatment. Girls or boys, same thing. You only ever got it once!

I never let it happen to me. I always told the truth . . . still do. When I was very small my father gave me a dose of cayenne pepper for lying to him. Just about killed me; burned my mouth to glory. My mother stayed up all night giving me drinks of water. But I never lied again, except for the odd little white lie. No, I've got no use for anyone who's dishonest or tells tales.

But one of the school girls, whenever she saw something going on, she'd pimp. She might find us out the back, smoking willow roots. We knew we weren't allowed to smoke, but anything we were told not to do, we had a go at. It's just human nature. All young boys do it, whether they're orphans or not. So we'd dig up willow roots, put them out in the sun to dry and then smoke them. Damn good smoke, too. We also tried dock leaves and tea from the tea-pot. No damn good.

Anyway, on with the story. I thought I'd better give this girl a lesson, so I sneaked out of school and put bird lime on the lavatory

seat. She always went to the lavatory on the way home. I thought
I was safe. Only thing was, instead of the girl sitting on the lavatory
seat, the teacher did. I was in for it then; the teacher broke three
canes on me at one go.

Mind you, meant I had my own heating arrangement — a warm
bottom from all the whacks. I never missed a day. Believe it or
not, when I left school the master said to me, "Percy, you've been
my most difficult pupil ever, but I guarantee you'll get on in the
world."

Darn cold at Whakarewa, though, down near the river and right
under Mt Arthur. The cold struck down. We were never ever warm
enough in winter — often couldn't sleep for the cold. No such
thing as hot-water bottles, never heard of them. We just had a
couple of hard, heavy sheets, built to last, one blanket and a
counterpane. One time there, just after I'd had rheumatic fever,
I got so cold I didn't know what to do. So I put my blanket on
the wires of my bed and pulled the mattress on top of me, to try
and keep warm. But then the cold struck up under me.

Just couldn't keep warm in the winter. At night we had to take
all our clothes off, and the ones who had pyjamas put them on.
I was growing fast, and the ones I had when I arrived were soon
up under my knees, so they got handed on. Then I had to go to
bed in my shirt. I tell you what, my bed now is a beautiful one.
I get in and go to sleep, no bother.

Another thing that used to stop us getting to sleep was the weather
— the terrific electrical storms rolling around the hills, crashing
thunder and forked lightning. There's not nearly so many of those
heavy electrical storms these days, what with the chopping of the
bush, and the aeroplanes disrupting the cloud formation. But those
storms gave nitrogen back to the soil and the crops. Nowadays we
put it in artificially, with fertilisers and that. It's certainly not as
good as the old natural way.

But I'll say it was cold — no fires at all in the orphanage. Nothing
you could do about it. No use complaining, it got you nowhere,
and most probably you got thrashed as well for being cheeky. Same
thing in the classroom — no fires, no heating, nothing. Only thing
that helped was the windows were all high up, to keep the warmth
in. That was also good because it meant the teacher couldn't see
the mischief we got up to at play-time.

We just went barefoot all day at school and even out in the paddocks,
working the horses and that. Shoes or boots were kept for Church
on Sunday. We got chilblains all the time. Mine got so bad I'd
get three or four tacks, drive them into the floor with a stone and
scratch the chilblains — tore my feet to pieces; they'd be bleeding

all over the floor. But it was the only way to get any relief, that bleeding. No singlets and gloves and scarves and hats and things. No way. We were orphan kids, hungry and cold. Little short pants and bare feet. I was one of the lucky ones: I had a suit jacket my mother gave me, but some of the boys only had a shirt. And everything got handed down when you grew out of it and patched again and again. Us boys had to darn our socks and jerseys and sew on buttons and that. Never ever saw new things.

We got a bath once a week — girls on Saturday afternoon, boys Saturday night. That great big bath with four of us in it at a time, to get the job over and done with quickly. No such thing as doctors and dentists to look after us. If you had a bad tooth you just went ahead and yanked it out. Only medicine we ever got was a terrible brew — Poo-Go-Like-Hell we called it — sulphur and treacle mixed up together. Once a fortnight we got it, a great tablespoon jammed in our mouth. The manager came round with a big enamel bowl of it. He'd dig in with the spoon and down it'd go. Mind you, it was a great mixture; kept the bowels open. It'd move mountains, that stuff. When you ran around and got warmed up, the smell was something terrible.

But that old Poo-Go-Like-Hell business kept us pretty healthy. Something did! And we were tough. We were so underfed we had no excess weight to encourage disease. We were built for speed, not for comfort! Wasn't too often we got sick, even though we didn't get the right vitamins and things. Mind you, I got rheumatic fever and got sent over to hospital for four months. Then it came back again and I was in hospital three more times. But I was lucky — it never affected my heart. I'm up to eighty now and I'm fit and well. I can do all the garden, mow the lawn, read the paper without specs, that sort of thing.

Those trips to the hospital were the only holiday I ever had. Christmas at Whakarewa was just like any other day. Only things I ever got for Christmas were little knitted things from my uncle — socks and that — and once I got a little toy from him. The other kids got nothing. No special meal, heck no. We didn't have to work though — just do out the dormitories and the kitchen, and we had to go to Church. Then we just mooched around. We had a big shed on the end of the chaff-room, so on wet days we'd get in there and play marbles and hopscotch, or draw with chalk on the wooden floor. We'd make our own darts — bits of wood with nails in — and draw a ring on the wall, or we'd make bows and arrows and have fights. One lot would put nails in their arrows; one lot would line up with bits of corrugated iron for shields. When you saw a head or a bottom, you fired. That was good, until one boy got an arrow stuck in his bottom and it got infected. Bows and arrows were stopped then. But we'd still do it, without nails.

We'd always think up something to do. My little brother could twitch his ears, cross his eyes and move his forehead up and down like a rabbit. The kids loved seeing him do that. Came in handy when the teachers were telling him off, too. He'd do his rabbit trick and they couldn't control themselves; they'd just laugh. Then there was another boy who was very strong. He could pick up three and a third bushel bags of wheat. He was only thirteen, but he had an enormous body, just like the Amazons you see in the magazines. We loved seeing how strong that boy was. Of an evening we had to go to our rooms, do darning and that till 7 o'clock, then Bible and prayers and off to bed. But if we had a few minutes in between, what we'd do was take our enamel tea mugs up, he'd take his shirt off and we'd hit him on the chest as hard as we could. I never ever saw him flinch.

Then there was another boy who worked on the farm and he used to wet his bed. The manager would thrash him for it. One morning this chap rebelled. He got sent to the bathroom, but he wasn't going to take it any more. He grabbed the manager in a fireman's grip, carried him off to the chaff-room, threw him in and locked the door. Left him there all day. "Don't you say where he is," he warned us. We were silent. In the evening one of the staff heard the manager yelling, so he got let out. But he never ever retaliated; he knew that boy would have killed him. But the boy was a hero as far as the rest of us were concerned.

Another thing we had was fire drill each week, going down from the upstairs dormitories on heavy ropes with knots in them so you'd get a grip — the same ones we got down at night to steal fruit! At fire drill us big boys would take a small boy on our backs, then we'd have to go back and get another one. We'd be timed at practice. We enjoyed that. The girls didn't have the rope drill — they went down the stairs — but they could use the ropes, too right. We taught them!

Other than that, if we weren't working we were at school. You went up to standard five at the orphanage, then a few would go up to a school in Motueka for standard six, so they sent me up there for a bit. I have to say this, our schooling was pretty good. It was ground into us . . . blocks, times tables, one times one equals one, two times two equals four. It was all recitation and learning by heart, but we learnt all right. If you didn't know the answers it'd be "Hand on the desk" and whack with the stick. Hurt like hell. But I always gave as much back; I'd distract the master and get whacked again. You couldn't really hurt old Stumpy.

Mind you, don't know where I'd have gone if it wasn't for the orphanage. I'd be out on my neck. When I was a boy I could never ever understand why I was an orphan, why our home broke up. I can piece things together now. My father was a hard man, one of the heaviest drinkers in Westport, whereas my mother was a dedicated church woman. Then the turning point came when her little baby daughter died, when she was only twelve months old. Mum couldn't cope with the whole situation any more; she had to get away from Westport. So she had us kids sent up to Nelson and put in St Andrew's orphanage, intending to come up to Nelson shortly after, pick us kids up and go on up to Auckland where she was going to set up house with her blind brother. But she only got as far as Nelson. She took ill and died there. A woman told me afterwards there was nothing wrong with her. They presumed she died of a broken heart . . . the breaking up of her home.

I was at Whakarewa, a young boy going on for twelve years old, when I got word that Mum was in the hospital. Over I went on the old boat, the *Koi* — five bob it cost, return. I walked from the wharf up to where my sister was at a branch of St Andrew's on Waimea Road. She said, "Don't go and see Mum, she's unconscious." But I went and sat by her bed. She was very thin, wasted away. Unconscious. The nurse said, "Your mother will speak to you soon," but next thing the minister came and knocked up a prayer. I got out of it then. I couldn't stand it any more.

She died next day — a cold, bleak day. I remember the funeral directors and the grave diggers, the matron, the minister and us kids. I looked down into the hole and thought, "Why did that happen to me?" Then later on, when I was hearing all the things happening in the war, seeing for myself the Depression and the whole hurly-burly of the world, then I understood. I thought how mean I had been. Mum was now out of all that; she was saved from all the things we were enduring. So I changed my attitude after that.

Yes, too right, I learnt a lot of hard things when I was very young. Bunged into an orphanage, fighting and starving my way through the week, losing my mum at twelve years old. My mum . . . I remember when I left Westport she made me promise her three things: that I'd never drink, never be a jockey and never marry. Well, I'd always longed to be a jockey — it was my big ambition. But I didn't. Worked a lot with horses, but never as a jockey. I didn't drink either. I made a vow when I married that my wife would never see mè come in the door the worse for liquor. Only happened twice in all my eighty years. Not bad eh? I never liked the stuff much, anyway — too bitter. I'd rather have a raspberry and lemonade any day.

Yes I did marry. Took me a long time, mind you!

If I was to go myself, tomorrow, I'd have no regrets, bar leaving the family. I've lived my life to the full. Had many laughs and accepted everything that's come along. I can say this: I've never regretted any moment of it, not even the orphanage days. Orphanage life affected my later life? No, I took it in the right spirit. I became bitter, though, because of the hypocrisy shown by the Church of England who ran the place. They were supposed to be representing Christianity; they were spouting it but not practising it. We were brought up with a Bible in our hands — had to read a chapter morning and night, and a prayer. The manager would be there, sticking his chest out, giving the Church service, pushing his concertina in and out. Then he did all those terrible things to us, behind the scenes.

Talk about it much since? Yes, I've talked a lot about the orphanage days, too right. I didn't hide it . . . let people know. Every detail I've told you is the truth. Tell you what, though: after I left the place I met up with different ones who'd served their time there. I wanted us to form an old boys' association. The answer was definitely no. They just wanted to forget Whakarewa orphanage. There was the whole stigma of the place; no one would go back to visit it. And then there was that whole business of the hypocrisy shown by the Church. They just wanted to wipe the whole outfit. Same thing when we had a reunion of Whakarewa in the 50s. I went there expecting to meet some of the boys and girls from our day. I went home sad and disillusioned. Two boys, two girls. The rest had died or didn't want to go near the place again.

But like I said, where else would we have gone, us orphans? And it's back to the old thing. I gritted my teeth and wouldn't let on they were upsetting me. I made that vow when I was ten years old and I stuck to it.

When I left Whakarewa in 1918 and started work at the post office, I was fourteen years old and earning fifteen bob a week. I got told there was two years owing on my brother's board at the orphanage, so for a long time I paid them twelve and six a week out of my wage. Left me half a crown to live on. I boarded free, in exchange for milking the cows, cutting wood, cleaning the pots, you name it, and I got half a crown from another boarder, for cleaning his shoes all week. He did it out of pity, you see. But without it I couldn't have managed.

I was on four pounds a week when I was married. We had to pay rent and live on that. We lived plainly but well. Brought up six kids. I'd have liked eleven, a cricket team, but we didn't get there. We struggled, the wife and me, paying off mortgages for years and years. I worked at all sorts: I was a scrub cutter, a farm hand, a drover, a bus driver on the old horse-drawn buses, and a groundsman at the boys' college. Ninety pound a week was my biggest wage ever. Took us until 1973 to get in the clear. It's taken us a lifetime.

There's plenty of money around nowadays, but it's no good. Everything's mortgaged; people are mortgaged. And the age of chivalry has disappeared. It hurts me to see that. I watch the kids today: they get on a bus, sit down. An old lady gets in and she has to stand. They just sit there.

Birching should never have been abolished either, for rape cases and that. Nor corporal punishment. That's my opinion. The original law says, "Eye for an eye, tooth for a tooth." I feel it's wrong to change that.

The world's getting worse, all right. Mind you, there's nothing we can do about it. It's got to happen, got to get so bad we reach a point, then burst, then purify. Everything's got to be destroyed before that can happen. Man will find he'll be done by as he does.

My one ambition now is this: when I leave this world I leave it a little better than I found it. I'd like my way of life to be felt, yes. If I've left something a little better, that'll be my greatest achievement.

How I'll do that? Through my actions. They speak louder than words, eh? I look after people, the old ones and the little ones. I don't go to Church. Couldn't do, with the hard feelings in my heart for the Church after my orphanage days. Haven't got a fortune to give away, either. Mind you, I should be better off than I am, but I'll never have a fortune because I feel there's others to be helped. So the main thing I do now is help the handicapped children ... that's my theme in life now. I do anything I can for them — unofficially, that is. I always put money in the boxes, wherever I see them. But there's something else I do, too. I go into pubs and halls and things, anywhere I happen to be, and do all sorts of tricks. I carry all kinds of gadgets and knick-knacks around with me; I put them up in the bar or somewhere and set them going. Get no end of money, and it all goes into the box for the handicapped.

Stemmed from the hard times at the orphanage? Yes, we should help those worse off than ourselves. I remember how, now and again, people used to call in and give us orphans biscuits and things. I want to do the same. I think somehow West Coasters always have that want to help people out. It's in them. If you arrive on the Coast, a complete stranger, the kettle goes on straight away. Well, that side of me has always been there — yes, even at the orphanage. I was always helping the little kids —

I always put everything I had into the job at hand — yes, even getting into trouble! I often think of a verse I had to learn at school:

If you've got a job to do, do it well,
There are other men can do it just as well.
Take a little time, give attention fullest share,
And then when done declare you've done it well.

It's a good one, eh? I think those words got stronger as I grew older. They gave me the will to do my best, even when I was down. But with my nature, phew! Life's been a struggle. I'm too pig-headed. But I've always been able to say I'm sorry. Never let the sun go down on your wrath, that's what I say; get it over and done with before you go to bed.

Anything I'd still like to do? Yes, but it's a bit of an impossibility. I'd like to see the Buller River dried of all that water that snakes down to Westport. I'd get in with a gold-pan and fish out all those beautiful nuggets. You bet. If ever that Buller changed its course, I'd be in there like a shot. The earth movements will come again. The hills will split open and the gold seams will be exposed again. All the old-timers know that's true. But I always was a bit of a romancer.

We've pretty well covered it now, eh? You've got a real insight into the boy they called Stumpy. Course there'll be some thinking, what old Stumpy says here is a bit far-fetched . . . maggots in the stew, that sort of thing. But it's all the truth.

And tell you what: all this talking relieves me. Lets out all the steam that's been in for years and gives me something to look forward to. When I see my life down on paper like this . . . phew! My friends will say, "By God Percy, was that *you*?"

AMY

'The seventy-year-olds —
they're just girls'

Amy's life had been a struggle. She'd been granted no room for self-indulgence, and she'd made no room for self-pity. She'd learnt to be frank and terribly practical, she knew how to make butter and cheese, how to chop down trees and build fowlhouses and skin possums. A friend down the road described her aptly: "I don't know anyone as tough as Amy. She really faces up to things and does things."

Amy was eighty-four, brown and wiry and very energetic; she had walked the Milford Track at the age of seventy-six. She had wispy, short white hair. She wore trousers or thick woollen stockings, and her long stride revealed the effects of her years in the north-Canterbury hills, west of Hawarden where she lived. Whenever I called she'd be out the back weeding the cabbage and carrot patch, or digging around the flowers or potting up plants — Amy loved growing things — or down the river in her 1950s Vauxhall, bagging up sand and shingle for the garden.

She would bustle us inside for a cup of tea, and it was action from start to finish. She'd be dashing around fishing out photos and letters and documents and treasures, poked in cups on the mantlepiece, behind pictures, under sofas, in drawers and bags and boxes. "If I die now," beamed Amy, "there'd be that much stuff to sort out. . . . "

In between all the fossicking she'd be whipping up sultana scones and talking — very fast. She was alert, devoted to living. Her hands and neck were worn out, but her face was still unlined and her eyes clear and piercing, like a sparrow's. A very earthy, slightly wild old lady.

Amy jumped at the chance to drive us back to her two old homes at The Peaks, up in the foothills of the alps. She spent the morning pointing out where the houses and the daffodils and irises used to be, poking around in the old barn where her father and brother had lived and inspecting the overgrown orchard. We picked plums and apples from her favourite trees. Amy gathered up her skirts and filled them till they sagged.

Amy had spent her life looking after people: her parents, a handicapped brother, an invalid husband, a bachelor uncle. She married late and she was alone now — a very lively yet very sane old lady, regretting this gap in her life: "I love people, love doing for them, cooking their dinners and washing their clothes. Now I feel I'm not doing anything worthwhile."

After each of our sessions I came away amazed at her exuberance and laden with goodies: fresh scones and bottled beetroot, lettuces and carrots from her garden, bones for the dog. There was no declining her hospitality because there was no doubting her sincerity.

I've always been wild, real harum-scarum. I can be a lady if
I want to, all dressed up in my frills, going dancing; but I
don't like being a lady. I'm not a city girl, living in those big
skyscrapers like a budgie in a cage. I'd sooner be wild, out in the
hills, out on the lakes.

Us wild types . . . we were never rough, but we always had plenty
of go. I've always been a worker — nobody's worked harder than
me — and it's kept me healthy. The ones who get to sixty and
then sit about in front of a heater watching TV, they don't last.
You see them in the old people's homes, sitting around the wall;
it'd drive me mad. I'd like to finish up here in Hawarden. But
I'm old as old now. The seventy-year-olds . . . they're just girls,
just out of school. Us real old ones joke about being ancient. I
meet them up the street and that and I say to them, "You still
above ground?" and they say it to me. We keep going. Stick to
the ship as long as you can, that's what I say, and when the ship
goes down, go down with it.

Nineteen hundred I was born, down the road at Hurunui in the
ruins of the Hurunui hotel, the old, original one on the other side
of the river. I remember our knife box when I was a girl was made
out of the bar of that hotel. And that's where we lived until I
was one or two, when we shifted up to Sandford Downs on Balmoral
station where my father worked as a rabbiter.

No school or anything up there — each Monday my father had
to drive us the eight miles down to the train bridge at Hurunui
in the horse and cart, down through all the manuka and scrub.
We'd walk over the bridge, then it'd be another four or five miles
walk to school at Medbury. We'd stay all week with our cousins
there and go home Friday. But I didn't go to school at all till I
was nine — didn't go till my brother turned six, the age for starting
school those days, then we both went. And I was always so homesick,
I'd stand at the fence and look and look. I could see the hills of
our place, way in the distance. I hated being away from my home.

I clearly remember that first day of school. Our teacher, Miss

Gillespie, she drove a grey horse eight miles down to the school, and us kids all used to look for a ride. And the smell in the school porch: leather school bags and sandwiches wrapped in newspaper — I can smell it all now. Everyone had the same lunch — two big pieces of bread with wild plum jam; no such thing as marmite and stuff, and if you wanted a drink you had to go to the pump. Us girls all wore lace pinnies and frilly panties, and that first day Miss Gillespie told me off for rubbing my slate with a hankie instead of a duster. No books at school except for a copy-book for handwriting, and yet I reckon we learnt more than kids do today. They have films and video this and that and they're always here and there and everywhere, away on school trips. No school sports at lunch-time or bus trips for us kids; we played hopscotch or tiddlywinks or we just stood around. If we wanted any fun we had to organise it ourselves.

My grandfather was quite famous for entertainment in this district because he had a monkey, a very small, cheeky one. When visitors came he'd jump on their shoulders and grab them by the cheek. He loved his cup of tea. It had to have sugar in it or he wouldn't drink it, and he loved the dogs; he curled up with them at night and always got around with them in the day. He loved to ride on the dogs' backs. They'd squeeze through a fence, the monkey would jump clean over the fence and land on the dog's back again. The kids all loved watching that. And he used to go down to school. He'd get into the porch, grab a boy's cap and race up a tree with it. He'd sit up there, grinning, then when he wanted to come down he'd wind his chain around and around his front legs, he'd find a space to drop the chain and down he'd go. All the kids would clap and cheer; everyone loved him. One kid at Medbury used to say his prayers, "God bless Mummy, Daddy, Butter's bull, Brooker's twins and Manning's monkey."

My grandfather . . . I remember driving down in the horse and cart to visit him at Medbury when I was about three years old. There was that long drive down in old Kit and the trap, a wedding present from my grandparents to my mother and father, and then there was Grandmother's great big long table, their fourteen kids and all of us. Grandfather was descended from the gentry. He had a white waistcoat and whiskers way out the side of his face. He'd sit at one end of the long table. They'd bring in the meat and put it at the head of the table, then he'd carve. I was terrified of Grandfather. I remember one time, everyone was there at the big table. He was there carving the meat and he said to me, "Have some of Grandma's nice apple jelly, Amy." I wouldn't eat it. I just sat and looked. "You naughty little girl," said Grandfather.

"I'll cut off your head with this carving knife." He was just having a joke. He was a real gentleman — never raised his voice, never swore, but I kicked and screamed and got put up in the bedroom. It was his whiskers and waistcoat; I was terrified. I was three when Grandfather died so it's a long memory, that one.

But any rate, I had very little schooling — left when I was fourteen and went out to work so I learnt everything I know in four or five years. No high school, nothing, but I can read and write all right. I went out to work on the stations around the district, cooking, washing, milking the cows, looking after the children, damming up creeks and taking them for swims; a maid I suppose you'd call me. Happiest days of my life, and I still keep in touch with all those kids I helped bring up. Some of them have grandchildren now. Then in 1920 I went on down to Elmwood in Christchurch and worked as a cook for a huge, rich family. They were real gentry — five of a staff, parlour maids, gardeners, ladies' maids, the whole shooting box. I was only twenty, but I did all the cooking. Had a kitchen maid to help me; I was a real working lady.

Nineteen twenty-two I moved on to cooking at Hanmer Hospital. I cooked for ninety at one stage there, on a great big coal range as long as that wall. For three years I worked there at Hanmer without having a whole day off; not even Sundays. We started work at 6 of a morning, had a couple of hours off in the middle of the afternoon and finished up round about 6 of a night and only got a half day off a week. Then after a year you got a month's holiday. The rules were very strict, too right they were. You had to wear a long dress and a hat in the kitchen and you had to be in by 10 o'clock at night. If you were caught out after that it meant instant dismissal.

I was there at Hanmer for years and years. Came back here to Hurunui for a bit after 1926, went back to Hanmer, and 1930 I came back here for good. I worked about the district a bit, did nursing and all sorts of things. I was jack of all trades, but you could say I was at home looking after my parents and the farm, looking after things. I gave a lot of my life to my family — my father, my invalid mother, my mongol brother. Then when I was thirty-nine my mother died. It was the greatest tragedy of my life. My mother gone. I loved her; she was a marvellous person. Coming home, my mother not there. . . .

My father had looked for her that day — couldn't find her anywhere. She'd had a bath, got out and that was it. I'd always banked on coming back home to look after my mother and father; never thought of her dying like that. Took me years to get over it.

I didn't work after that — stayed at home and looked after father and my invalid brother. That was my life, ups and downs. And I didn't get married till years later when I was forty-two. That was *very* late in life those days — disastrous. Twenty-two or so was the average. My husband had been badly wounded in the first war — one arm was paralysed — but he could run the farm okay. He dug ditches, dug the garden, drove the car. Then when he was fifty-seven he had a stroke and was paralysed for twenty years, so I looked after him and ran the farm.

And even after we got married we had my bachelor uncle living with us, until he died at the age of ninety-five; and I had my cousin living here in Hawarden with us till she died at ninety-two. We're a tough breed, our family — live a whale of a long time. My brother was here for the last couple of years, too. He lived with us till he was ninety-five. He went just a couple of months ago. I miss my brother now. I loved the company, getting about together, someone to cook for. Not now. He's gone right out of my life.

I've spent all my life looking after people. I hate living on my own — no one to look after. I feel I'm not doing anything worthwhile now.

You see, I've got to be moving around, in the garden and up the hills and that. I'm fit for my age — walked the Milford Track when I was seventy-six; had a marvellous time, loved it. I practised here for weeks beforehand — walked four or five miles up the road with my boots and pack on. Then I led the way, on the Milford Track.

Walk! I ran everywhere when I was a kid — ran like a hare — and I'd go out shooting hares and that with a shotgun; I was always out with the boys. I knew how to rough it, too right I did. When we first went up to The Peaks, when I was twenty-six, I slept in a tent for three or four years. There was only a little two-roomed cottage, a kitchen and a little wee bedroom. My mother slept in the bedroom, I slept in the tent and my father and brother slept out the back in the shed, with the mice and things!

Sleeping in the tent? Yes, I did that for years and years, but it was all right. It had a board floor, a little black stove and a nice bed, nice counterpane, dressing table, everything. Cold in winter? Oh yes, snow everywhere, but when you're young. . . .

And look at you: you're even more primitive than me, lass. I slept in a tent; you're travelling around and sleeping outside under the trees. Talk about us being pioneers! I'd say you're a breakaway from the young generation, lass.

But any rate, we were all so thrilled to get that little farm; somewhere of our own — we didn't have to rent a house any more. Very happy years, those ones. We lived in the kitchen, played cards at night, then went off to bed. My father was away a lot. He worked on the Lakes road, and he'd often be out there for weeks on end, so I'd have to stay at home and milk the six cows, keep the whole place going. When I think now what we did those days. . . .

There'd be no water in the dry summers. I'd have to ride our mare down to the Hurunui River for a drink once a day, and all the other animals followed, the foal and all the cows and that. Then I had hens, ducks, geese and turkeys everywhere up there at The Peaks; sold them to keep the place going. I'd put live hens and chickens and crates of ducks' and hens' eggs and cream on the train; it came way up here those days. And I chopped trees, put up fowlhouses. . . .

I was an extension of the dog, or an extension of the old man's right arm — everything a female should be in a farmer's eyes! We made all our own soap, bread, cheese and butter — I always made my own butter until I came down here sixteen years ago to retire — and we put in plenty of fruit trees and veges, grew peas up the back to sell at Christmas. Nowadays you have peas any time of the year you want them — frozen ones. Yes, only things we really had to buy were flour, tea, sugar, raisins and that.

We all lived up there at The Peaks until I was thirty-nine, when we bought a real house, up the road a bit. It was beautiful — had three bedrooms, hot and cold water, everything — and I put in acres of lilies and daffodils. It was just like fairyland. One of the happiest times of my life, up there. But the grief to me was we were only there twelve months, then my mother had the stroke. So I came home to look after my father and brother and I stayed home, never went out to work again.

Then suddenly my husband had a stroke, too, so we shifted down from The Peaks, shifted into town. We had to be nearer things, for him. It was too far away up The Peaks, too lonely; we were getting old. But it broke my heart, selling up our home. The new people chopped down the garden, changed things around. And I didn't like living down in Hawarden; I wanted to be back in the hills. At the beginning there I'd say, "Blow, I'm not stopping here. I'm getting out of it." I didn't like the flat and the frosts and the clay. The ground gets that hard, it's no good for gardening. But you can't just live for the garden, and I'm used to it now. And I'm too old to shift. My friends are here, and my bowls. . . .

Sixteen years ago it was we shifted down here to Hawarden. We'd been here six years together — got the garden going, everything going, then suddenly my husband dropped dead at bowls one night. Finish. And I don't like it here, looking after just myself. Need to be looking after someone. . . or else out in the wilds, that's me.

241

But Hawarden! We're slipping up now. Used to have a butcher, a baker. Nothing here now; it all comes up from town, Christchurch. Now they're even saying they'll take away our shop . . . don't know what us old ones will do. The young ones have great big cars and they go to town, fill up the back with groceries from the supermarket so the little places are squeezed out. I'm afraid it's a think-big world. We're getting too clever; we'll blow the whole place up.

I'd say we had the best of the world. I feel sorry for the young ones today with all the pressures and worries. They have so many decisions to make. The kids come home from school and their mothers ask, "What do you want for tea tonight?" That's another decision they've got to make. We were just glad for what we were given. And we had no toys and things, but we kept ourselves entertained the whole time. None of this, "I'm bored," and "There's nothing to do."

We'd tear around the hills looking for wild raspberries and great big black Kentish cherries — we'd pick buckets of them — and alpine strawberries. We knew where all the patches were. Or we'd get a thrill out of seeing the moon at night from the horse and trap, or Dad would take us out to see a storm. We'd be listening to the wind, listening for the thunder. That was our entertainment. I remember the night Haley's Comet came across the sky. Everyone said it might be the end of the world, its tail was going to reach the earth and burn it up, set the world on fire. I was terrified the night the comet came. Dad took us out to see it. I was on his back and I was so frightened I couldn't look at it.

But we amused ourselves all right; couldn't go anywhere for entertainment, took a whole day to get anywhere. If we went to Christchurch once a year and saw a punch and judy show we thought it was marvellous.

Yes, I'm the old generation now, I can go way back. And we've been around the district a whale of a long time now, our family. My grandfather came out from Medbury in England, bought a piece of land here, and then when they were putting the railway through they wanted a bit of his land. So they said to him, if you're willing to let us have it you can name the railway station. They couldn't have stopped him anyway, could they? But anyrate, he named the place Medbury, after his home in England.

Then my great uncle built the old Hurunui hotel which has become quite a landmark now, on the main road between Christchurch and Nelson. John Hastie was granted a licence to run the hotel in July 1860 and that was the start of the Hurunui pub. It became quite famous as an accommodation place for gold diggers going to Westland or for drovers bringing stock from Nelson and that. Hastie charged the drovers two and six a night and that included a bath, dinner, bed and breakfast, a cut lunch for the road, a stable for the horse and a feed of chaff, and a paddock for the sheep. Then if you wanted a billy of beer, that was sixpence extra.

It was a great little pub, there was no doubt about it. Somewhere in all this mess there's a record of the rules of the place. Ah, yes. One of the rules said Hastie had to: "Provide a shed sufficiently weathertight, and fit for the accommodation of at least six horses" and to: "Keep at all times a proper supply of oats, and oaten or grass hay. Oats to be charged for to travellers at not more than sixpence per quart measure." He had: "To keep a lamp burning with two burners from sunset to sunrise, giving a sufficiently bright light, and being so lighted as not to be visible from the Northern bank of the Hurunui." And take a look at this one: "The licence to be cancelled . . . if any drunkedness be proved to have been allowed on the premises, or if any spirits shall be supplied from the house or premises to any aboriginal native of New Zealand."

And this one, too: "To keep at all times a horse for conveyance of foot passengers across the Hurunui between the hours of daylight in summer and winter at a moderate charge. To afford every assistance in his power in directing strangers to a safe fording across the river."

There were no bridges at all over the Hurunui those days. You just came across on your horse or in the coach and your only help came from the ferryman who surveyed the river for depth, checked if the bottom was rough and got a good place for you to cross. The river could change its course a terrible lot from day to day. The ferryman would go across on his horse and, besides the normal bridle and saddle, he had some other gear. If his horse got washed off his feet he'd put this harness on himself and let the horse swim and tow him to the bank.

There was one very well-known ferryman, old Harry. He worked the Parnassus crossing of the Waiau, before it was bridged. Harry lost one leg when he was an eleven-year-old boy, working one of those old chaff cutters — a big wheel turned by a horse. He was in the centre flicking a whip to keep the horse going. He fell in and the two big cogs at the bottom mashed his leg up. No artificial legs those days; he had to have the whole leg off, and he'd get about with a crutch, yet he became a very good horseman. He'd put one hand on the horse's mane and spring up on his one good leg. He'd vault onto the horse's back like lightning, or he'd swim alongside the horse, holding on to the saddle.

One day Harry was guiding a coach across the river. There were several women inside, very nervous of the whole business and wanting to go back. Harry said, "No, no return. The coach has got to go over." One woman piped up, "What'll happen to us if you get swept off your horse and can't show us where to cross?" Harry said, "I'll make it all right," and set to work. The coach was swaying all over the place, the water was that high, almost coming inside. Harry was sometimes on his horse, sometimes in the water, but he got them all across. Then when they were all having a walk around and straightening themselves out this woman asked Harry, "Why did you suddenly get off and start swimming?" Harry told her: "You were so cocksure that a man would be useless in that deep water without a horse, so I got off and swam, with only one leg. Let that be a lesson to you lady. Never underestimate the capabilities of other people."

Old Harry was a ferryman for years and years, then later on he got a truck and ran a carrying business between Cheviot and Christchurch. He'd roll drums of kerosene and stuff around, throw sacks of wheat and flour up, hop up himself and off he'd drive, all with one leg.

But very few motor vehicles about when I first knew the Hurunui hotel. The publican had to get his kegs of beer up to the Medbury railway station but he had no dray, no vehicle of any sort. What he'd have to do each time was take a horse up to a chap's place two and a half miles away from the pub, put her in his spring dray, drive back to the station, load her up, drive up to the pub, unload, then take the dray back. A whole day's work just getting the beer stocks in. Then at Christmas-time he'd have an eighteen-gallon keg of beer sitting on a platform out the back. You could go up to the pub, fill up your stone jar of beer, pay up and then go out the back and help yourself out of the big keg. And those days there was no difference in price between a small and a big glass of beer in the bar — six ounce or twelve ounce — they all cost sixpence. Then if you wanted spirits, the barman just put the bottle and a glass and a jug of water on the bar and you helped yourself.

You'd think they'd make more of a profit now with those gadgets that squirt out a certain amount and that's that, but the old publicans reckon they're making less money. In the old days the blokes would come up to the bar at the beginning of an evening, they'd tip up the bottle and half fill the glass. But by the end of the night they'd be practically drinking water. They'd be taking that little whisky the publican might as well have left the cork on the bottle. Yet they could keep face because it looked like they were drinking with the boys. These days . . . hell's teeth . . . they'd just keep drinking till they fell over.

The local policeman used to have a look in maybe once a week. One chap came from the West Coast. He had his own way of dealing with people drinking after hours. He'd drive up to the pub, turn the car around, then he'd get out of his car, turn his back on the hotel, straighten his coat — which didn't need straightening — then he'd slam the door, look up the road and down the road, open the door and slam it again, and finally turn around and go straight into the bar. The men'd all go out the back door. They'd be going for their lives. If he found anyone in the bar he'd take their names, and next thing they'd be in court. He'd given them fair warning. He was damn strict if you got caught, but very fair.

You could say that the policeman and Hastie between them, they ran a good pub. But Hastie was an epileptic, and in 1868, when he was forty-three, he had a fatal attack and died, leaving behind his wife Margaret, one son and three daughters. Margaret and her younger brother John then took over and managed the hotel, and when work started on putting a bridge over the Hurunui and the road had to be changed, in the late 1860s, they built the present Hurunui hotel, nearly a mile from the original one. This partnership lasted eight years until John bought a piece of land and moved away and Margaret went down to Christchurch.

After that several different people leased the hotel. On and on it went, everyone having a go at it. At one stage there the cook had a great swag of cauliflowers growing in the garden. You never got a meal without cauliflower, and you'll find all the old locals around here still call the Hurunui pub "the Cauliflower" today.

Then one of the publicans' wives got nicknamed "the Magpie". She was always in the bar and she couldn't stop talking . . . worse than me! An old joker who lived around here, an old Irishman, went into the pub one day and he had something in a sugarbag, hanging over his shoulder. The publican's wife said to him, "You've got something in that bag and it's moving. You've got to tell me what it is." The old joker laughed and laughed. He wouldn't say. Then in the end he did tell her what it was. He said, "Ah, namesake, namesake." It was a magpie, a chatterer; he was taking it home for his kids, and the nickname stuck. You could get those birds to talk very easily, and you had to be very careful — they'd hear you swear at the dogs, and then if they wanted to tell you something and you weren't listening, they'd let fly. If we had visitors we'd lock them up, away from earshot!

The old Hurunui pub had a parrot, too. It'd go into the bar and do the rounds, talking to people. It'd say, "Who are you?" and chatter away. The men would feed all sorts of language in; it'd learn anything. Then when the drovers were up early getting their breakfast they'd be banging pots and plates and scratching at the fire and they'd hear, "Stop that bloody noise." The parrot's rest had been disturbed. He'd be screeching and flapping around and telling them what he thought of it.

Yes I'm as old as old. I know all this ancient stuff about the old Hurunui pub. Next thing you'll be calling me "the Magpie", too, I'm doing that much talking. But the Hurunui . . . it suits me. I'd like to finish up here.

Let's go and see where the old pub was, and the school and the bridge. No time like the present. And how about going up to see where I used to live? Righto, we'll go. I haven't been up there for years, up The Peaks.

I know all this country so well, up here, I could go around with my eyes shut. This car knows her way up here on her own. I used to drive up and down this road in a horse and trap. Lord yes. Cars now . . . I mean, it's convenience. You took a hell of a long time to get anywhere in the early days. I've had this little Vauxhall for years. It's a 1950-something model. I've had it darn near thirty years; it does me. I don't drive far — down to the river for sand and shingle for the garden, that sort of thing, but I'd be lost without it. And it's all I want. Everyone says I need a new car. I don't want a new one.

There you go, that's where our little two-roomed cottage was, and the old orchard, it's still going, the plums and early apples. That's where my tent was, out there in the orchard. Nineteen twenty-six we came here, and there's still signs of us all over the place. There's one of the old spring carts we used to ride in, and this is the shed where my father and brother slept, in here; see the old dressing table and the mirror? It was all papered and nice those days. Here's my old school slate on the floor. You have it. Slates . . . children today wouldn't know what you were talking about. We used to shear the sheep here, just outside the shed, and we planted all those trees. Those were the days. . . .

Now we'll go up to our other house.

I came here in 1939, planted all those trees and the garden. It's all different now. They chopped down the trees, put up bridges; we always left the car on the other side of the creek. This place has got too many memories. The fowlhouses I built were up there on top of the bank. There were turkeys running everywhere, and all that bank by the creek was daffodils and lilies. This brings out a lot of sadness in me; the happiest days of my life were here. Imagine, coming from this to a bare paddock down on the flats at Hawarden. I feel terrible. It's all overgrown; you wouldn't know it. It doesn't do to come back to a place. . . .

246

I'm the old generation now; I'm ancient as hell. But I hope I don't peg out right away — I'd like to see this book of yours. It won't be out for a couple of years! Hell's teeth, I'll be pushing up daisies by then. But they're having a jubilee at the end of next month for the centennial of Hanmer Springs. I'm going up to that, too right I am. I said to my doctor, "You've got to keep me alive till then." "I'll do my best," he says. "Oh," I said, "that doesn't sound very hopeful." I said to myself, he thinks I'll be dog tucker by then.

But I'm going to that do at Hanmer. I say to them all round here, if I don't see that jubilee I'll be really upset. Everyone thinks I'm mad, because of course if I do peg out I won't know anything about it. But any rate, I've booked in for everything — the socials, the ex-staff party, the ball. And they're having a beauty contest. I'll have to take my bathing costume!

Any rate, I've got a new dress for the jubilee. If only I could get a new face.

16-97.   (17) Wattie.

WATTIE

'Know what I call you? My korero girl'

Wattie was the unofficial grandfather and sage of Stewart Island. He was born on the island in 1892, he'd spent most of his ninety years there and had no intention of moving. He was the ranger for the Departments of Lands and Survey, Forestry and Internal Affairs for thirty-four years and earned part of his living from fishing. In 1963 he received the M.B.E. for his services to natural history.

But perhaps above all, Wattie was known as a self-taught and widely respected naturalist. He knew instinctively when certain birds were nesting, or moving south, and always he watched the plants and the sea. He was devoted to the wild, wet Stewart Island environment and proud to confess it: "I'm a sort of a bush type, you see. Fires and camp ovens suit me. Everything I needed was on Stewart Island." He'd been happy living an isolated life, without the frills we expect today: "Ever had a car? Not really. A boat's my thing. I didn't need a car."

Wattie's special words and phrases echoed his bond with his surroundings. He always preferred to go "windward" of me as we walked, and he'd point out things "fore" and "aft". His thoughts would turn "inland" rather than "inward".

He was sharp-eyed, brown and lean, and strode around the tracks and shores of Stewart Island in sandshoes and corduroys, checked bush shirt and beret. He was long widowed and living with his bachelor son, a fisherman. They were not a bit domesticated. The food was left out in handy heaps on the table, the dishes were piled up on the bench, the tea towel blackened and the washing waited.

We'd sit around the coal fire in the kitchen and talk, fortified with big, chipped cups of strong tea, chunks of bread and cheese or fruit cake donated by the hordes of relatives and friends and strangers who popped in to see Uncle Wattie. Some days we'd dip through the inlets and bays in his cluttered old boat, or potter over to Thule or Deep Bay, out to Ringaringa and down onto the spit where his ancestors were buried. Wattie was fit and very determined to stay that way. His stamina was astounding.

At first he was sceptical of our talking about "this folk history business", about personal opinions, thoughts and feelings. He preferred to be remembered as a practical, scientific sort of a chap. But my stubbornness was ingrained, like Wattie's. I knew all those personal responses were there inside him, waiting.

Trust grew between us during our weeks of conversation. Wattie spent three days talking about his "performance" in World War I, confessing he'd returned to the island a wounded hero, and he'd nourished that image, but he hadn't been a particularly brave soldier. He wanted to get it all out, before he died. Wattie discovered the pain — and the ultimate relief — of vulnerability: "All this talking, it's baring the soul too much. I don't tell anyone about this as a rule, but you've got me talking."

I left Stewart Island with deep respect for Wattie, for the partnership he'd formed with his raw, unrelenting surroundings, and with much gratitude for our special friendship. He always called me his "korero girl", his talking girl, and whenever we said our goodbyes we'd exchange a blessing:

> Haere ra. Go in peace.
> E noho ra. Stay in peace.

This story first appeared as a Lands and Survey publication.

My life? I don't often tell people about that sort of thing, but you've got me talking.

Yes, I've lived a long time and I've done a lot of things. I was born here on Stewart Island, at Ringaringa. December 1 it was, 1892. Granny Harrold got me into the world. She was a half Red Indian woman, wife of a seafaring man, and I'd say she got most of my generation going in this world. She was the nearest thing to a midwife that we had on Stewart Island those days. No doctor, nothing.

Tell you what, I think my first year at school would be 1899. We'd all walk a couple of miles over to the school at Halfmoon Bay, me and my brothers, over the Deep Bay hill and over the rata log, then over Peterson's Hill. Mr Peterson was my teacher. He was from the Shetland Islands and he came to Stewart Island on the *Rosa* cutter; I remember seeing her hull down the bay. As a matter of fact, Mr Peterson was the teacher there at Halfmoon Bay practically the whole time I was at school. He had two daughters: Annie helped him in the schoolroom; and the other one, Bina, helped out with the singing and ran the post office, which was just a few drawers and boxes in the porch of the old schoolhouse.

What I remember about that first day at school? I remember I sat with an older brother all day, and I do remember sitting outside at playtime and seeing Charlie Marklund shooting shags in the bay with a muzzle loader. Shags weren't protected those days, and Charlie was probably getting them for a museum or something. He was looked upon as an authority on birds and that.

Any rate, that was my first day at school. And I remember we had those old long desks, all joined up together in a row with the seats joined up to them — old things, with ink wells. We just used slates and pencils, of course, and we weren't meant to spit on the slates to clean them up; we were meant to have a sponge or something, but it was quite easy to spit, then wipe your sleeve along it.

I'd say the biggest incident in my school days was seeing a great big four-masted barque lying outside Halfmoon Bay. She'd come out from Britain and America and her crew had mutinied — that's what we heard. I remember she looked so weird out there in our bay — transparent like crystal. Yes, something like *The Ancient Mariner*; I can recite that poem word for word. That's a good way to get to sleep, too! But I've got another system for getting myself off to sleep: I try to memorise the track going overland to Pegasus, to get all the bends and rises in the right order. It works; I've never got to Pegasus yet.

I'd say we had a fairly good education. Those days we were educated in things that mattered, things relevant to life — the three Rs, and woodwork and sewing and cooking, that sort of a thing. Today ... I don't know ... they swot for School Certificate. You hear Selwyn Toogood ask those people on the TV a simple question and they're bogged down. I'd say we had a better all-round education. But I'll tell you one thing that was no good — I laugh to myself about it nowadays — the natural history lessons we got. No such things as nature trips; Mr Peterson had a little notebook and he told us about whales and things. All we learnt was "whales are warm-blooded", things like that. But us kids didn't know a thing about what was really happening in the natural world, with the plants and birds and that on Stewart Island — right outside the back door!

Mr Peterson kept pretty good control. We all got belted with a bit of supplejack from the bush or with the leather strap, doubled and knotted through itself. Mr Peterson would sit in the corner, he'd throw the strap at you and yell out, "Bring that up." Then he'd whack you. The girls got it too, those days. Mind you, it saved us a lot of bother. Mr Peterson didn't have to keep us in after school. He wanted to finish early and so did we, so he just belted us.

At lunch-time us boys would go down the beach or up Mill Creek. We'd jump off the rocks and swim around; no such thing as bathing trunks. Or we'd go round the point and play games, kicking a football into the water and that. Now and then we'd have to wade right out and get the ball, or grab a dinghy from the wharf and pull out. You could say the beach was our playground. It was all we had; nothing was laid on those days. We'd do skipping with long bits of kelp or we'd play hopscotch. The tide always came in and cleaned our mess up. We'd also carve cricket balls out of the thick seaweed and chop a bat out of the bush — we never thought of having a bought bat and ball — or we'd drag up some of that thick bull kelp and make temporary shoes. We'd hack them out and slop around the place.

Well, at any rate, after the school years I went away to high school in Invercargill, then when I was about sixteen or seventeen I started work at the Union Bank over there. Stayed there less than a year. I was a bush and hill lad; it didn't suit me there in a bank in town. I didn't suit them either. I kept blotting the stamps they used!

My next job was just knocking around the country, working on farms here and there. I learnt to ride a horse, got myself a stock whip and I'd gallop around the cattle helping with the mustering; or I'd do menial jobs, plucking sheep and that sort of thing. Then I came back and did a year's fishing here on the island, but I still wanted to see more of the country at that stage, so off I went up the North Island, doing station work and fencing. I learnt how to make North Island fences — they're miles ahead of the South Island ones. Any rate, I stayed up there for nine months, then one day I was down the wharf at Gisborne and I saw this big schooner. I was interested in the rigging on her, so I had a talk to one of her crew. Well, next day I was up the street and this young bloke came after me. He says, "You want a job?" So I sailed up to Auckland on that schooner — *Awanui*, that was her name. Took us three weeeks, landing stuff off all the way along. Sometimes there'd be little bits of wharves, but often we'd just send the stuff ashore in a big open boat they called a surf boat. We'd pull ashore while the schooner lay at anchor in the bay. The cargo? Mostly stores, I think.

The crew was just the captain, the mate, one able seaman, the cook and me, plus another couple working their passage. My wages were five pound a month, and I was to be paid off when we got up to Auckland. I remember I found this place to stay. Ninepence for a good feed, that's what it cost me — steak and kidney pudding and vegetables and all the trimmings.

Then I heard my brother Charlie, who was a half-trained surveyor, was doing railway extension work up near Whangarei. I said, that'll do me. I remember that day very well. I was standing in front of the *Herald* office and the bulletins came in. They'd just get put up in the *Herald* office . . . no radios those days . . . never heard of them. Any rate, they said France and Germany were at war; Britain wasn't. The First World War was under way.

So off I went with a whole crowd of other blokes to do relief work on the railway extension. I can see it now. We all lined up and got tents and wood for bunks and iron and stuff to put up chimneys. That's what we had to live in. And this fellow came up to me, he says: "I like the look of you. What about coming and joining up tents with me?" He said there was a creek down a side road, plenty of room to pitch a tent. I thought that sounded all right, and the other blokes were all squabbling and stealing, so we set up camp down there. This chap knew the ropes. He knew some bloke who put us on a decent gang and next thing we were at it. We just worked with picks and shovels and barrows; never heard of bulldozers. We had to cut into the hillsides, shovel them into barrows, fill in the gullies. . . .

And up there at the railway camp, that was one of the few times in my life I let people down. At the back of my mind, all along, was the thought that as soon as I could get enough money together, I'd go off and enlist. So when Easter came, work knocked off and we all went down to Auckland, where I got onto a little steamer and came south to Dunedin. But I hadn't paid for the stores I'd bought up at the railway camp. I felt bad about that. I always meant to send something up, to cover those stores, but I never got round to it.

As soon as I got to Invercargill I went to Doctor Richie Crawford. I knew I was healthy, and he gave me a ticket to be a soldier. I presented this at the recruiting place at Invercargill and got accepted, so I came home here to the island for a few days before going up to Trentham for three months' training. And I tell you what, that's the last time I remember being excited about the war. Off we went on the troop ship and we had a miserable time. The conditions were all right, but the tucker was no good — any amount of it, but it was always a bit smelly; the cook wasn't too fussy. The frozen stuff was always slightly thawed. It'd been shifted from one ship to another, and the tucker wasn't cooked through enough. You needed paint brushes to eat the eggs, they were that watery. But sailors and soldiers always complain about tucker.

And I remember on that troop ship they tried to stop us men from smoking cigarettes. They said it'd spoil our wind when it came to charging the enemy! This caused terrible trouble from time to time. Us soldiers would tell the officers to go to blazes or take a swipe at them when we got ordered to quit smoking. Then someone'd end up in clink.

Any rate, we were the Fourth Reinforcement, off to the war. Right from the start I thought I knew how I'd handle war. I said I'm going to brace myself to fight fear. When the trial comes, I'm going to face it. But I wasn't much of a soldier. I died every day at that war. And better men than me were killed every day.

Then right from the start I found the heat unbearable. We're not used to that sort of thing in Stewart Island! I got badly sunburnt, moped around and didn't feel hungry. Anyhow, we marched up and down, getting inspected, then one time when we halted for an inspection I just couldn't stand up any more. An Aussie bloke had stopped his mule cart on the track behind us. I was in the rear rank, so I slipped out of line and got into his cart. No one took any notice. Then the officer bellowed out, "Parade attention!" and I jumped out of the cart and back into line. Same thing happened next day. Then after inspection I was slumping over my rifle and an officer screamed out, "Pull yourself together," but I couldn't do it. I'm not a weak man . . . am I? But I couldn't do it.

Lucky for me, another more sympathetic officer came up and said: "Fall out. You look pretty crook." I marched down to the camp and on the way I saw a big tent. It looked cool so I just lay inside it for the rest of the day. It was damn hot all right. Another bloke back at the camp died of the heat.

I should be dead myself from what happened to me over the next few days. I eventually got myself back to the camp. I remember stripping off and getting under the cold shower; my teeth were clattering. I don't remember anything else until I woke up in the Australian hospital four days later. I saw I was in a different place, somewhere I'd never been before. I thought I must be hallucinating. What had happened, some chaps had found me in the tent and thought they'd better do something about me, so they dragged me along to the New Zealand first aid area, but the orderlies said I was drunk and wouldn't have anything to do with me. I was just drooping around and vomiting the whole time, so these chaps took me over to the Aussie first aid base. The officers said, "He's sick all right, but take him across to the New Zealand base." Back they dragged me again, but still the New Zealand doctor said I was drunk. At this stage the blokes got het up. They threatened to call the guard, and in the end it was the Aussies who took me in. I woke up in their hospital. I'd been there four days!

I've never told anyone about all this. I was that ashamed. There I was languishing in one hospital, then another, when I should have been out in the field, fighting. I never even wrote home, I was that ashamed.

What was wrong with me? No one seemed to know. Later on someone told me it was some sort of a heat stroke. I'd overheated without perspiring and more or less burnt up inside. I never did like the heat; still don't. I got thin as a rake — around seven or eight stone. I was as skinny as those pictures in the paper of famine children in India. Then, with so many soldiers coming in wounded from Gallipoli and that, I had to move out of the Aussie hospital. I got put into one French hospital, then another, with all sorts of queer food I didn't understand. I said, "I've come here to be a soldier, not to lie in hospital," and they said, "You're not fit to be in the desert just yet."

On and on it went. They put me out into an Aussie detail camp, but then one morning I woke up crook. I tottered back to the New Zealand lines and slumped down in a tent; no one took much notice. Then someone bandaged my eyes and took my temperature — 104. I had a temperature of 104.2°F for days on end. One of the few things I remember was the doctor saying to me, "For goodness sake, get your temperature down!" In the end I started perspiring and coming right, so they decided to send me off to England. The doctor said I wouldn't last another bout, so they'd better get me away from the place.

There I was in hospital again — an English one this time, near Waterloo Bridge in London. People would come and take us on outings. It was a great thing to cultivate New Zealanders and Aussies, and I saw things I probably wouldn't have seen otherwise — St Paul's and that. Then one day I spotted Sir Winston Churchill. He was crossing the corner of Hyde Park and I spotted him. I'd seen pictures of him before. I knew him all right.

Next thing, someone thought it would be nice if I went up to see my ancestors in the Orkney Islands, so off I went up there, but I was out of place with that crowd — they were all lairds and ladies and things. It was interesting, but I was damn glad to get out of it. I went back to London on the fleet mail boat and then back to Egypt. I was there only about a month before we all set off across the Mediterranean to Marseilles, and then we had four days in narrow little carriages, going up to Flanders. Cold! We'd had plenty of blankets in Egypt, but up there in the north of France we had just one blanket each. I've never been as cold and miserable in my life. We'd have to lie down at night on the board floors with our blanket. We'd lie there too cold to sleep and scared to swear because all the others would wake up.

I was in the trenches up there for a while, too. I was in the great fighting at the Somme, the bath of blood. I wasn't in the front lines — like I said, I didn't have a very exciting time in the war — but I was there, all right. Shelling, shelling everywhere, crashing all over us, just like a gale. And they'd used tanks for the first time in that war. Everywhere was just like a great ploughed paddock with stranded tanks scattered around and corpses everywhere, and swollen dead soldiers, mouths open, flies crawling . . . people don't want to hear about that sort of a thing. But that's where I got wounded.

What happened? This night we marched back to a deep trench with the shells still crashing all around, and we were all desperately thirsty but there was no water handy. Well, we knew some of those stranded tanks had water in them — oily old stuff, but water. We used that lot up, then I said I was game to go back and get some

256

more, so we ducked over to a tank, me and another chap, Bill. We filled our tins and started back again. On the way my hat was blown off with a shell, and by the time we got back to the trench the rest of our bunch had moved! I got my gear together — they were starting to shell like blazes by this stage — then someone yelled out we were expected at the front line. I went to help fasten my mate's gear. There were shells crashing all around. We were just crouching there, sheltering. Suddenly, there was a shattering crash. The same shell got us both. I thought, this is it. I said to myself, I'm dying now. I didn't panic. I said, "Never mind, Bill. We've done our stuff."

The shell got me on the shoulder, smashed it up to pulp. My boots were shot through at the toe and my feet were splintered everywhere. I couldn't *move*.

And I knew my mate was dead. I made it; he didn't. I looked at him. He had a hole in his head. And I knew he was going, by the few words he tried to say about his mother. He was probably saying, "Tell my mother," or else he was jolted back to being like a little boy and he wanted his mother. He was a better man than I was, and he died. He's buried somewhere there on the field.

Other than this, all I remember is the terrific, shattering crash. I couldn't see how I could live, with my shoulder smashed to pulp. I felt resigned. The other fellows said they saw me fly in the air and land, face down. One of them turned me over. He had a look and said, "Wattie's had it." By this stage I'd just gone blank. I said to myself, "That's good. I'll die now." The stretcher-bearers came and got me. I said to them, "Put me on my feet and I might get myself out," but then I went a black colour, so they got me onto a stretcher. Off we went, bumping over the shell-shot roads to the ambulance wagons. Shelling all around, all the time. I'd say they were the really brave men in the war, those stretcher-bearers.

Well, at any rate none of my mates thought they'd see me alive again. I wasn't suffering much, but I was extremely thirsty. I got looked at briefly and put onto an ambulance train. The number of times that train stopped and waited, goodness knows what for, and I remember that for eats we were given great lumps of cheese, thick as slices of bread, and great big wads of bread — all us smashed-up men, all so sick we couldn't eat much of the most delicate sort of food! Any rate, next thing was we got to some sort of hospital. They fixed me up a bit and dug out some of the shell, but I didn't get well. The food came in from the far end of the ward, but by the time it got to me it was lukewarm, and I wasn't hungry enough to enjoy it. I just didn't eat it. Yet the doctors didn't want to shift me because I was too weak.

In the end I said to myself, blow it, I'll die of starvation at this rate, so I got out of the stretcher and walked down to the hospital ship crossing the strait. Four hours we lay in Dover Railway Station. Kind women brought cups of tea and little things to eat, and finally we got over to Walton-on-Thames and into the hospital there.

I began to get better there, but I was still a mess — all one side of me. My arm would have hung out sideways, but the surgeon put it into a splint. That was very painful at the time. There was no meat on the shoulder . . . just bone, it was that shattered. There were still bits and pieces of shell in my hand and that. I'm not going to show you all my wounds! They kept digging some more of it out, but my hand, especially, wouldn't get strong. My thumb was no good. They'd get hold of a pair of forceps and haul a whole lot of splinters out, but it didn't get strong until they finally cut me right open and cleaned the whole lot out. As a matter of fact, there were still small splinters in other parts of me, even when I got back to New Zealand. They'd be busy hauling bits of bone out, and metal out of my back.

My arm now? It gets sore if I put a strain on it. But it doesn't matter.

I was in hospital there in England, dashed if I know how long, until I got back here. They didn't want to send me back home just then — I wasn't better — but that's the way things happened. Like I told you, I never seemed to get anything exciting in the war! And I'd say this, men do a lot of exaggerating about the war anyway. It's just like when a man comes home from hunting, the wife's busy poking around cooking and looking after the babies. He can't just say he's been hunting. He has to say the boar charged him and it was all touch and go, to try and get the story *across* to her. Well, us men tend to do the same thing about the war.

Any rate I don't like all this; it's baring the soul too much. Let's korero about something else. I came back to New Zealand on a hospital ship.

Would I have lived my life out here on the island if it wasn't for the war? No, probably I wouldn't. What with my wound and all that, I had to take it easy, fishing and part-time rangering. Stewart Island suited me. When it was so terrifically hot, in Egypt and that, I used to think, if I get back to New Zealand alive I'll make damn sure I go back to Stewart Island — a nice, *cool* place.

So I ended up being the ranger for the Lands and Survey, Forestry and Internal Affairs Departments here on the island. Nineteen twenty-five it was, when I started. I got a salary, a very small one, and I did the job single-handed for all those years. In the possum hunting days it involved an awful lot of work — not just the protection of wildlife, but also checking licences, stamping skins, signing papers for hunters, putting up notices. I had to keep a general eye on the reserves, put a stop to things like burning and illegal taking of firewood. Plenty of things I wasn't told to do, but I did them anyway; I enjoyed just poking around. I made it my business to look after things. It wasn't my work to cut and mark tracks, but I'd do it anyway, for my own use.

What I set out to do as a ranger? I'd say the most valuable thing I did was to stop respectable people from helping themselves to the birds. When the pigeons were thick everyone would shanghai them and put them in the pot. Well, they gave it up, out of consideration for me. Of course, the toughies didn't give it up; they'd taunt me by shouting out, loud so I could hear, "That'd look well in the pot." Then there'd be the odd bloke blatantly destroying the birds, shooting a tui in the fuchsia tree every morning, for the cat's breakfast! Sheer ignorance.

Yes, protection of the birds was a hard job all along, because even the Pakehas thought of birds as something you could help yourself to. There'd be hundreds of pigeons in Deep Bay or around the Church of England, great flocks of fifty and 100 or more coming over. Same thing with lots of the other birds that are scarce, or gone, today. . . .

Why? The thing is, we've upset the balance of nature. My own opinion is that the rats are the main cause; they're thick in the bush here. Everyone nowadays reckons that the cats are killing off the birds, and especially the kakapo, but I reckon the wild cats are doing more good than harm, killing off the rats. All the old identities here know that if we didn't have wild cats in the bush we wouldn't live ourselves; the rats would take over.

I'll say this: there've been about six bird species disappeared from Stewart Island in my lifetime, or nearly disappeared. We used to see the kokako frequently in certain places, especially where the bush was short but not stunted. Another bird that used to be quite common but isn't around now is the bush canary or yellowhead. Some of the "experts" say they've never been here, and others say we've got them mixed up with yellowhammers. That's insulting. My older brother remembered them well, and I've seen plenty of them on the mainland; they were common around Dunedin at one stage there. But not on Stewart Island any more.

Then there's the little teal duck, which some people call the brown duck; I remember counting a flock of seventy-five once. We used to say there was a pair of them in every puddle on Stewart Island! I began to make notes because I noticed they were on the decrease, and now, if they're not completely extinct, they nearly are. I think the wekas got their chicks. People? Yes, of course, we ate them . . . *murdered* them. Those days we didn't think about birds getting extinct; they were just part of the food supply.

But I'll tell you what, all due respects to the Forest and Bird people, and they did make me an honorary member, but they do get very starry-eyed. Half the time they don't know what's going on. And half of them don't go out in the bush; they have slide evenings instead!

Yes, I've noticed that small birds like riflemen, cuckoos, larks, moreporks and owls are generally less plentiful these days. Then there's another thing that's happening right under my nose: the little red-billed gulls are being chased off every breeding place on the island. At one time they nested on the nugget at Lonnekers, in Golden Bay and Ryan's Creek. I'd actually see the eggs in the nests, then a week or two later they'd be gone. I have an idea, and there's some evidence now to back this belief, that the harrier hawks are the culprits; the eggs are easy picking for them. And the harriers may also be the reason the blue shags so often change their nesting places. At any rate, the Forest and Bird people should be protesting about the little red-billed gulls by now.

I'd say the only birds holding their own are the bellbirds and kingfishers, and perhaps the tuis. Maybe you could include the grey warblers and parakeets — they were at least holding their numbers until recently. I heard a parakeet yesterday. Kakas used to be thick, then they got very scarce indeed, maybe through parrot disease, but I think they've made a fairly good recovery.

The tokoeka, the Stewart Island kiwi, is an unusual case; it's *increased* recently. When I was a kid you'd hear one just very occasionally, over the other side of the Rakeahua River. We always said there were *none* this side of the Rakeahua. Then when I was a young man I saw a few tokoeka tracks at Mason's Bay and Hellfire, way down the west coast of the island. Now you can come across a tokoeka on the back track to Horseshoe Bay, and they've even been seen in the village.

Kakapos? I've never seen one. I do remember hearing how Jim Murdoch saw some kakapo feathers; and Arthur Ford, an old goldminer had a dog that brought one into camp. Then a deer culler once found one asleep in a tree down at Kopeka; he grabbed it and got a few feathers.

What I think about the recent kakapo searches? I've been ditched on issues I *do* know a lot about, so I can't say what we should do now about the kakapo. I learnt a long time ago that living in the territory where the birds *are* doesn't count. You've got to live in a town and have a degree to be a bird expert!

No, I don't fight with people about their views, nowadays.

They're taking wekas off Codfish Island, too — an elaborate operation to try and keep the petrels going. It's a good thing, if it's saving the petrels. But my point has always been, when they save one species by destroying another, those people who have the benefit of seeing the saved species are only a favoured few. How many people get to Codfish Island? The other thing is, they went to the trouble of building an enclosure to get the Codfish wekas acclimatised before they liberated them. The locals just laughed. Why go to all that expense and silliness? A weka will live anywhere. Now they just throw them ashore on Stewart Island! Then the experts say the wekas might swim back to Codfish Island. They're not that silly, although I do think that from time to time they swim across to Ulva, about three-quarters of a mile from the island.

But many of the locals did have a laugh at the expense of the weka project on Codfish. A lot of the old weka-eaters would still like to cook up a few. They're tough as old boots — they've got thick, oily skin to keep them happy on rainy days — but I could live on weka stew myself, just like it says in one of our old songs:

What would a Maori do
For a good old weka stew.

I just quartered the birds and cooked them up with a little bit of onion and salt, sometimes rice as well, that's about all you want. What it tastes like? Like weka! I don't think it's strong-tasting, myself. I like the gamy flavour of those sorts of things, and weka oil is looked upon as a great thing for rheumatism — it's so penetrating, keeps the old joints going. But you do have to cook it quite a long time to make the skin edible. Not like those town types, though; they cook things to a rag. They come along and fill the stew up with veges and they boil it to nothing. A lot of those townies think if you go two days without veges, that's the end of you!

Yes, we ate wekas all right. My father was very strict about the game rules, but wekas were so plentiful and we ate any amount of them, mainly when we were out camping. Kaka stew's very good, too — very sweet eating. You can't imagine parrots being good to eat, but they are, and same thing with tuis — they're very good eating. Sounds a terrible thing to do, nowadays, but not then— they were just the natural things to eat. Captain Cook said tuis were the finest thing the bush afforded.

No, my father didn't mind us shanghaiing thrushes and that, but he always said don't touch the natives. We did, though — pigeons and tomtits and tuis. We had this rhyme:

All through tea the boys did mutter
That tuis taste better than bread and butter.

We just made use of what was around us, the birds and deer and fish. The old Maoris were very fond of eel and mutton birds, and I like a feed of it myself — too right.

Then the old-timers would get a drink out of the matai, the black pine. They'd bore a hole, let the moisture build up, and there's your drink. Same thing with the manuka — we boiled up the twigs and made tea. It's meant to be good for backache, but I don't know what causes that backache it's meant to cure! Bidibid made you a cup of tea, too, and for diarrhoea we'd boil up koromiko leaves and drink the liquid, or at a pinch you just chewed the young leaves. Same process with manuka or rimu leaves, if you got constipated. Then if you had a sore you'd heat up some ngaio leaves. They go moist and oozy and you can make yourself a poultice. The Maori families here used ngaio rather than bother with the district nurse.

We made use of the seaweed on the beaches, too. We just dried the carrageen and made it into a slippery kind of jelly, like ordinary milk puddings — semolina and that. Then during the war there was a great carrageen trade here when they couldn't get hold of Irish Moss to make cough mixture, toothpaste, leather dressing and paint emulsion and that kind of thing. The Dominion Breweries also bought it to make beer.

Where the devil's my hat? I started wearing a hat on chilly mornings years ago, and now I can't do without it.

The deer problem? What I do know is this: they're all playing around and asking each other, "Should we stop the deer or shouldn't we?" But I say, it's fifty years since the deer did the damage. It makes me wild. People come here and do surveys and write articles. They all say we must stop the deer, and the deer are damaging the bush. But even before I was married, way back in the 1920s, there were signs of deer damage. You could see changes just twenty years or so after the deer were first released.

The "experts" also say we must stop the deer getting down to the south and west of the island. But the Virginian deer were liberated down at Pegasus, in 1905! As for the red deer, I actually remember seeing the first six arriving on Stewart Island. That was in 1901 when I was just a boy. I can remember the deer crates on the Halfmoon Bay wharf. I'm the only one left who can remember that.

Our reaction? We were grateful. The deer gave us a good meat supply when times were hard, and they made travel easier in the bush. I always used to say that if the changes made by the deer could have remained static, they could almost be regarded as a benefit. But the changes went disastrously onward to their present stage.

What we should do now? My statement is this: it's not just the start of the problem. There's hardly any Hen and Chicken fern left in the bush now, yet young Stewart Islanders don't know that the bush *is* eaten out; it's always been like that in their lifetime. But what I'd do is protect Ulva. It's a sort of a show place, the finest bush area we've got left. So I'd say, clean *all* the deer off Ulva. They reckon they've cleaned the deer off the island, but I've seen tracks there. They have reduced the herd, but only a couple of deer can keep a place like that eaten out.

I'm not arguing about the main part of Stewart Island; it's pretty well impossible to deal with the deer there now. They've reduced numbers there, too, but the point is this: you go round the inlet on a fine day and you see several deer. They're not shot out. I don't think the Government deer hunters did much more than keep ahead of the natural increase, so then the survivors thrived because they could get more food. In my opinion, the deer numbers have reduced not because of the deer shooting, but because the numbers increased so much that they've eaten themselves out.

Yes, the problem of deer on Stewart Island is too big an issue, so it'll get shelved. But for goodness sake save Ulva; that *can* be saved.

My other statement is this: I've kept the deer off the islands in the Bravo group, Tommy, Crayfish, Groper, Goat and Refuge Islands and some of the other little islands. It wasn't my job, but I did it, I've been very keen on those islands all along. I'd take my dog over and occasionally we'd drive a deer back into the water. Those islands are particularly interesting, pretty well virgin bush. The deer must not get onto them. And they're pretty good still, far as I know.

But me? I'm dropped from the deer issue, too, these days. I can't assert myself now. And why fight? It's like trying to make peace between England and Ireland . . . or between the Lands and Forestry Departments here!

What I think about fish farming on the island? I think the fish farms should go to Port Adventure and Pegasus. I'd be quite happy with that. I don't say everyone else would be happy, mind you! But fishing is all part of life here. The island wouldn't have been settled in the first place if it wasn't for the fishing and sawmilling. So we've got to have the new marine farming; it's just a continuation of the old-style fishing. There it is. I've never been in favour of stamping out commercial fishing in the inlet.

But what I say is this: don't put the fish farms on Bravo Island or in Big Glory. That's the most interesting part of the inlet. They both should be left intact; they're too beautiful to be ruined by marine farming. One side of Big Glory is all beautiful native bush with sheltered water and a pied shag nesting rookery. The other side is more windswept, but there's lots of nice little bays. Yet the council don't know about that. Half of them have never been down there; they don't understand it. They're going to have a tour and a meeting to decide what to do about it, but who is allowed to go? There are certain people they're going to ask. They won't ask me. Never have. Why didn't I get asked to go along on the tour? I've got the background. I know what I'm talking about. But people make a great fuss of me, then they ditch me.

What I'd do if I was ranger today? I'd say, in the interests of the adjoining lands, build the fish farms somewhere else. If they *have* to be in Paterson Inlet I'd even sooner see them near my place, in the North Arm. I'm not keen on opposing things. I don't like writing letters to the paper or getting mixed up in protests because there's such a lot of fanatics in those groups. But I think I'll have to put a letter in the paper. I'm honorary ranger still. I feel I ought to stir myself up and write. The local council is ignoring me. I don't know if it's much good going to any of their meetings. I don't hear half of what they're saying now, anyway. I'd get overlooked. The best idea would be if I could get up and have my say, then go home. But what difference would it make? I'm disillusioned.

But I'd say I've had a good life as a ranger ... a strenuous one, mind you. I've walked over most of this island, keeping an eye on the reserves. I was tough all right, those days. I could leave home, get to the far end of Bungaree and come back the same day, just using the old abandoned tracks cut by the sawmilling people. But I know nothing about tramping like they do it these days — dehydrated this and that and sleeping bags. I know nothing about that. Some of them take the town into the bush with them. One young chap I came across was cooking up tea and I heard him say: "I don't know what we're going to have for a third course!"

Me? For a day trip I'd just carry a couple of little jam tins, one inside the other, a mug, some tea and sugar and a good lot of lunch. Those jam tins were my billies, homemade billies, and they'd last far better than those bought ones, too. Then if I was away for two or three days I'd also take a couple of spuds or some rice, some oatmeal and bread and a few tins of bully beef. You just stick a tin of bully into the billy, heat her up and there you have a hot meal. I didn't worry about veges; they're for the town people.

Stewart Island people aren't so mad about vegetables. I like the old condensed milk, though. I'd take along a tin or two. And once you've put a hole in the tin you just stick your mug over the top and it's perfectly sealed.

First job in the camp is to get the rara, the kindling wood, and get a fire going. You've got to get good rara — kamahi or manuka. No torches those days to help you out if it was dark . . . only matches and candles. So if it was raining while you were still out in the bush you were stuck for a light. No such things as sleeping bags either; never heard of them. I just carried a couple of blankets, or sometimes I didn't even take the blankets, just a tent. I'd build up a great big fire and just curl up in front of it. Cold? Yes, a bit. Even when you're in one of those old huts with iron on the roof, the frost strikes right through the winter. Some blokes reckon the tea froze hard in the billies! And you've got to make sure your trousers are strong. The Stewart Island scrub soon carries your trouser knees away. It's no good taking your oldest worn-out trousers; I soon found that out.

Know what I think? With the track and hut system nowadays, we're not letting people be tough enough. And we're wasting public money, too. We're spending money like water, for no one's benefit. The trampers come to Stewart Island, they bring their dehydrated food with them and they get free board in the huts. The tourists come on the ferry for the day. Half of them even bring their *lunch* with them. Us islanders don't benefit from them at all.

But especially, what with all the flash huts and that, we're not letting young New Zealanders learn to live in the bush. All that's really needed is an overhead shelter, a big roof. As long as it's good, dry land you can block one end off from the prevailing wind. You put up your tent under it and you're right. You do need a couple of decent fireplaces, that's very important, but those modern huts have silly little fireplaces designed in Wellington, and they have no decent bar to hang your billy on. You need a good, big fireplace, big as that table, so you can all sit round and dry your sodden clothes. Know how the old Maoris did that? They'd rip off their trousers, throw them right on the fire and whip them off. They'd do this once or twice and they'd be dry in no time. Works well; I've tried it. Mind you, you've gotta be quick!

Too right, I went all over this island. I'd go overland to Pegasus on the south coast. I did that whole track up, clearing and marking and that. Just used the material that's there — bits of stick from the bog pines and piles of stones, or I'd blaze the trees. My idea was, I didn't cut right through to the wood so I didn't damage the tree. Today they use big red discs and things. It's all right.

My point was this: I didn't always cut a track to get from A to B as quickly as possible. I like to get down to a beach now and again, makes it far more interesting. But people today want to go the shortest route, so they cut off bits of my old tracks. Tell you what though, my hands are like a society lady's now, from doing no work.

The other thing is, when I cut a track I always cut a good one, so people don't get lost, and those old tracks of mine come in useful for search and rescue work. A fair few chaps go missing in this wild part of the country.

Wilderness? Should we control it more so people don't get lost? I'll tell you what, the Lands Department treats all of southern Stewart Island as a wilderness. But I say we've got all those old tracks from the early times; it doesn't make sense to blot them out. They should concentrate on keeping a few of them in order so people can get about the place, and for historic purposes, too, not get carried away with cutting new tracks. Take that route overland to Pegasus: it's a wonderful trip down to the south coast; I must have done it dozens of times. How long would it take me? All depends. On a very long summer day you can get to the Rakeahua River very early, have a feed, set off and get to Pegasus by night-time. But you're striding it out to get there in one day. The last section is a bit tiresome, always another ridge. Then finally you get to the top of the Tin Range and drop down to the old mining claims in the valley. But more often than not I'd spread the trip out a bit.

At Pegasus you came out where the old Pegasus pub was in the early days — just a tiny little hotel; the bar was about the size of that sink top. But the whole thing got pulled down, to make a hut somewhere else. Any rate, from the old pub you could look across to where the people lived in the bay. You'd coo-ee out and someone would pull across in the dinghy; saved you a long trek around the bay.

There were just a handful of people living down here. They'd give you a meal: fish and mussels and oysters — Port Adventure and Pegasus oysters are the best in the world — or tinned meat, or sometimes frozen meat from the fish freezers. I can never forget one lady down there: she was a town sort, had a nice natty little house with screens on the door to keep the flies out, way the billio down there!

Hard to imagine now, that little settlement — houses, boatsheds, jetties and the fish freezer. Tell you the truth, I don't know what's down there now. But no buildings and no people, that's one thing certain. And another thing that sticks in my mind: there was this old draught horse down at Pegasus. There were actually two of them at one stage when they were forming the roads and laying down tramways. I think they'd been at Mason's Bay and got taken down there by boat. Then when the whole works at Pegasus was abandoned, the two horses were put out on the open hills where they could get a decent feed. There'd always been a bridge here and there, across the creeks and dips, but they rotted away, so then the horses couldn't get back. One died; one was up there for years. I always looked out for her. She'd be outlined on the hills — just her, nothing else. She looked queer in the light.

Then one time I didn't see her. And I couldn't find her hoofmarks here and there. She must have got down into a gully in the winter. Someone found her bones. . . .

The actual discovery of the tin down south there was way before my time, and the goldmining was before that again. But no one got rich down there. As a matter of fact, the only ones who made any money were the ones who sold their gold claims and got out of it. As for the tin, the old goldminers couldn't make out this black substance in their claims. Then in the late 1880s and early 1890s people arrived from Australia and the locals poured in. They got a bit of tin, then gradually the whole thing petered out. There was a revival of interest when the value of tin increased just before World War I — they put in jetties and tramways. But they soon realised there just wasn't enough tin around to make it worthwhile, so the whole project was dropped.

However, news of the gold and tin discoveries caused quite a rush for a time down there, and the miners made little camps in the valleys. Some of them built huts. Others camped in tents, but they made them homely; they'd raise the tent a little off the ground so there'd be headroom, then they'd wall up the sides and put a fly over the whole thing. And there'd be a fireplace in the front, so they could cook in comfort with their billies and camp ovens and frypans. Camp ovens are the thing; they do any job you want.

Yes, it was quite a little camp. Now? Nothing there at all. That's what is ridiculous. Our country was built up out of places like that, and now we're not allowed to build there.

I was down there at Pegasus for four months, fishing, way back before 1924 when I got married. The blue cod spawned about August, and there was no good fishing in the north after that and only a little crayfishing, but down at Pegasus they bite longer and better. They're bigger, too, because it's not fished so much . . . lovely big cod and groper and trumpeter. So I thought to myself, I'll go down there for a while. I had my war pension, but I thought I needed a little more, so off I went in a little twenty-footer. I remember it took me four or five hours. I stayed down at Pegasus at Big House, a sort of a hostel place, with a group of fishing fellows and one other chap who drove the turbine engine. We just lived there, four or five of us together. Tommy did the cooking in the old colonial oven. He'd make lovely soda loaves for us and we bought bread whenever a boat came in, but I remember he'd always be saying, "If you fellows don't help me a bit more I'm going to give up the cooking." He always needed wood for the fire, that type of thing. In the end Tommy left and we had to do our own baking. That wasn't so good.

Entertainment? You didn't worry about that. Things just fell into line. I don't remember much about what we did in the evenings . . . playing cards and that, having a yarn or two and drinking. I only came up to Halfmoon Bay once in those four months, I do know that. No, I just spent my time working away on my own. Independent. When I wasn't fishing I was exploring the island, climbing around. Big Charlie was the same. He'd pull out in his dinghy and get a fish. The others just sat around.

Gold? I've prospected all over the place. Never got much — just a few bits of reef gold, the stuff that hasn't travelled far. Plenty of places I've struck gold on this island, but it's always in isolated places, too hard to get at. Some places you just haul out a tussock and get a few colours. But no, the gold fever never made me drop my job and everything and head south.

Better days then? I'd certainly turn the clock back myself. Certainly simpler, those days. But what can you do about it? I'm still going along strong just yet, any rate. I hope I'm still alive next time you come. I can't go on living for ever!

Tell you what, though: you almost missed out on this session with me. I nearly did myself in the other day. I had a tip into the sea, down Deep Bay. I always thought it'd be a nice way to go, drowning, but then when it happened I fought like blazes. No, I'm not ready to go just yet.

What happened? I was half in the water and half not in the water. Everything that shouldn't be happening was happening. The damn water shouldn't have been over my head, but I couldn't get my feet on the bottom. And it all seemed sinky and muddy, and it was pouring into my gumboots! Anyhow I managed to wade ashore. I kicked off my gumboots and I said to myself, what now? Common sense said, get yourself home before you catch pneumonia; the law of the sea said, put your boat right. So that's what I did.

When I got back home here I just chucked the sodden clothes off and had a hot whisky. I dabbed myself a bit with a towel and put on some clean clothes. I had a feed and I felt fine. Then I was just thinking about getting a couple of hot water bottles and turning in, and some visitors turned up, so that was that!

But then I started shivering ... shock. I got carted up to the ranger's place and put to bed. I got pumped up with drugs and speared with injections. I wanted to come home. I had no pipe, nothing.

I'm not scared of dying. Sometimes I think it'd be a darned handy thing. And like I said, I don't ever want to be in a hospital with bedpans and all sorts of sorrowing people around.

I had to keep going. That's the thing how it is. Let's have a brew and then korero a bit more. . . .

We never ever did have a permanent doctor here on the island, although every now and then one retired here. In the past, if we needed a doctor we went to Bluff by fishing boat. Those boats went whatever the weather. Nowadays the doctor comes once a month. He flies in and out. There's usually a notice on the board. I just go to him and get my cramp pills; nothing to it.

Ever had a car? Not really. I'm not a driver, never have been. A boat's my thing. One stage there when I was about sixty I did buy a motorcar — fifty pound it cost me. I drove it around the paddock at Invercargill, to get the feel of it, and I drove it a few yards down the road. What I wanted it for? To learn to drive, mostly! What sort of a car? I can't remember that. It's like Mark Twain's dog. Someone asked him, "What sort of a dog's that?" and he said, "Mostly dog." Any rate, it was just an old, worn-out thing. And I remember the bloke who sold it to me tried to drive it to Bluff. She ran out of petrol and he didn't have the money to buy any more. Everyone was hard up those days.

In the end I got my motorcar over here to the island, and my friends learnt to drive it. I never ever learnt. I was going to, but I didn't get round to it. I didn't *need* a car. It wasn't worth bothering about, so I sold it.

I remember the first motorcar that ever came to Stewart Island. Mr Stone, one of the early taximen in Invercargill, lifted it out of the ferry. I was a grown man at the time. It might even have been after I'd seen war service. I remember the kids raced after it for fifty yards or so; it was a real novelty. People lived plainly those days. You pushed your stores home in a hand barrow, and I clearly remember the first time I came across a telephone. My father arrived home one night and said he'd talked to the mainland!

Yes, I suppose there's some interest in all these little old details. Most people today do have a telephone and a car and can't imagine anyone not ever having them. Any rate, me and Alex, we've got a chain-saw and a lawn-mower now, so we're rising socially!

But, see, I've been different in lots of ways from most people. I've even been different from some of the old Stewart Islanders. My outlook, that's what's different. Lots of the people here on the island aren't interested in things away from Halfmoon Bay. Their husbands go fishing, and if they ever go for a picnic, they go to Ulva. Same place, every time. Not terribly much imagination.

But even when we were kids we were different from the Bay kids. They just stayed put in the Bay; we thought they were townies. But us kids way out here at Ringaringa and that, we went all round the place. We had shanghais and when we got the chance, we were off. Then my father saw that we did a trip away every school holiday, up a mountain or up to one of the huts at Rakeahua or somewhere like that. A bit of natural history. We always got a trip away, even if we didn't get across to the mainland. In fact, we never went to the mainland, really. Nowadays I only go over there because I'm old and stupid. I don't belong. When I have to go to, say, the dentist, I've got to locate him. Then I forget his name. He says come back in the afternoon, and when I go out in the street I'm lost ... bewildered. I can't see the street crossings, can't see if the lights say go or stop. I have to ask someone.

But Stewart Island ... I've been very happy here. If I had my time again, would I live here? Yes.

What I missed, from the mainland and that? Nothing that I regret. Everything I needed was on the island. I never made much money, but enough, and plenty of interesting people come over here. I've been quite happy. The place is getting overcrowded now, houses everywhere, but it's all right still because we're still cut off to a certain extent. One old man at Ruapuke used to say, "It's looking bad weather over there at New Zealand," but that's simplifying our views too much. We say "mainland", and we do know what's going on over there. We say "over there at New Zealand" as a joke nowadays.

Same thing with many people's views on the size of Stewart Island; they have a fantasy about us. One foreigner asked this daft question: "Why can't you set off walking from Halfmoon Bay in the morning, walk down to the south coast, herd all the deer back to the north and catch them that evening? And the Navy could help out by going around with search lights." My comment is this: he's never *been* here. It's so ridiculous. People just don't know what goes on down here. They don't realise how big and wild the island really is.

I like the smell of what you're cooking up for our lunch. I'd sooner have it than the M.B.E. and I like eating off a piece of newspaper; I can smudge away. . . .

Let's korero a bit more. . . .

Entertainment? I've never been much of an entertainments man. I've always been happy without pictures and dances and that; I've always been on the outside edge of modern life, although I've always mixed with educated people. At one stage there nearly every naturalist that came to the island came straight to me, because I had a reputation for practical knowledge . . . which I still have, whether people realise it or not.

No, on the island we're so busy we haven't time to think what to do for entertainment. We're busy doing. But I'll tell you something that's died out now, something we used to do down here before the days of social welfare: we did lots of fund-raising, especially to give a woman a help to make a fresh start when she was widowed. We'd have a dance, just with accordions or a piano for music, or we'd have a concert with songs and recitations. *Down By The Rio Grande*, someone always recited that, and *Lucky Jim*. Same thing if someone had a fire, and they were very common in the old days of cooking fires and candles; the locals would take up a collection for anyone who lost their home. I said at the time, it's getting that way now the insurance companies will be complaining!

Then the county council would have a concert, and each of the churches would have theirs. The Plymouth Brethren were very strong those days. They'd come to school and preach to us kids and show us pictures, then we'd all sing songs — *The Band Of Hope* and that sort of thing:

> *That's the way to win the day,*
> *Work a little longer.*
> *Drink shall fall with tyrants all*
> *When bands of hope get stronger.*

We all used to sing that. There were two sorts of people those days: people who drank and people who didn't.

But tell you something: I don't know half the people here in the village now. People know me better than I know them. I don't know half the ones who give me rides in their motorcars, when I'm walking round Lonnekers to the Bay. I'm the oldest one around here now.

Yes, we're isolated by choice over here. My uncle was thirty-one years on Ulva without going over to the mainland. He had a wee shop over there — sold ropes and ships' gear and provisions, that sort of thing, and he also ran Stewart Island's first post office. It was opened in 1872 and called the most southerly post office in the world. There was never a very organised system. A cutter would come into Halfmoon Bay, and if there was any mail aboard for Ulva a chap would go over to Ringaringa and put up a smoke signal. Today someone would say, "Why are you lighting a fire!" Then my uncle would sail over to Ringaringa and pick up the mail. At one stage there you could post mutton bird tree leaves from my uncle's post office over there on Ulva. You just wrote on the leaves and posted them. Then later on the authorities banned this practice because the dampness of the leaves wrecked the rest of the mail! I also use those mutton bird tree leaves for a cup. If I come to a creek and there's a nice tree handy I fold the leaf a certain way, give it a tricky twist and I've got a cup. Handier than bending right down and sticking your mouth in the water. Yes, I like these old ways.

Any rate, my uncle was happy to stay put over there on Ulva. He'd just come across occasionally to Halfmoon Bay. He couldn't be bothered to go over to Bluff. We like the solitary life. And it's inertia, too. Look at me, I used to stride around the streets of Invercargill. Now I go over there and I just sit in the RSA!

No, I don't object to the tourists. It's nonsense to say Stewart Islanders don't like visitors; we're friendly people. But one thing I'm not too enthusiastic about is all these skin-divers about the place. They clean up everything — the pauas and scallops and mussels. The crayfish are getting scarce now, too; crayfishing is a real rat-race these days. The idea is, there's a crayfish down there and they're all trying to surround it with pots. Me and Alex, we throw away the little ones that the others grab. It's a sad thing, but I think nowadays a crayfish is born to be caught.

Same thing with the flounders — the people come over here and get a big swag, then they waste them. The old island types would go and get just what they wanted, plus a few for the old lady up the road and someone else who couldn't get them himself. The old islanders were natural conservationists, but outsiders don't always operate that way. Same story with the birds in the old days. You took them whenever you wanted them, pigeons and kakas and that — they were all on the game list. But they were plentiful, and they stayed that way because we didn't ever take more than we needed.

What the rangers should be doing for the island today? Put it this way, it's not for me to lay down a thing like that. They have a very difficult job these days, very different problems, what with the deer and the marine farms . . . *and* the private rows and rivalries! I'd suggest to the Lands and Forestry Departments today that they *can* work together, there's a place for both of them on Stewart Island. Lands can get on with survey and map work, kakapo searches, trips to Codfish Island, that sort of thing. The Forest Service can look after the tracks and noxious animals and that side of things.

I'd also say this: the Forestry Department has spent money like water, as though they're a tourist department. There's been too much money spent on tracks and huts, and they've goaded the Lands Department into keeping up with them.

Should we leave the old whaling relics and bits and pieces from the shipbuilding and fishing days? Or revert the place to the wilderness it once was? I'd just leave things as they were, especially the old huts and tramlines and sawmills. They're better left out there than stacked in a museum. As for the new stuff, the concrete bases for radio aerials for the oil rigs and that, it's hard to say what to do with those sorts of things. I'd say if the deer don't keep the second growth back, it's soon all covered up anyway.

Pollution? The pollution problem generally? I don't know what we're going to do, unless we kill off all the people! Halfmoon Bay is polluted; everything drains out to sea. But I'm a bit of a romantic. . . .

Why I resigned as ranger? I was over sixty-five years old. The Commissioner of Crown Lands said he'd keep me on, on a year-to-year basis. I thought, well, I can carry on fishing without any headaches. What headaches with rangering? The many ignorant people, and things ending up in court cases. The Departments have treated me well, and they didn't interfere with me much, but with working with all three Departments there were always letters to attend to, almost every mail. I'm a practical man. I made it my business to look after things on the island. I enjoyed just poking around.

I wear my ranger's badge still. It's handy. If you speak to a man and you haven't got a badge of authority, he can tell you to go to blazes. Yes, if I have occasion to I still say something, if I see a bloke blatantly destroying the birds or misusing firearms, that type of thing. But most people aren't hard on me nowadays. I've got to that age now when people are inclined to be nice to me!

The biggest achievement in my life as a ranger? I'd say there were two things: helping people go out and look at things, all those people who've come here, naturalists and ordinary people from all round the world — I've helped them all; and keeping the deer off the Bravo Islands.

I think I got the M.B.E. for my general services in helping people. Off I went up to Wellington to get my medal. Nineteen sixty-three I think it was I was ordered up there. I remember I went up the steps and across the stage. I hove to and stood to attention. Got my medal, from the Queen — she hooked it on.

High point of my life? No! The people here, the old Stewart Islanders, couldn't have been more warm-hearted about it, but I knew they'd soon forget I had an M.B.E. It had no significance for them. They just liked me, so they were generally pleased about it, but by the time I got orders to go to Wellington they'd forgotten all about it. One couple saw me off on the boat; one lady sent a telegram. But no one came to meet me when I came back with my medal!

So what was the highlight of my life? I'd say, helping the people. The point is, I *wanted* people to understand Stewart Island. I still do.

I don't tell people about all these sorts of things as a rule . . . but you've got me talking again!

Know what I call you? My korero girl.

Haere ra.

E noho ra.